More Praise for *A Rebel's Journey*

'Deeply informed and passionately engaged, this is an exceptional work of scholarship, reconstructing the life and thought of pre-revolutionary Iran's most exceptional figure on the left. The book's intriguing protagonist was not only a leader of armed struggle against the Shah's dictatorship, but the guerrilla movement's sharpest and most devastating critic from within. Lacking access to canonical revolutionary texts, he fashioned an autonomous intellectual perspective defiant of all established canons, including those sacrosanct to Iranian and global revolutionaries. Vahabzadeh has done a wonderful job of intellectual restoration and remembering, while showing an intriguing path forward to the revolutionaries of our time.'

**Afshin Matin-Asgari, Professor of Middle East History,
California State University, Los Angeles**

'An outstanding interpretive and critical overview of the vast body of Mostafa Sho'aiyan's writings. Peyman Vahabzadeh masterfully reveals Sho'aiyan's cosmopolitan and frontal theory of rebellion, and his singular and uncanonical leftism.'

**Mojtaba Mahdavi,
Professor of Political Science, University of Alberta**

RADICAL HISTORIES OF THE MIDDLE EAST

SERIES EDITORS

Dr Mezna Qato, University of Cambridge

Dr Siavush Randjbar-Daemi, University of St Andrews

Dr Eskandar Sadeghi-Boroujerdi, Goldsmiths, University of London

Dr Omar H. AlShehabi, Gulf University of Science and Technology

Dr Abdel Razzaq Takriti, University of Houston

OTHER TITLES IN THIS SERIES

Khalil Maleki by Homa Katouzian

Contested Modernity by Omar H. AlShehabi

For more information and details of forthcoming volumes, please visit
oneworld-publications.com/radical-histories

A Rebel's Journey

Mostafa Sho'aiyan and Revolutionary Theory in Iran

Peyman Vahabzadeh

ONEWORLD ACADEMIC

Oneworld Academic

An imprint of Oneworld Publications

Published by Oneworld Academic, 2019

Copyright © Peyman Vahabzadeh 2019

ISBN 978-1-78607-620-5
eISBN 978-1-78607-621-2

Typeset by Geethik Technologies
Printed and bound in Great Britain by Clays Ltd, Elcograf S.p.A.

Oneworld Publications
10 Bloomsbury Street
London WC1B 3SR
England

MIX
Paper from
responsible sources
FSC
www.fsc.org   FSC® C018072

In memoriam

Mostafa Sho'aiyan (1936–75)
Theoretician, Practitioner, Rebel

and to

his comrades who cherished his friendship
and preserved his legacy with exemplary fidelity
in the unkindest of times

At this time, 'rebellion' (shuresh) *grew stronger, and aside from the movements that appeared in Tabriz and other towns in Azerbaijan, a movement rose among Iranians and their Georgians and Russian comrades in Caucasus and it was during these days that... they cre- ated the basis for the rebellion of Gilan.*

Ahmad Kasravi, *History of Iranian Constitutionalism*, p. 852

Forty years after Guevara's death, the international climate and discourse about political change has changed out of all recognition. The heroic guerrillas in the mountains and jungles of Latin America, fighting for a better life against repressive dictatorships, would today, in the world after 9/11, be demonized as 'terrorists'. Yet they were once seen to belong to that long-established and honourable tradition of those who picked up arms to fight for national liberation.

Richard Gott, *Guerrilla Movements in Latin America*, p. xv

The monster of yesteryear that has been slumbering in the deepest grounds of social relations for... centuries awakens to every flick of tomorrow and charges at the blossoms of the future with its enormous and fiendish force.

Mostafa Sho'aiyan, 'Open Letter to Mazdak,' p. 13

Error is first a passer-by, then it becomes a neighbor and eventually the landlord!

Mostafa Sho'aiyan, 'Open Letter to Mazdak,' p. 61

We are the product of 500 years of struggle: first against slavery, then during the War of Independence against Spain led by insurgents, then to avoid being absorbed by North American imperialism, then to promulgate our constitution and expel the French Empire from our soil, and later the dictatorship of Porfirio Díaz denied us the just application of the Reform Laws, and the people rebelled and leaders like Villa and Zapata emerged, poor people just like us. We have been denied the most elemental preparation so that they can use us as cannon fodder and pillage the wealth of our country. But today, we say ENOUGH IS ENOUGH.

Subcomandante Insurgente Marcos,
Our Word Is Our Weapon, p. 13

[The] adversaries… [that this] book combats in different ways [are]: […] The political ascetics, the sad militants, the terrorists of theory, those who would preserve the pure order of politics and political discourse. Bureaucrats of the revolution and civil servants of Truth.

Michel Foucault, Preface to *Anti-Oedipus*, p. xii

CONTENTS

ACKNOWLEDGEMENTS

This book is born out of an invitation by Siavush Ranjbar-Daemi, and I thank him for this unique opportunity. Many thanks also to Eskandar Sadeghi-Boroujerdi for his support through this process and Novin Doostdar, Jonathan Bentley-Smith, and Paul Nash at Oneworld for their encouragement, support, and professionalism. As well, I thank Richard Collins for the meticulous editorial work on the manuscript. I would like to acknowledge the late Cosroe Chaqueri, the original publisher of Mostafa Sho'aiyan's works through Edition Mazdak in Florence in the 1970s. After my initial interest in Sho'aiyan's works in the late 1990s, Professor Chaqueri shared his personal archives of Sho'aiyan's writings (fairly rare at the time) with me and thus directed me to the path that I have taken to Sho'aiyan in the past two decades—a long journey that culminates in this book.

I am eternally grateful to Reza Farnoud who graciously helped me with the enormous task of securing and moving historic sources for this research. I thank A. Rad who brought me some key sources, S. Sarabi for sending me an unpublished article by Sho'aiyan, and Afshin Matin-asgari for providing important articles of the 1960s and making suggestions. I am indebted to Asghar Monajemi, Mostafa's long-time friend, who shed light on the many aspects of his life and works, as well as Mostafa's comrade, Gh. Farhang Forutan (Abbas), who shared with me some key original documents of the group and clarified some aspects for me. I am indebted to Nasrin Yari Saidkhanlu for sending me some of Sho'aiyan's earliest unpublished writings. I also acknowledge Anahita Sho'aiyan for providing useful information. A visit to Hoover Institution in Stanford University in summer 2006 allowed me a careful review of the original writings in the Sho'aiyan Archives. Finally, many thanks to the staff at the Interlibrary Loans Desk at University of Victoria Library, in particular Dave Pretty, for their efforts to supply me with the scarce sources necessary for this study. As is clear, a work such as this is never an individual's feat, although its shortcomings are entirely mine.

Last but certainly not least, this book is yet another product of the loving support of my exilic life companion Giti and our intellectually curious son Emile. They provided me with the much-needed time and peace of mind to work on this manuscript, while posing challenging questions to me—questions that mysteriously found their way into this book in various ways.

ABBREVIATIONS FOR
SHO'AIYAN'S MAJOR WORKS

For full citations, please see the bibliography. Titles in square brackets are given to unpublished works or letters by the author of this book.

HSW   *Half-a-Step on the Way: The People's Liberation Front*
IIME   *On the Role of Israeli and Iranian Regimes in the Middle East*
IRJS   *Injudicious Replies to 'Judicious Steps'*
OLM   'Open Letter to Mazdak'
PFB   *Poems from the Battlefield*
Rev   *Revolution*
RRC   'Responses of Red Comrade'
SOLF   *The Sixth Open Letter to the Fadai Guerrillas*
SOLI   *Six Open Letters to the Organisation of Iranian People's Fadai Guerrillas*
SURMJ   *A Review of the Relations Between the Soviet Union and the Revolutionary Movement of Jungle*
SW   *Selected Writings*

TCE   *Two Critical Essays on the People's Fadai Guerrillas*
WBD   *What Is To Be Done?*
YGNF   *The Younger Generation and the National Front*

NOTE ON TRANSLATION
AND TRANSLITERATION

T he absolute majority of the sources used for this study have been published solely in Persian, and, as such, the unenviable task of providing the reader with readable English translations of the Persian texts fell to me. In translating some Persian polysemic words, I chose to accede to their contextual meanings by introducing the word's etymological significance or historical context, or simply by inserting the Persian words in parentheses. In transliterating names of persons or places, or certain Persian words or concepts, I followed the simple rule of approximating the sound of Persian letters to those in the English alphabet. I eliminated the typographical ciphers and diacritics that are used to designate Persian letter sounds involving scanning and accentuation, in the manner used by *Encyclopedia Iranica*. The exceptions to this rule pertain to the Persian or Arabic proper names that have a certain norm of spelling owing to their appearance in English (e.g. Mohammad, Mahmoud, Muslim). I have ignored the distinction between long and short vowels in Persian, but I have used the inverse apostrophe to mark the vowel

Ayn in Persian words when Ayn appears in the middle of the word (e.g. *tab'id*) but simplified that rule in the one prominent case: Sho'aiyan (which should be Sho'a'iyan). I have dropped the apostrophe when the Ayn appears as the first vowel of the word (e.g. Ali or Elm). I have also used diacritic to mark the Hamza in the middle of the word (e.g. Fada'i), with the prominent exception of 'Fadai.' My main objective has been to negotiate between a readable English and the writing styles of the authors of these texts, in particular Sho'aiyan's highly idiosyncratic prose. I have aimed to maintain a style of writing that captures the nuances in a discourse as a subset of language that locates, conditions, and makes possible the articulation of the subject matter.

INTRODUCTION

Reactivating Distorted Histories

My heart is a fire-temple that'll never grow dim,
not at night and nor in the day,
nor through the years,
nor even through centuries.

Sho'aiyan (1974)

Once upon a time, an eighteen-year-old student walking through Sohrevardi (formerly Farah) Street in Tehran around June 1979, a few months after the Revolution, noticed a rather rare and small poster, printed on cheap yellowish paper, on a wall, the only one of its kind, as if an orphan. The poster commemorated the martyrdom of anti-Shah militant communists known as *Goruh-e Rafiq Sorkh* (The Red Comrade's Group). Of that poster the piercing images of two men stood out. The young man, who by this time had already educated himself about the underground resistance against the Shah, asked himself why he had never heard of this group and those militants. Thirty years later in 2001 in Paris, this man discovered that the images were those of Nader Shayegan and Nader Ata'i, comrades of Mostafa Sho'aiyan. I was that passer-by, clearly no longer young, and I had gone through the character-building (the verb 'survived' is meaningless for me) waves of post-revolutionary repressions and the war with Iraq in which I participated as a conscripted soldier, among many other adventures and displacements thrown at me by life. The question that intuitively dawned on me back in 1979 still nags at me but it now has a more universal reach: why is it that some phenomena dominate the public view and grow mainstream at the expense of others? It is the question of marginalisation. During the eleven years it took me to research, write, revise, and rewrite *A Guerrilla Odyssey* (published in 2010) on one of Iran's most popular leftist organisations, People's Fadai Guerrillas, I encountered many lives, opinions, works, and events that had been marginalised as though their contribution to our present-day lives did not matter. In any case, the images of Shayegan and Ata'i on the yellowish posters have been permanently carved in my memory: they look at me as though they are command-ing me to write their story. I think it was due to my sensibility toward the marginalised that the study of what turned out to be a 'mainstream' dissident group in *A Guerrilla Odyssey* led to the discovery of Mostafa Sho'aiyan. Through that discovery I became aware of the global implications and contributions of the works of Iranian thinkers, in particular Sho'aiyan.

This book offers a detailed and analytical study of the life and times of one of the most singularly important figures of the Iranian Left and one of the most original intellectuals of twentieth-century Iran. Mostafa Sho'aiyan (1936–76) was a pro-lific writer, poet, Marxist theoretician, revolutionary practitioner, and critical thinker. In the international collective memory of the revolutionary age of the 1960s and 1970s, aspects of Sho'aiyan's life remind us of the Brazilian Marxist revolutionary Carlos

Marighella (1911–69), famed among world revolutionaries for his *Minimanual for the Urban Guerrilla* (1969), although Sho'aiyan's life trajectory remains more complex than his, and Sho'aiyan exceeded Marighella exponentially when one considers Sho'aiyan's ample works—over 2,300 pages. In addition, for a thinker who only had limited access to the global revolutionary literature, since by his own admission he did not have the reading knowledge of any language other than Persian, certain aspects of his ideas remind us of the works of Leon Trotsky, Antonio Gramsci, and Herbert Marcuse. A Tricontinental spirit is also evident in his theoretical writings.

This book aims to present an *intellectual biography* of Sho'aiyan, but this task would not be possible without delving deep into his *lived experiences*.[1] More ambitiously, I will *reconstruct* a theory of rebellious front for our twentieth-first-century reality *through a critical interpretation and reassembling of his thought*. Anything relating to Sho'aiyan remains unsettlingly controversial, as he often defied conventional wisdom and logic. The reader should expect that my attempt at bringing his works back to life will be equally controversial but moderated through the wisdom granted to me by hindsight. I want to show that, once reappropriated, Sho'aiyan's thought has a broader appeal to international audience interested in the defiant movements of not only the 1960s–1970s but also the myriad anti-establishment movements today—from the Zapatistas in Mexico to democratic confederalism in Rojava, from the Arab Spring to Occupy Wall Street. Sho'aiyan's work offers useful insights about (neo-) colonial reality and hegemonic construction of resistance and liberation, not to mention his defiance of conventional political discourse that hides certain realities and experiences. His ideas, I believe, can be teleported into our collective resistance today against a global neoliberal assault on the planet and its inhabitants and allow us to reflect on the importance of marginality as potential enclaves of defiance. To some extent, this book emulates the way researchers have brought the experiences of the Latin American movements to the global venue and thus contributed to the movements elsewhere.[2]

My objective is therefore to contextualise Sho'aiyan's theoretical contributions within his concrete life and times, so that I show the gestalt of his intellectual development. In addition to some public venue interviews, I have already published several scholarly articles examining Sho'aiyan's contributions, analyses, and pathology of the Iranian Left.[3] But this book is *not* a reworked version of my published papers. It provides an original rethinking and reworking of my engagements with the unparalleled contributions of Sho'aiyan, as I systematise his thought and show its merits and flaws. My objective is to show how Sho'aiyan offered new ways of rethinking the complexities of Iranian politics under an authoritarian state, as he aimed at forging a liberatory, non-doctrinal Left. My interest in Sho'aiyan is, in part, a reaction to the systematic disregard of his work that was afforded to him by both the leftist parties and personalities that had rejected his approach and those who nowadays shed crocodile tears for him in their futile attempts to appropriate his untameable thought.

The study of Sho'aiyan's works is, of course, a worthwhile exercise in its own right, and it constitutes legitimate scholarship as a part of registering the Iranian intellectual history in the twentieth century. And yet, as a scholar from Iranian origins teaching classical and modern European thought in the West, I have become increasingly weary of the way the contributions of the thinkers of the Global South (Iran, in this case) have been systematically relegated to the limited fields of Iranian Studies and Middle Eastern Studies. Such a trend—that is, to deploy the study of the non-Western Other to the designated realms of scholarship and 'area studies'—reveals the often surreptitious *orientalist epistemologies* that have become hegemonic in the academy, and, precisely because of the hegemonic status of such orientalism, it goes unnoticed by those who find a niche in the 'area studies' of the South. In this hegemonic epistemological universe, as Walter Mignolo has shown, the South produces the case while the North provides theory and analysis.[4] I therefore emphatically want this book to offer an analysis of the works of Sho'aiyan *as an international and internationalist thinker* and to bring to light his potential contributions to the revival of the Left in this age of savage globalised capitalism, democratic pretense, mass surveillance, pacified resistance, digital slacktivism, and common despair.

In a previous work on Iran's Fadai Guerrillas, I advanced the thesis that, despite their rhetorical adherence to Marxism-Leninism, Iran's most celebrated urban guerrilla organisation in the 1970s was in fact a militant hub for diverse ideas, multiple political tendencies, and activists from various, even diverging, cultural and class backgrounds.[5] This book follows a similar trajectory but at a different level. I will show in this book the political, intellectual, and discursive contexts of Sho'aiyan's unparalleled and maverick thought by dwelling on the intertextuality of his writings as well as the rhetorical means through which he himself dwells on multiple discourses available to him at the time in order to forge his unique theory of the revolutionary front. It is hoped that, in addition to registering Sho'aiyan's life and thought, this work contributes to scholarship on the saga of an age of searching for new ways through plurality and debate, of a rich and collective intellectual universe traveling through its trajectory, and of an Iranian cosmopolitan culture.

*

For about twenty years after his death Sho'aiyan remained the forgotten revolutionary of the Iranian Left. Asghar Monajemi who smuggled his writings to Europe in the early 1970s, the late Cosroe Chaqueri who published these works in Europe after Sho'aiyan's death through his Edition Mazdak, as well as a handful of dedicated comrades, in prison and at large, were about the only people who not only cared about Mostafa but loved him deeply and were devoted to him. This close-knit network of comrades selflessly safeguarded Sho'aiyan's writings and his memory. The Iranian Left, before and after the 1979 Revolution, totally disowned Sho'aiyan whose massive corpus of original writings on history, theory, and policy reviews outweighed by a large margin those of every other leftist writer and thinker in Iran. The only exceptions to this systematic marginalisation are the two documented debates between Sho'aiyan and Marxist theoretician Hamid Momeni, the theorist of the Organisation of the Iranian People's Fadai Guerrillas (OIPFG) in 1974–5.[6] Paradoxically, though, these debates only contributed to Sho'aiyan's marginalisation, the extent of which cannot be exaggerated. In the years following the 1979 Revolution, the Left was too caught up in the fast pace of unfolding events, and its theoreticians from various shades of Marxism, as is evident by the vast leftist literature of this time, felt more comfortable working with the borrowed ideas from Russian or Chinese Marxists than trying to extract ideas from their own compatriot. He was such a forgotten revolutionary that only a handful attended the sole event organised by his loyal comrades on the anniversary of his death and held at his tomb in Tehran's Behesht-e Zahra Cemetery in February 1980 as the short-lived 'Spring of Freedom' withered away (see Chapter 1).

On a warm summer afternoon in 2008 in a café in Paris, Professor Chaqueri related an anecdote to me: he told me he had published Sho'aiyan's *Revolution* in 1976 in a print run of

1,000 and had taken the copies with him to various Iranian venues and opposition gatherings in Europe. The book was sold out within a year, but not a single review of the book was ever published anywhere. This is the extent, Chaqueri reflected, to which Sho'aiyan's work was systematically ignored by the activists of the Left (SOLI 16). It is interesting that no one took Sho'aiyan's *Revolution* seriously but Momeni's rejoinder to it, also published as a book, was reprinted many times. In other words, the activists only became aware of Sho'aiyan through Momeni's refutation of his ideas. Interestingly, Cosroe Chaqueri (Khosrow Shakeri, 1938–2015) himself was a rather marginalised figure within the leftists. He was a student activist with and co-founder of the National Front branch outside Iran in 1961 and a leading figure of the Confederation of Iranian Students-National Union (CISNU), elected to its Central Committee between 1965 and 1968. Later, in 1982, he received a Ph.D. in History from the Sorbonne. Chaqueri was the publisher of over twenty volumes of 'Historic Documents of the Workers', Social Democratic, and Communist Movement.' Through his father's export business based in Florence, he had established Edition Mazdak. He told me that when he received Sho'aiyan's works, mailed to him anonymously with unsigned instructions on how to get in touch with Sho'aiyan's contact in Europe, he was immediately impressed by his work, and although he remained unwaveringly critical of several aspects of Mostafa's work he decided to publish them under the alias *Rafiq Sorkh* (Red Comrade or Comrade Red). Monajemi told me that when Sha'oiyan received Chaqueri's critique he wanted to write a serious rejoinder but then changed his mind when Monajemi discouraged Mostafa, reminding him that at the time, when no one would publish his writings, Mazdak's willingness to bring Sho'aiyan's ideas to the public was a unique opportunity not to be jeopardised by theoretical disagreements.

In any case, in a handwritten note that I have seen, Mostafa conferred upon Chaqueri the exclusive right to publish his writings, a right that led to Chaqueri's conflict with some of Sho'aiyan's comrades when they published some of Mostafa's works in post-revolutionary Iran. Chaqueri was an equally controversial figure among the activists and shunned by them. He was known for his blunt criticisms and uncompromising positions. Life is curious: by a twist of fortune, the two maverick activists crossed paths and become comrades without ever having met one another.

Sho'aiyan led no party and he was not a member of one. The two small underground groups he co-founded were discovered and dismantled by security forces before they had a chance to carry out any significant operations. He never wrote within the established jargon of the Left. I shall show in this book that one of the most genuine aspects of his work was that his ideas must have been affirmed through his experience. As such, he remained a singular figure, only to be misunderstood and labeled by the leftist activists, if they ever bothered to read him at all.

All of Sho'aiyan's major works were published in the mid-1970s by Mazdak in Florence and were mostly distributed among the dissident students in Europe and the United States, although a limited number of these books were taken to Iran after the Revolution. Within a few years after Sho'aiyan's death, the Iranian Revolution of 1979 changed the country's political scene forever. Some of Sho'aiyan's works were also published by his dedicated comrades around 1980 who founded the short-lived *Nashr-e Enqelab* (Revolution Press). With the Revolution, after a short period of the Left's flourishing in 1979–81, there came the dark decade of the 1980s in which leftist and other dissident activists of all shades and inclinations, including the Muslims outside the state orbit, were purged in their thousands in Iranian prisons, while tens of thousands more fled the country, becoming self-imposed exiles, and many more sought refuge in the anonymous layers of society. With the repression of the women's movement and national minorities that preceded the purges and the continued crackdown on intellectuals and silencing of writers, the Iranian social and cultural scene grew very quiet in the 1980s and 1990s. A few copies of Sho'aiyan's works survived this decade, thanks to hiding places of Mostafa's loyal comrades. These were mostly but not exclusively members of the group Sho'aiyan and Nader Shayegan had founded, but their connection with Sha'oiyan and his legacy is personal: they loved him and believed in him. They revered Mostafa's intellectual feats and praised his personality, his attentiveness and kindness in particular. When I talk to them more than forty years after Mostafa's death, they still speak of him as if he is alive, with great love and admiration.

In any case, the political scene seemed fairly barren and intellectual pursuits under tremendous pressure until the 1997 electoral victory of reform-minded Mohammad Khatami who won the presidential election through the mass support of women and youth. One of the outcomes of Khatami's reforms was easing the rigid publication regulations (read: censorship) imposed by the previous governments through the Ministry of Culture and Islamic Guidance—regulations that implemented strict guidelines over the publication of the books and magazines, as well as films and music, scrutinising these media methodically for the content that might be regarded as potentially 'harmful' to the state-sanctioned Islamic values or political views. During Khatami's presidency, the publishing industry thrived and numerous titles, previously banned, were published. In the absence of the Iranian Left, ironically, this relaxing of publication regulations ended Sho'aiyan's obscurity and gradually brought his life and works to the view of the educated public and to an entirely new generation. The forgotten Mazdak publications of

Sho'aiyan's works some twenty years earlier now gained currency. The internet also immensely helped Sho'aiyan's emergence from obscurity. But why did Sho'aiyan's works make a comeback? The answer is complex but I will try and answer it here.

Apart from a limited number of commemorative notes published in the journals of Iranian expatriates in the 1990s,[7] the first work that brought Sho'aiyan to public view was Houshang Mahrooyan's book (2005), dedicated to one of Mostafa's closes friends, Asghar Monajemi, in which he published one of Sho'aiyan's last works in addition to his own long laudatory introduction.[8] Then another book emerged, edited by Cosroe Chaqueri (2007), containing a preface by this author, an editor's introduction, and eight open letters from Sho'aiyan to the leaders of the OIPFG, criticising the latter's internal policies.[9] Both of these books distinctly offered Sho'aiyan's critical reflection on the OIPFG (or PFG), an urban guerrilla group founded in 1971 and the most popular Marxist organisation in Iran in the 1970s and 1980s, with a formidable legacy that continues to this day, notwithstanding the group's near total eradication before the Revolution and the failed politics of its many splinter groups thereafter. The intention of the authors of both of these volumes was, quite judiciously, to offer a critical view of the doctrinal Left, and in Chaqueri's volume, with the hope of forging a new, democratic Left in this potentially historic opportunity for a leftist renewal. But the fact that both books contained Sho'aiyan's sharp critique of the Fadai Guerrillas, a group that, despite its possibly irrecoverable political decline, was still dear to an entire generation of activists, certainly had something to do with the granting of a publication licence for these books. In other words, these first publications staged Sho'aiyan's intellectual legacy only in opposition to the Fadai Guerrillas, and not as an original and independent thinker. In particular, Mahrooyan depicted a toothless Sho'aiyan—in contrast to the uncompromising, radical revolutionary he really was—only understood in terms of his disagreements with the Fadai Guerrillas. These books' publication must be viewed within the context of the changing cultural and publication policies of Iranian intelligence: by the turn of the millennium the Iranian state confidently considered itself to be solidly in control and thus, instead of repressing the cultural presence of the leftists, the state opted for opening up the publication domain to works that were 'critical' of popular leftists groups the state had repressed in the previous decades. The Ministry of Intelligence itself published volumes of historiographical works, based on SAVAK and its own documents, on various dissident groups, but it welcomed works critical of the leftists that came from independent scholars. Not surprisingly, these two books inadvertently set the stage for Iranian 'yellow journalism' to appropriate Sho'aiyan—framing him primarily in terms of his critique of the Left in their pages, a project on a par with the cultural policies of the state intelligence—and thereby once again marginalising Sho'aiyan.[10] But here was Sho'aiyan's unwitting mystery: the distorted and abused figure of Sho'aiyan in the pages of the yellow magazines gave birth to a whole new interest in his work by the post-revolutionary generation that not only appreciated a much-needed reckoning with the Left's past—with its ashes and diamonds—but was also eager to bring into view the breadth of Sho'aiyan's ideas as much as publication regulations in Iran allowed. Young leftists, coming of age in the postcommunist era, could not have returned, for the most part, to doctrinal Marxism-Leninism (of various shades) that defined the pre-revolutionary Left. Sho'aiyan offered this generation the possibility of a new sort of leftism.

The new interest in Sho'aiyan therefore appeared, once again, in journalistic dimensions. The first was a well-received, voluminous biography, *Mostafa Sho'aiyan and Revolutionary Romanticism*, first published in 2010 in Sweden and then in 2015 in Tehran (where it had a second printing).[11] Although the book shines a light into the rather obscure corners of Sho'aiyan's complex life, it lacks the principles of historiography and biography, and in many cases it mixes fact with fiction, takes the claims of activists either at face value or stretches them, and falls seriously short in presenting and engaging with Mostafa's thought. Next was young journalist Sam Sarabi's dedication of the 'Political Thought' section of an issue of the Tehran daily newspaper *Shargh* (12 May 2012) to Sho'aiyan, which contained several articles and interviews on Mostafa's ideas and activism.[12] Recently, the journalist Ali Nili dedicated an unprecedented fifty-three-page exposé to Sho'aiyan—in an unmistakably positive tone and sharply critical of yellow journalism's derogatory views of the militant left—through several interviews and documents, in the Tehran monthly *Nasim-e Bidari* (December 2016).[13] These works have contributed to transforming the image of Sho'aiyan, bringing to the fore, within the existing publication limits, his multidimensional character and complex mind. To these must be added a short political biography, written by this author, of Parviz Sadri, one of Sho'aiyan's closest comrades and one of Iran's most prominent disappeared dissidents,[14] a volume that also attends to Mostafa's underground activism.

In light of the *reactivation* of Sho'aiyan's works, a task to which this book is dedicated, it no longer seems plausible to seriously consider the twentieth-century intellectual history of Iran—let alone the history of the Iranian Left—and overlook Mostafa Sho'aiyan. This book intends primarily to bring his theories of revolution and frontal politics, and in conjunction with that, his political thought, to the fore, to show how in response to his existential and historic frames Sho'aiyan succeeded in offering a political theory that is still vibrant and relevant in our age of homogenising and globalised injustices.

THE ROAD FROM HERE

To achieve its objectives this book will take the following trajectory. Chapter 1 offers a political biography of Sho'aiyan in as much detail as is necessary to provide the appropriate contexts for the following chapters. It situates Sho'aiyan's coming of age in the context of the 1950s, before and after the CIA–MI6-engineered coup of 1953 that toppled the popular government of Mohammad Mosaddeq and instated imperial dictatorship. This formative experience planted the seeds of 'frontal thinking' in Sho'aiyan's mind, a thinking that directed his activities and research in the 1960s and then his underground activism in the 1970s. This chapter emphasises the key turning points in Sho'aiyan's life within its historical and intellectual contexts, and, as such, this is the only 'biographical' chapter of the book, since the book's prime objective is to offer an analytical account of Sho'aiyan's singular thought and his unique politics.

Chapter 2 highlights the key positions Sho'aiyan took in the 1960s, the decade during which he became the thinker and theoretician of the 1970s. His engagements with the Tudeh Party, the Second National Front, the Shah's reforms, and his research on the Jangali movement are discussed in this chapter. Chapter 3 chronicles his short but bitter experience as a member of Iran's leading armed underground group, the People's Fadai Guerrillas, in order to trace and discuss his critical engagements with the Fadaiyan, and how he emerged as an unwavering critic of Stalinism and doctrinal Marxism within the Iranian Left. Chapter 4 also offers his written debate with the Fadaiyan's mid-career theoretician Hamid Momeni on the subject of the revolutionary intellectuals, their ontology, and their role within the liberation movement.

The next two chapters bring to the fore his intertwined theories of the front and rebellion. Chapter 5 goes back to his formative experiences of the front during the 1950s and 1960s and documents the way he conceptualises the liberation front and how he proposes to put it in action. Chapter 6 probes his magnum opus, *Revolution*, and offers his theory of the rebellious essence and rebellious action. In conjunction with his frontal thinking, this chapter brings together the key elements that constitute Sho'aiyan's thought. The Conclusion will show the relevance of Sho'aiyan's thought for today's world.

One important note: this study probes those writings of Sho'aiyan that he identified as his own and sent to Edition Mazdak in the 1970s, especially in the last two years of his life. Thus, the pieces he wrote upon the request from Mojahedin (and possibly others) have been excluded from this book.

1

THE MAKING OF A SINGULAR REVOLUTIONARY

*A full-fledged historic war is upon us. Whether we want it or not. So one must confront the past by relying on the simultaneously destructive and generative forces of the futures—the forces that are presently few but also the greatest and most creative forces of being. There is no other road to salvation (*rastgari*).*

Sho'aiyan, RRC 14

U nlike his contemporaries, Mostafa Sho'aiyan wrote quite extensively about his own life, activities, and concerns even at the time when he lived underground as one of Iran's most wanted men. He introduced to the Iranian political culture the uncommon legacy of openness, inasmuch as such openness would not jeopardise dissident activists. Thus, Sho'aiyan challenged the long-cherished inclination toward secrecy, an unfortunate consequence of living under a dictatorship. In fact, by bringing out into the open the inner life of militant activists of

1

his time—and this is rather counterintuitive—he promoted the struggles of a generation of Iranian activists who, having come of age in the 1960s and lost all hope of challenging the authoritarian rule over their country through legal-constitutional means,[1] had embarked upon an armed struggle to untangle itself from the 'repressive development'[2] that imposed upon the young, educated women and men the dim horizon of becoming soulless function-aries living in a rapidly changing society devoid of democracy, participatory political life, and social justice. It is partly thanks to his documented reflections that today we are able to reconstruct the highlights of his life and offer a fairly accurate biography. It emerged as a feminist motto in the 1960s, but Sho'aiyan lived the truth that 'the personal is political.'

EARLY LIFE

Mostafa was born in 1935, during the reign of Reza Shah (1878–1944; reigned 1926–41), into a lower middle-class family in the old neighborhood of Abanbar Mo'ayer in southern Tehran. His mother, Sakineh, came from a deeply rooted Tehrani family that had lived in the city's traditional neighborhoods for a few generations. His father, Mohammad, had moved with his broth-ers to Rasht at a young age and later joined the ill-fated Jangali movement (1915–21) led by Mirza Kuchek Khan. With the movement's defeat in 1921, eighteen-year-old Mohammad fled to Tehran where he opened a tailor's shop and married Sakineh some years later. The family lived modestly. Mohammad died in 1942, leaving behind four children, Parvin, Khosrow, Mostafa, and Pari.[3] Mostafa's mother—called Khanom Jan—was a literate woman, raised, after her parents' passing when she was a child, by her grandmother and paternal aunt. Childless, Khanom Jan's aunt had left her the property that sustained the family in the absence of Mohammad. Parvin was one of the first Iranian women to receive nursing education from England; she married a physician, Naby Gheselbashiyan, and they both worked in Masjed Soleiman in Khuzestan Province for the National Iranian Oil Company. She now lives in Tehran. Khosrow joined the Iranian army after secondary school and reached the rank of sergeant. He became ill during his service and was honorably discharged from the army. He passed away in 2011. Parvin and Khosrow were Mostafa's older siblings. Pari was his younger sister who held a postgraduate degree in education, although she never worked in that capacity. She married Mr Salari and immigrated to the United States, where she passed away in 2015.[4] Anahita Sho'aiyan, Mostafa's niece, points out that it is true that Mostafa lived in an small, old house in southern Tehran with his mother, but this does not mean his was a poor, underprivileged family. In fact, the family enjoyed formidable 'cultural capital': all but one of the four siblings had a university education.[5]

Mostafa was still a child when, during the Second European War (World War Two), the Allies occupied Iran and forced Reza Shah to abdicate on 16 September 1941 in favor of his twenty-one-year-old son, Mohammad Reza (1919–80). The occupation of Iran by British and Soviet forces, ironically, brought about relative political freedom in the country, allowing social and political groups, repressed by Reza Shah's authoritarian regime, to flourish. Within a few short years, Iranians were experiencing a diverse and lively political scene they had never seen before, with many political parties emerging, newspapers and magazines mushrooming, and labor unions forming and expanding. Within days of the occupation, the Tudeh Party of Iran was founded in October 1941, and it played a crucial role in organising labor and women in the country.[6] Also founded in 1941 were the nationalist

Iran Party and Pan-Iranist group,[7] followed by Socialist Theist Movement (*Nehzat-e Khodaparastan-e Sosiyalist*) in 1944.[8] Also established with the encouragement of influential clerics, including Ayatollah Kashani, was the conservative militant Shi'i group, Fadaiyan-e Islam (est. 1946).[9] Aside from the organs of these parties, multiple newspapers and magazines introduced to society an enormous array of ideas and ideologies pertaining to amplified contested views within the international political climate of a world that seemed destined to re-emerge in the bifurcated Cold War era. Iranian political life was now jovial, vivacious, and colorful, but also precarious. The monolithic and repressed social scene under Reza Shah was no more. With his connections to the dominant classes and elite within the country still too weak and his status still not fully registered with the western powers, Mohammad Reza Shah's position was too feeble during these years to allow him to try and emulate his father's heavy-handed rule, which he achieved in the post-1953 era.

Sho'aiyan witnessed first-hand a rapidly changing Iran while attending school and working simultaneously, often catching up with sleep and study between the two places. Mostafa grew up in this world of heterogeneous ideas and was deeply influenced by the experience of the National Front led by Dr Mohammad Mosaddeq, a character whom, despite his critical reflections, Sho'aiyan unwaveringly cherished to the last day of his life.

THE FORMATIVE YEARS

Sho'aiyan's first experience as an activist took place, he recollects, during the premiership of General Haj Ali Razmara (1901–51; premier, June 1950–March 1951). Mostafa must have been fifteen when he 'was drawn to politics,' joining the

Pan-Iranists, an alliance founded as a loose group in 1941. In 1951, Pan-Iranist members Mohsen Pezeshkpour (1927–2011) and Dariush Forouhar (1928–98) founded the Iranian Nation Party Based on Pan-Iranist Principles (*Hezb-e Mellat-e Iran bar bonyad-e Pan-Iranism*). The Party contained three cliques: one was royalist while the other two were pro-Mosaddeq and anti-imperialist. Disagreements soon forced the Party into a split, with Forouhar leading the Iranian Nation Party and Pezeshkpour and others founding the Pan-Iranist Party.[10] In any case Sho'aiyan 'became a member of the Pan-Iranist Organisation under the flag of Mehrdadiyun' (OLM 52). He refers to the pro-Mosaddeq faction within the Pan-Iranist Party, led by Mohammad Mehrdad (d. 2005), known as the *Parchamdaran* (literally the 'flag-bearers'). Sho'aiyan parted ways with the Pan-Iranists after the popular uprising of 21 July 1952 that forced the Shah to reinstall Mosaddeq as premier (SOLI 13; OLM 52). But this was not because his professed 'chauvinistic attitudes' had diminished. On the contrary, he reflects sardonically, 'Later, with a few class-mates and neighbourhood friends, we organised a circle whose slogan, as we offered it in absolute humility, was "Iran Above All"!' (OLM 52). At this time, he attended Tehran Industrial Secondary School, was a top student, and worked night shifts to support himself (SOLI 11).

The 1953 CIA–MI6-engineered coup overthrew the demo-cratically elected nationalist government of Premier Mosaddeq and smashed the dreams of a nation for democratic self-govern-ance. This was when Sho'aiyan began his self-didactic process—a mode of existence that he steadfastly continued until his last day. This is also when he began leaning toward Marxism. As he sarcastically recollects, 'My becoming a Marxist was truly extraordinary! How glorious is our modesty, we who become Marxists—and a pure Marxist, too, one who [suddenly] enjoys a thorough grasp of [Marx's] philosophy and philosophical contributions in a lived fashion—without even reading one of Marx's writings!' (OLM 52). 'In any case, I also acquired this humble character of immediately regarding myself a knowledge-able and full-fledged Marxist' (OLM 52). In the post-coup years, young Sho'aiyan found his way to Mesgarabad Cemetery in the south-east outskirts of Tehran where he spent extended periods of time alone writing poetry, short stories, and reflecting.[11] Over a decade later, in an exchange with his former comrade Marzieh Ahmadi Oskui (1945–74), Sho'aiyan recollects:

> I have frequented for years, even the most fertile (*ruyande-htarin*) periods of my life, in the cemeteries and especially in the 'silent expanse of Mesgarabad' in sorrow… But my dear, I am not 'buried' in Mesgarabad. The events of social life pushed me to Mesgarabad to bury me there. On the shoulder of my legs, my dead body fell upon Mesgarabad. But behold the magic of dialectic: Mesgarabad hurled me out of its tombs alive.[12]

The years between 1951 and his admission to university consti-tuted his key formative experiences. Everything he wrote and the activities in which he partook acquired many shapes and forms later, but they can all be traced back to his support for the National Front, living through the post-1953 years, witnessing the failure of the Tudeh Party (which neither effectively supported Mosaddeq nor mobilised the Party's Officers' Organisation against the coup), and of course, his choosing Marxism.

Simultaneous with his newly acquired Marxist worldview, in 1958 Sho'aiyan was admitted to Tehran Technology Institute to study welding engineering; originally known as the Higher Technical Academy (est. 1929), it was renamed the University of Science and Technology in 1972. Attending the university provided Mostafa with the fertile ground for thinking and activism. He found like-minded friends on campus, some of whom he bonded with through long-lasting camaraderie. They were affected by the experience of the oil nationalisation movement and the coup. These friends included Ali Golesorkhi, Siavush Sami'i, Anushirvan Bojnurd, Sirus Niknafas, Nasrin Sadri, and, notably, Behzad Nabavi and Parviz Sadri (1943–d. unknown) who joined Mostafa in the late 1960s to create an underground militant group.[13] The trials through which these friendships were forged and polished primarily involved participating in protest action over various student grievances as well as street protests at several important occasions: these protests bore an 'educational' character in that they always involved the raising of political awareness.[14]

Now in his mid-twenties, attending the university and involved in the student movement, Sho'aiyan became associated with a small circle of disillusioned members of the Tudeh Party who had set themselves the task of critiquing the policies and politics of their former party. This circle was reportedly founded on 7 December 1956 (16 Azar 1335),[15] on the anniversary of Iran's Student Day (*Ruz-e Daneshju*), the day that commemorates the student protest against then US Vice President Richard Nixon's official visit to Iran, just four months after the 1953 coup. The protest at Tehran University left three students dead and many injured when troops raided the campus. The circle emerged when remaining members of a small Tudeh splinter group called Hajjar and several disillusioned Tudeh members converged following the total eradication of the Tudeh Party cells, including the underground Officers' Organisation (containing 600 officers) by 1954. The circle called itself Jaryan—Persian for 'process' (literally, 'current'). It was an intentionally informal designation, signifying a reading and analysis circle, as Jaryan did not regard itself as a political party, although in its early communiqués the group, actually calling itself Jaryan, had ambitiously regarded itself as the nucleus of a future communist party, aiming at creating an organisation fit for activism under Iran's police state.[16] Having joined Jaryan a few years later, Sho'aiyan contradicts this claim, stating that 'since we had no particular designation, in our conversations we referred to ourselves as *"jaryan."* Obviously, our name [the name of this group] was not "Jaryan"!' (SOLI 23, n. 3). The heart and soul of Jaryan, and the writer of its hallmark analytical treatises, was a former Tudeh revolutionary officer, Mahmoud Tavakkoli (1927–2007). Other associates included Ali Akbar Akbari, Houshang Keshavarz Sadr, and Massoud Rahmani; prominent writer Mohammad Ali Farzaneh and eminent sociologist Amir Hossein Aryanpour are also said to have been connected with this group.[17] Tavakkoli had lived a turbulent life: born in Rudbar in the Caspian Gilan Province, he attended military school and later military college. He had not yet finished the four-year college program when Reza Shah abdicated and he joined the Tudeh Party. He joined the leftist officers supporting the Soviet-backed Autonomous Azerbaijan Government (*Azerbaijan Melli Hokumati*; November 1945–December 1946), and after its downfall as a result of the Soviets' withdrawal from the Azerbaijani territories (following their pact with the Iranian government), Tavakkoli was among the nine officers who crossed the border into Iraq in April 1947, seeking asylum. He spent three years in Iraqi prisons where he further developed his initial disappointment with the Soviets' opportunistic attitude toward Azerbaijan—a maverick and rather 'forbidden' thought at the time. He and his comrades were extradited to Iran in 1950 and processed by a military trial, but, because Tavakkoli was technically a military student and not a ranking officer at the time of

8

his defection, the military court dismissed the charges against him and he was released. He joined the now semi-clandestine Tudeh Party, this time as a civilian, but because of his criticism of the Soviet Union and unwavering support for Mosaddeq and the oil nationalisation movement, which contradicted Party policy at the time, he was expelled from Tudeh. He offered extensive and compelling analyses of the Tudeh Party (1959) and the oil nationalisation movement (1961). Jaryan continued as a loose intellectual circle until 1966 when it entered a hiatus, only to be dissolved in 1968. In the late 1950s, Tavakkoli received a Ph.D. in psychology and was given a part-time teaching position at Tehran Technology Institute where the engineering student Mostafa attended his classes on social psychology.[18] According to Sho'aiyan, he became associated with Jaryan in the spring of 1961 (OLM 52). Later in life, Tavakkoli began to develop schizophrenia, living out the last decades of his life in isolation in his family house in Andisheh Street in Tehran.

In light of his lived experience of the oil nationalisa-tion movement, and his youthful, heightened nationalistic sentiments, and witnessing the coup first-hand, Sho'aiyan's association with Tavakkoli and Jaryan deeply influenced his thinking in the years to come. The author of critical analyses about the Tudeh Party,[19] Tavakkoli enabled young Sho'aiyan to see that there were ways of thinking through Marxist theory other than those sanctioned (and imposed) by Soviet social-ism and thereby the Tudeh-style leftism. Sho'aiyan has been credited for having co-authored this work with Tavakkoli,[20] but he categorically denies this, specifying in his letter to Mazdak (his publisher in Europe, run by Chaqueri) that Tavakkoli was the sole author of all Jaryan literature.[21] When viewing Jaryan's critique of Soviet socialism, we should note that the Sino-Soviet split had not yet fully developed, and, while China was undergoing the rapid building of socialism, it had not yet emerged as an influential pole contesting the Soviet monopoly of world socialism. Put succinctly, the split emerged as the People's Republic of China regarded the process of de-Stalinisation in the Soviet Union, initiated by Nikita Khrushchev in 1956, as a deviation from Marxist orthodoxy. The disagreements only developed when the Soviet Union increasingly turned toward 'peaceful coexistence' in its foreign policy, in the eyes of Chairman Mao Zedong a heretical compromise with imperialism. Cults of personality and leader worship contributed immensely to the split. At this time, however, the phenomenon known as Titoism—à la Josip Broz Tito (1892–1980)—had already been around since 1948, when Yugoslavia was expelled from the Soviet-led Communist Information Bureau (Cominform). The positions of the Tudeh splinter group known as the Third Force (*Niru-ye Sevvom*), led by Khalil Maleki (1901–69), resonated with this phenomenon.

Maleki had studied chemistry in Germany where he met Marxist intellectual Taqi Erani (1903–40). He returned to Iran without finishing his degree.[22] Later in 1937, he was arrested along with a group of socialist intellectuals known as Group of 53 that included Erani, who died in prison. Maleki and his comrades were freed after the abdication of Reza Shah. He hesitated for a year before joining the Tudeh Party. Upon joining, though, he aligned himself with the Party's 'Reformist Wing,' became the head of the Party's Provincial Committee in Azerbaijan, and grew intensely critical of the Tudeh's policy toward the Soviets and Azerbaijan. After the collapse of the Autonomous Azerbaijan Government, he led the famous split from the Tudeh in January 1948 (along with Jalal Al-Ahmad and Eprim Eshaq). When Mosaddeq came to power, in May 1951, Maleki and Mozaffar Baqa'i, a National Front founder, formed the Iranian Nation's Toilers' Party (*Hezb-e Zahmatkeshan-e Mellat-e Iran*). The Toilers' Party supported Dr Mosaddeq. But in October 1952 Baqa'i (making a U-turn against Mosaddeq) split from the Toilers' Party, and Maleki and his friends continued under the Third Force Party, publishing *Niru-ye Sevvom* (*The Third Force*; 1952–3). The Third Force Party grew modestly and unwaveringly supported Mosaddeq. The coup put Maleki in jail in 1953.[23] Upon his release, he published *Nabard-e Zandegi* (*Life's Combat*; 1955–6) and then *Elm va Zendegi* (*Science and Life*; 1959–60), propagating his Third Force ideas. In 1957, after serving another prison term, Maleki founded the Socialist League of the Nationalist Movement of Iran (*Jame'eh-ye Sosiyalistha-ye Nehzat-e Melli-ye Iran*). In 1960, he returned to politics, with the Socialist League being a critical part of the Second and Third National Fronts. At this time, Maleki published his views anonymously in the Socialist League journal *Sosiyalism*, published in Europe (editor, Amir Pishdad).[24] He was arrested in 1965 for 'planning to overthrow the regime of constitutional monarchy.'[25]

Maleki offered a theory of humanist, democratic socialism, independent from the Soviet hegemony.[26] But Tavakkoli and Jaryan, who were uncompromisingly critical of the Tudeh Party, also clearly distanced themselves from Maleki's ideas, and their critical stance against the Tudeh was inspired neither by Titoism nor by Maoism and the Sino-Soviet split. This might explain why Sho'aiyan did not choose from the existing strands of Marxism—Soviet Union, Maoism, Titoism—that to varying and changing extents dominated the world at the time and influenced Iranian Marxists. Having joined Jaryan, Sho'aiyan began to develop a maverick way of thinking from this point onward, thanks to navigating intellectually through the flickering nuances of non-doctrinal Marxism in Iran.

SOUL-SEARCHING IN THE 1960s

This book pursues an *intellectual biography* of Sho'aiyan in the context of modern Iranian political development and intellectual history. I must therefore pause on a key existential moment in Mostafa's life: between 1958 and 1962 he was an engineering student at Tehran Technology Institute and engaged in student protests and activities, and by 1961 he had joined Jaryan (OLM 52) and met Tavakkoli. At this point in time, history also provided a nourishing context, a third element in the alchemy of Sho'aiyan's thought: between 1960 and 1961, the suffocating, post-coup political atmosphere was somewhat relaxed.

Having secured his grip on power and eradicated the opposition, the Shah now needed to launch his ambitious national developmental plans in order to catch up with the economic expansion of the commercial and industrial bourgeoisie, a process delayed by the occupation of the Allies, the oil nationalisation movement, and the resistance of the old and obstinate landowning class. The Shah's proposed reforms primarily concerned building infrastructures and institutions for the state-owned corporations that would then feed the Iranian capitalist class through subcontracts and regulated private expansion of manufacturing sector. For such grand plans, the Shah faced funding shortages, and to remedy that he approached the United States and the World Bank for loans. The Kennedy administration sanctioned the loans pending structural reforms. Not trusting the Shah to carry out the reforms, however, the ruling Democratic Party in the United States pushed for the premiership of Dr Ali Amini, Iran's ambassador to Washington. The Shah initially refused, and, paradoxically, that led to a fragile 'controlled freedom' that rejuvenated the country for three years.[27] Political parties (except for the outlawed Tudeh Party) were allowed to run for the Twentieth

Majles (Parliament) elections in 1960. These included the two 'rival' state-sponsored parties (*Hezb-e Melliyun,* or Nationalists' Party led by Manouchehr Eqbal, and *Hezb-e Mardom,* or People's Party led by Asadollah Alam), as well as the Second National Front.[28] The latter was formed in haste in July 1960 by and out of the individuals and parties associated with the original National Front, and thus it lacked a clear political strategy or platform. Election irregularities caused public outcries and legal actions against the government. The Shah dismissed two successive loyal premiers (Eqbal and Ja'far Sharif Emami) in response to public concerns before acceding to the premiership of Amini—the Americans' favorite. Amini convinced the Shah to dissolve the Majles in favor of new elections and exile General Bakhtiar, the notorious head of SAVAK (*Sazman-e Ettela'at va Aminyyat-e Keshvar;* National Intelligence and Security Organisation; est. 1957). Furthermore, Amini started negotiating with the Second National Front and introduced land reform. In 1962, disagreements over the military expenditure, however, led to Amini's dismissal by the Shah, who had now assured the United States that he was capable of carrying out the promised reforms. Amini had already prepared the groundwork for land reform, which the Shah took over, and upon the ratification of the Majles and a referendum (26 January 1963) he implemented his six-point 'White Revolution.' As the reforms began to restructure the country's economy, the short-lived period of political renewal came to an end as epitomised by the crackdown on the clerical opposition to the reforms—in particular, Ayatollah Khomeini's opposition to land reform and women's suffrage—in June 1963. Opposition leaders were once again arrested, tried, and sentenced to prison terms.[29]

These three elements—Sho'aiyan's experience of Mosaddeq's National Front in his youth, his association with Tavakkoli during his university years, and his activism in relation to the Second National Front—*originally* cultivated the particular thinker that Mostafa became later when a fourth element of revolutionary, liberatory theory, redefined his thinking by the late 1960s. The student movement regenerated with the relative opening of the political field and the formation of the Second National Front (*Jebheh-ye Melli-ye Dovvom*) in 1960 and the Student Organisation of the National Front (*Sazman-e Daneshjui-ye Jebheh-ye Melli*) emerged as the umbrella organisation that contained student activists of different ideological and political inclinations. At this time, as Sho'aiyan's comrade Behzad Nabavi recalls, 'in the campaigns of this period, although Mostafa held Marxist inclinations, he did not show them and was better known as a nationalist figure who felt close to nationalist and religious forces.'[30] Sho'aiyan was a leading figure among the radical students who intended to challenge the moderate leadership of the Second National Front at its First Congress (25 December 1962–1 January 1963). Another leading student leader was Bizhan Jazani, an original theorist of armed struggle in 1965 and an indirect founding figure of the future *Cherikha-ye Fadai-ye Khalq*, People's Fadai Guerrillas (PFG), created in 1971, while Jazani was in prison, by his followers and another group of student activists.[31] Since the politically conservative leadership of the Second National Front did not recognise a student organisation under the Front's rubric, student activists created the Organisation of Tehran University Students-Followers of National Front (*Sazman-e Daneshjuyan-e Daneshgah-e Tehran vabasteh beh Jebheh-ye Melli*) and published *Payam-e Daneshju* (Student Courier) under Jazani's editorship and management. 'Although Bizhan [Jazani] was not a member of the University Committee, he was one of the leading few in directing the tasks and making decisions… There were three main cliques: that of Jazani, that of Mostafa Sho'aiyan, and the clique of Iranian Nation Party.'[32] Founded in 1960 and published until 1965, *Payam-e Daneshju* was the publication of this student body. Jazani held various key roles for the organ, and Hassan Habibi, Houshang Keshavarz Sadr, Hedayatollah Matin Daftari, Majid Ahsan, Mansur Sorush, and Nabavi were involved in its publication and distribution.[33]

The students wanted to utilise this unique political opportunity to push for what they regarded as key demands: reviving oil nationalisation, pushing the government to leave CENTO (Central Treaty Organisation, aka Baghdad Pact, formed in 1955 by Iran, Iraq, Pakistan, Turkey, and the United Kingdom), and demanding free elections and land reform. In this context, Sho'aiyan and Jazani met several times between 1962 and 1964. The student activists also deliberated several times on how to proceed with creating a student caucus in the upcoming Second National Front Congress. Sho'aiyan was a delegate of students of Tehran Technology Institute and Tehran Polytechnic, but he ran as an independent. Alarmed by the student presence, the conservative leadership of the Second National Front disqualified Jazani and his comrades from Congress participation. As an independent, however, Sho'aiyan did manage to participate in the Congress, but he found the atmosphere dominating the Congress so apprehensive of police infiltration that the leadership banned the delegates from voicing what were regarded as subversive ideas.[34]

Meanwhile, though, Sho'aiyan and Sadri were present outside the student movement as well. One 'Top Secret' security document (dated March 1963) reports that Sho'aiyan and Sadri had attended meetings of the Socialist League in which many known dissident figures associated with the group, including Maleki and Al Ahmad, were also present.[35]

With the failure of the Second National Front (1960–64) and then the Third National Front (1965–6) to effect any meaningful change and the return of dictatorship after the June 1963 crackdown, the then invisible embryo of a new generation of activism began to take shape. Already in 1961, due to disagreements with the leadership of the Second National Front, Mehdi Bazargan, Yadollah Sahabi, and Ayatollah Mahmoud Taleqani had broken away, forming the Liberation Movement of Iran (*Nehzat-e Azadi-ye Iran*).[36] The Liberation Movement brought together liberal-leaning religious figures formerly associated with the National Front who were distinct in their politics compared to the dominant clerical opposition to the Shah. In particular, the Liberation Movement figures emphasised freedom and social justice. The high school and university students who had participated in the National Front and the Liberation Movement at this time and witnessed the political opening and repression of 1960–63 were radicalised. Many of them, including future members of one of the two founding groups of the PFG, had become political activists at this time. These are the activists who later envisioned, theorised, founded, and manned the urban guerrilla groups of the 1970s. In his last statements in his defense at the military court, Bazargan had prophetically anticipated the emergence of a generation of rebellious young men and women that would redefine Iranian political life in the 1970s: 'We are the last to have struggled politically through the constitutional means. We expect the judge to convey this point to his superiors...'[37]

But we must now step back and revisit Sho'aiyan's activism and association with Jaryan, which did not serve him well in the eyes of the leftist activists of the time. Tavakkoli and Jaryan were called 'American Marxists' (OLM 52)—a label that stuck in the collective memory of the militant Left in the 1970s and was later used to discredit Sho'aiyan's theoretical contributions (see Chapters 2 and 3).[38] It was during his association with Jaryan and after Tavakkoli wrote and distributed his *What Is*

To Be Done? (1961) that Sho'aiyan emerged as an analyst.[39] As early as 1960, Sho'aiyan began using several pen-names for his writings: Yoldash (comrade in Azeri), Sarbaz (soldier), Rafiq (comrade in Persian), Serteq (stubborn), Sorkh (Red), Doost (friend), Timar (care). Later in the 1970s, he was identified by his comrades as *rafiq Sorkh*, the Red Comrade (or Comrade Red). By this time, Sho'aiyan had already been the (unpublished) writer of poetry and fiction.[40] He had also taught himself to draw, having left behind several sketches. But it was at this historic moment that the theoretician was born: in the months preceding the National Front Congress, Sho'aiyan wrote his first political treatise: *Nasl-e Javan va Jebheh-ye Melli* (The Younger Generation and the National Front), signed by Sarbaz and dedicated to the first Congress of the Second National Front (see Chapter 2). The Congress did not allow a reading of this treatise, fearing its radical ideas. The treatise, however, was copied and distributed among students and some leaders of the National Front.[41]

During these years, Sho'aiyan had forged strong friendships with like-minded students at the Institute, namely Sadri and Nabavi, with whom he created an underground cell in the second half of the 1960s. They were involved, along with other students such as Hossein Sadri (Parviz's younger brother), in student protests inside and outside the university, although not always in the front row of the action. Security reports from this time regarded Sho'aiyan as a ringleader of the student protests.[42] Meanwhile, Mostafa graduated with a master's degree in welding engineering as the top student in the Class of 1962, which qualified him for a state scholarship to the University of Oklahoma, USA—an offer he refused for obvious reasons.[43] In the context of the return of dictatorship after June 1962, upon graduation he had to work for the government (for a certain period of time) as a way of repaying the free university education he had received. He was assigned a teaching position at the Industrial Secondary School (*Honarestan-e San'ati*) in the town of Kashan. In this traditional and religious town, he felt isolated: his heart lay in Tehran and with the projects, not to mention his comrades, he had left behind. Almost immediately after moving to Kashan, he began challenging the uncompromising bureaucracy for his transfer to Tehran, writing numerous letters to the Ministry of Culture. He asked his medical friends to provide him with the medical documentation confirming his 'depression' and that he needed to be close to his family.[44]

This teaching position kept him in isolation, away from the centre of action, and it was most likely the handiwork of SAVAK to informally exile Mostafa. He may have felt cursed at being stuck in the provinces, but Kashan sheltered Mostafa from the growing intrusion of SAVAK into the lives of activists who were identified in the period 1960–3, many of whom were arrested, interrogated, and/or imprisoned after 1963. Feeling isolated in Kashan did not diminish Sho'aiyan's zeal for reflecting on post-crackdown conditions, offering strategies to counter dictatorship and being involved in activism. Inadvertently, Kashan provided him with the time to read and educate himself. Viewing the new situation from afar gave him a bird's-eye view. Being away from Tehran also helped Mostafa cut out the unnecessary contacts he had accumulated during the past years, contacts that under the new police conditions could potentially expose him further to Iranian intelligence. Sho'aiyan maintained his contacts with his select comrades from his student years at the Institute, above all Parviz Sadri. The two met regularly, at least once a month, discussing new ways of reviving the movement. From out of these discussions, according to Hossein Sadri, the seeds of Sho'aiyan's 'negative resistance' strategy were planted.[45] In the absence of any viable option for popular mobilisation, he wrote 'A Thesis for Mobilisation' and implemented it, advocating an economic boycott of the regime's financial institutions as a way of revitalising the nationalist movement (see Chapter 2).

As a result of his endless barrage of letters to all official levels, he finally managed to push the reluctant bureaucracy to transfer him to Tehran in 1966, where he mostly taught history and social sciences in various secondary schools for the next two years (SOLI 11–12). Although he had monitored the political climate unceasingly, Sho'aiyan returned to a different Tehran. Disorganised, disoriented, and failing to win Dr Mosaddeq's endorsement, by 1964 the Second National Front had disintegrated. Avoiding the mistakes of its predecessor, the Third National Front was formed in the spring of 1965 through the convergence of the Liberation Movement, Socialist League, Iranian Nation Party, and Iranian People's Party, but shortly after, the security forces arrested a number of leading figures of these parties, thus effectively terminating the Third National Front. Indicative of the regime's tightening grip on the opposition, the imprisonment of the leading political figures and intermittent debriefings of (and threats to) many other activists by SAVAK had now forced the majority of dissident activists and intellectuals either to turn to the cultural venues and literary and intellectual magazines to express their ideas or rethink their future move toward creating clandestine groups that aimed at initiating the only option remaining to achieve democratic rights and meaningful political participation: armed struggle. In Sho'aiyan's case, these two alternatives were not mutually exclusive. On the contrary, he cleverly used the former as a means of contributing to the latter.

Many of the intellectuals and writers associated with the past movements gathered around the influential intellectual magazines of the 1960s, often short-lived or with changing editorship.

These included: *Ketab-e Hafteh* (Weekly Book; editor, Ahmad Shamlou), *Ketab-e Mah* (Monthly Book; editor, Jalal Al Ahmad), *Andisheh va Honar* (Thought and Art; editor, Nasser Vosuqi), *Jahan-e Naw* (The New World; editor, Reza Barahani, then Amin Alifard), and *Arash* (editor, Sirus Tahbaz, then Eslam Kazemieh). Aside from the latest literary works from all over the world and from Iran, these magazines offered translations of the ideas, observations, and theories pertaining to the Cold War, non-Soviet socialism, and national liberation movements. The works of Jean-Paul Sartre, Aimé Césaire, Milovan Djilas, Isaac Deutscher, Frantz Fanon, Michel Foucault, and Antonio Gramsci, among others, appeared in Persian in their pages. Personally knowing many intellectuals and writers of these magazines, Sho'aiyan received many ideas from them, while publishing his own articles and poems in the pages of these magazines—*Jahan-e Naw* in particular. These ideas, as I shall show later, re-emerged in his works.

Sho'aiyan was also among those activists who began rethinking the future strategy of Iran's liberation movement, a project halted by the 1953 coup. The ambition of revitalising the movement in 1960–3 was conclusively lost in the aftermath of the Shah's heavy-handed crackdown on peaceful opposition and protests. Strategically, repression was rather unnecessary and unwise on the Shah's part; it showed his conviction that he was divinely chosen to rule the country and take it on the path to the Great Civilisation. For this to happen, he needed to monopolise Iran's future development, a phenomenon I have called 'repressive development' that characterises Iran's economic and political modernisation in the 1960s.[46] But in order to understand the turning point in the 1960s, attending to this generation's perceived *hope* is important. The crackdown, *primarily* aimed at the constitutionalist Second National Front and the outspoken but still peaceful clerical opposition (before Ayatollah Khomeini rose to prominence) that had positioned itself not against the Shah at this time but against land reform, women's suffrage and the legal exemption of citizens of foreign states residing in Iran (Vienna Convention on Diplomatic Relations, April 1961, known as *capitulations*), abusively extended to all foreign nationals. The 1963 crackdown irrefutably proved that all avenues for peaceful and legal change had been blocked, just as prophesied in Bazargan's defense statements quoted earlier.

Thus, the 1960s turned out to be a decade of militant experiments by various activists from different shades of the political spectrum. For two major reasons, these 'experiments' proved unsustainable and were thus short-lived. The most significant cases (and their key operational dates) included the cell from the Maoist splinter group from Tudeh called Revolutionary Organisation of the Tudeh Party of Iran (ROTPI) (1964–5), the Qashqai uprising (1965–6), Islamic Nations Party (early 1960s), and Association of Allied Islamic Societies (1965). The ROTPI cell had entered Iran to instigate a peasants' uprising, a tactic similar to Maoist-instigated uprising among the Qashqai tribe. Following Mao's doctrine of 'surrounding the cities from the countryside,' the idea of a peasant uprising indicated ROTPI's illusions about the realities of rural Iran or its tribal culture. The Islamic Nations Party consisted of militant Muslims inspired by revolutionary Algeria and Latin America, but it lacked any notion of secret organisation: its members were arrested en masse before ever seeing action. The Association of Allied Islamic Societies consisted of traditional Muslims for whom resistance meant assassination: members of this group killed Premier Hossein Ali Mansur on 20 January 1965, which brought about the demise of the group.[47] Of notable significance, however, was the 1968 Kurdish uprising, an event largely ignored by historians, which mobilised hundreds, even thousands, and led to the militarisation of Kurdistan for months.[48] These attempts failed to generate a living, dynamic, and nationwide *grassroots* support movement because, first, in some cases their actions largely involved inapplicable duplication of other revolutionary movements due to the differences between Iran and other countries where these actions originally took place, and secondly, these groups were detached from the student movement. The Kurdish case, however, must be treated with greater care in this regard, but it falls outside the focus of this study. The first factor behind the failure of these groups (duplicating revolutionary blueprints), of course, can be blamed on their leaders. The second factor, however, involved a demographic shift: between the early 1960s, on the one hand, and the late 1960s–early 1970s (the heyday of the urban guerrilla movement in Iran) on the other, the student population had grown exponentially: as the country embarked upon the Shah's ambitious developmental plans, the need for training specialists to man the newly created economic and administrative sectors had dramatically increased. Thus, new higher education institutes and universities emerged: the post-secondary student population alone grew more than tenfold between 1953 and 1977.[49]

By 1965, the activists had come to terms with their new repressive reality. Inspired by the revolutionary movements in Vietnam, Algeria, and Latin America, as well as a liberationist reading of Islam, by 1964, several young members of the Liberation Movement of Iran—chief among them Mohammad Hanifnezhad, Said Mohsen, and Abdol Reza Nikbin (his name was later replaced with Ali Asghar Badi'zadegan)—had reached the conclusion that militant action against the regime was in order. They became founders of the Organisation of Iranian People's Mojahedin (OIPM; *Sazman-e Mojahdin-e Khalq-e Iran*), a group that launched guerrilla operations in August 1971, only after it was heavily raided by the police.[50] The group had spent the 1960s recruiting and acquiring weapons, funds, and supplies clandestinely and without attracting attention. It was also preoccupied with ideological training, an arduous task that involved reconciling specific radical readings of the Shi'i tradition with modern revolutionary ideas, especially Marxism. As it turned out, the melange of Shi'i teachings and Marxist-oriented revolutionary action (the 1960s-style) was not as easy as Mojahedin's original founders had envisioned: the group went through a coup-like split in 1975 in which a Marxist faction that dominated its leadership (known as the 'central cadre', or CC) tried to confiscate the organisation and committed acts of murder in its attempt to purge Muslim comrades. Despite that, when OIPM re-emerged following the 1979 Revolution, it became the most popular political group nationwide outside the groups and parties associated with the post-revolutionary state. But then a questionable armed uprising by OIPM in 1981, in response to the state's continued repressive measures, led to its bloody repression by the Islamic Republic, causing the death of thousands of its members and supporters up to 1988. Between 1979 and 1981, as OIPM and its organisations were growing fast, the group and its members were continuously attacked by pro-regime thugs and cadres of revolutionary *komiteh* (post-revolutionary, state paramilitary, later to be organised into the Revolutionary Guards Corps). In addition, the new regime had alienated OIPM when the group's leader Massoud Rajavi was banned from running for the Constituent Assembly, and the Iranian Revolutionary Court arrested OIPM member Mohammad Reza Sa'adati, charged him with carrying out espionage for the Soviet Union, and sentenced him to ten years, only to summarily execute him after the June 1981 uprising.[51]

Back in the 1960s, sensing the imminent repression of all opposition by the regime, in March 1963 Jazani, Manouchehr

Kalantari, Dr Heshmatollah Shahrzad, and Kiumars Izadi created the core circle in Tehran that later grew into Group One, as Jazani later called it, one of the two formative groups of the People's Fadai Guerrillas (PFG, later renamed the Organisation of Iranian People's Fadai Guerrillas, or OIPFG; or Fadaiyan, the plural of 'fadai') that instigated full-fledged urban guerrilla warfare in Iran. After the arrest of Jazani and his comrades in 1968 (fourteen members in total), the group's surviving members attacked the gendarmerie post in the village of Siahkal in the Caspian province of Gilan in February 1971. It was a small but daring operation that finally broke the myth of the invincibility of the regime and became the epic founding moment of the urban guerrilla movement. In 1970–1, the surviving members of Group One joined a group of younger revolutionaries from Mashhad, Tabriz, Sari, and Tehran—to establish the PFG. Massoud Ahmadzadeh, Amir Parviz Puyan, and Abbas Meftahi were the founding figures of this group. Known as Group Two, it contained university students who were half a generation younger than members of Group One, and unlike most members of Group One who had lived between the 1953 coup and the 1960–3 opening and crackdown, the shared formative experience of Group Two members went back to 1960–3 and various religious groups. They were influenced by the Latin American revolutionary literature,[52] as particularly evident in the momentous treatise of Ahmadzadeh, *Armed Struggle: Both Strategy and Tactic* (1970)—a book that became the manifesto of Fadaiyan in their initial couple of years. Therefore, in retrospect, the PFG is widely deemed to have been influenced by Latin American revolutionary theory—that of Ernesto Che Guevara, Carlos Marighella, and the Tupamaros of Uruguay (*Movimiento de Liberación Nacional-Tupamaros*, or MLN-T).[53] This observation is not incorrect, but it suffers from a parallactic vision, and accordingly it partially eclipses the truth that—while inspired by the heroic resistance of the Vietnamese against American imperialism, the triumphant Algerian war of liberation led by *Front de Liberation National* (FLN), Cuban Revolution, and Latin American movements—the turn toward armed struggle in Iran was actually rooted in this generation's experience of repression and its yearning for freedom, dignity, and meaningful political participation. Urban guerrilla warfare gained widespread momentum among world revolutionaries after Che Guevara's death in Bolivia in October 1967: it achieved increasing popularity after the international revolutionary year of 1968 and with the spread of the New Left,[54] crystallising in Marighella's 1969 *Minimanual of the Urban Guerrilla*. Less known is that the idea behind urban guerrilla warfare and the first experiments in this regard go back to 1962 when the National Liberation Army (*Ejército de Liberación Nacional,* or ELN) was founded in Peru by militants from various ideological inclinations and theorised by Héctor Béjar.[55] It is frequently mentioned that Che Guevara's *Guerrilla Warfare* was first translated by the National Front activists in Germany and published in *Iran-e Azad* (1963 and 1964).[56] This translation later ended up in the hands of Ahmadzadeh and Puyan in Mashhad and influenced them.[57] What is usually ignored, however, is that by 1963 Jazani and his comrades had already reached the conclusion as to the inevitability of guerrilla warfare. Their decision *precedes* their exposure to the Latin American revolutionary theory. This is why they originally decided to organise *both* urban and mountain teams. By 1967, Jazani and Hassan Zia Zarifi had already authored a treatise about their new strategy, summarising the earlier debates within the group.[58] Thus, one cannot easily attribute Jazani's turn to militantism to the influence of Latin American revolutionary literature and movements. Having observed the success of the Algerian experience, I argue, Jazani and Zia Zarifi had come up with the idea on 'their own,' if one can split hairs here. In this, we must recognise them as originators.[59]

Also original was Sho'aiyan. He, too, had reached the conclusion, by 1964, that breaking the suffocating silence imposed by dictatorship required militant action. And while influenced by the revolutionary movements of his time, he, too, had arrived at the idea on 'his own.' He was destined to cross paths in the 1970s with both Fadaiyan and Mojahedin. That is why, while associating himself with Tavakkoli and later with the intellectual magazines of the time, he inevitably had to part ways with them, but maintain his public presence until the right moment. His turn to militant action became decisive after his economic boycott strategy fell on the deaf ears of the leading clerics. It was then that he realised, as Mosaddeq had already cleverly anticipated, that there was no potential for such strategies for popular mobilisation. The crackdown of the opposition only confirmed his intuition (see Chapter 2). So, along with friends from the Institute, Sadri and Nabavi in particular, Sho'aiyan took part in the key events of the late 1960s. They engaged in, or guided, student protests. Hossein Sadri often functioned as a liaison between Parviz and Mostafa and the student activists from Tehran Technology Institute and adjacent universities, in particular in the school year of 1966–7.[60] Meanwhile, two important events took place. The leader of Iran's oil nationalisation movement Dr Mosaddeq died on 5 March 1967 at the age of eighty-four in his family estate in Ahmadabad where he had been under house arrest since 1956 (following a three-year prison term). The state did not allow a funeral to be held for him, but Sho'aiyan had been present at Mosaddeq's residence on 10 March along with key figures of the National Front and other dissidents.[61] On the occasion of the fortieth day of the National Front leader's passing, Sho'aiyan praised Mosaddeq in a piece that was published only after the 1979 Revolution. This article ends with a shocking warning: 'Tremble, you hangman (*dezhkhim*), a terrifying future awaits you!'[62] In January 1968, members of Sho'aiyan's circle actively participated in the funeral mass rally for world wrestling champion Gholam Reza Takhti (1930–68) who, it was said, had committed suicide at the peak of his career, but was widely believed to have been murdered by SAVAK. In the political climate when no public protest was tolerated, dissident activists turned Takhti's funeral processions and memorials into protest rallies. In particular, the student movement exploited the rallies to turn the mass mourning into protests against the regime.[63]

Nabavi graduated in 1964 and Sadri in 1965, so the group could not have formed until the two had completed their mandatory military service—that is, until 1967. While his comrades were busy in their uniforms, Sho'aiyan took several 'exploratory' trips to the provinces to witness first-hand the conditions in Iran's countryside after the land reform. Aside from teaching, Mostafa had joined Social Studies and Research Institute (*Mo'asseseh-ye Motale'at va Tahqiqat-e Ejtema'i*) as a part-time researcher. Annexed to the University of Tehran, the Institute was founded in 1958 by Dr Ehsan Naraghi (1926–2012), a former Tudeh supporter who had renounced communism after working for UNESCO early in his career. The Institute funded two trips for Sho'aiyan—to Kerman in the autumn of 1966 and Shiraz in the summer of 1967.[64] Mostafa's long-time comrade Asghar Monajemi, also took him on a trip to Khuzestan in the summer of 1968.[65] As evidenced by his diaries, he returned from these trips with the assessment of an Iran that was suffocated and corrupt, a country whose people lived in undignified conditions.

It was in 1967 that Sadri returned from military service with the idea of setting up a metalwork shop. The shop served as a rendezvous hub for his comrades, and, as it began to attract the attention of Iranian security, Sadri shut it down and sought employment in the industry and in teaching. Later in 1967, however, with the financial support of his brother-in-law Ali Golesorkhi, a former National Front activist and an engineer, Sadri created a metal casting shop (his engineering degree was in metal casting) in southern Tehran. Using his contacts in the industry, Golersorkhi facilitated orders for industrial fittings, clamps, and clips. The shop ran for about a year before it was shut down due to financial losses.[66] But in that period it had already served its secret purpose. Of course, the idea behind this enterprise was not entirely Sadri's own. The two engineers, Sho'aiyan and Sadri, were thinking about the logistics of prolonged guerrilla warfare. During the time it operated, the shop produced hundreds of pieces that, when assembled, became cup-like grenade shells.[67] These shells reappear twice in the subsequent history of Sho'aiyan's activities. Golesorkhi was not privy to this idea, of course, but in retrospect he reminisces that Parviz's project 'contained this pretty mischief [producing grenade shells] in it. He must have started [the metal casting shop] with this purpose and this idea and plan from the very beginning.'[68]

All the while, as the plans for creating a clandestine, armed cell were slowly and cautiously underway, Sho'aiyan gradually emerged in the intellectual venues with a public persona of the critical and non-doctrinal Left. Among the venues with which he associated, as mentioned, was the Left-leaning cultural-intellectual magazine, *Jahan-e Naw* (The New World). The magazine was originally published in 1944 under the management and editorship of Hossein Hejazi, until it ceased publication after the coup, in 1954. It was relaunched in 1964, when the then sixty-five-year-old Hejazi invited poet and literary critic Reza Barahani to take over its editorship. As a monthly magazine left to the vision of Barahani, it emerged as recognisably dissident-critical, promoting national liberation and postcolonial ideas as well as criticisms of the Soviet bloc socialism. Until its publication stopped in 1971, *Jahan-e Naw* featured the works of such international figures as Boris Pasternak, Franz Kafka, Aimé Césaire, Friedrich Nietzsche, Michel Foucault, Martin Heidegger, Isaac Deutscher, Oswald Spengler, Karl Jaspers, Paul Valéry, Allen Ginsberg, Fidel Castro, Jacques Prévert, James Baldwin, Pablo Neruda, C. Wright Mills, Virginia Woolf, Jaroslav Hašek, Mao Zedong, Ho Chi Minh, Léopold Senghor, and Martin Luther King Jr—to name but a few. The Iranian intellectuals associated with *Jahan-e Naw* included Jalal Al Ahmad, Manouchehr Hezarkhani, Dariush Ashuri, Mostafa Rahimi, Nader Naderpur, Ahmad Ashraf, Yadollah Royai, Heshmat Jazani, Goli Taraqi, Samad Behrangi, Esmail Khoi, Mahnaz Afkhami (later Minister of Women's Affairs, 1976–8), Homa Nateq, Baqer Parham, and Morteza Saqebfar—again just to name a few. Within a year, Barahani was removed from the magazine and replaced by Amin Alifard. But the journal continued in more or less the same style.[69] *Jahan-e Naw* represents the most prominent example of the dissident-intellectual magazines that reflect the cosmopolitan ambiance of Iran's intellectual life in the 1960s. Other such magazines—*Ketab-e Hafteh, Arash,* and the short-lived *Ketab-e Mah*—also brought together the concerns of Iran's writers and intellectuals with those present in the international scene. Sho'aiyan's intellectual and theoretical development took place within this atmosphere: as an avid reader and an unassuming, perpetual learner, Sho'aiyan read and absorbed many of the ideas published in these magazines as well as the underground literature such as the translation of Che Guevara's *Guerrilla Warfare,* and from this cosmopolitan culture he emerged as an internationalist revolutionary theoretician. He published two articles and a poem in *Jahan-e Naw*—enough to register him publicly as a published author. His poem, clearly political, reads:

Interrogation
– ......
– ......
– that the night is dark
    – but...
  – that have fallen from the branches
  yellow leaves, in silence.
    – but...

– what will you say now?
– I'll still say
   – but...
– I'll still say
  – but...[70]

His association with *Jahan-e Naw*, in particular, turned out to be productive in more than one way: it allowed him to recruit several university students for his armed, underground group (Chapter 3).

Aside from his public engagement, Sho'aiyan had researched the Jangali movement during the late 1960s. The result was his voluminous historical-analytical study of the peasant-based liberation movement—known as the Jangali movement—led by a former junior Shi'i cleric, Mirza Kuchek Khan (1880–1921) in the Caspian Gilan Province. The movement was a response to the failure of the Constitutional Revolution (1906–11) to bring about social justice—in this particular case, land redistribution. It led to the establishment of the short-lived Gilan Republic or the Soviet Socialist Republic of Iran, 1920–1. Kuchek Khan's movement was defeated as the state, weakened in the post-constitutionalist years, gradually asserted its rule over the country. Colonel Reza Khan, who founded the Pahlavi dynasty in 1926, suppressed the movement conclusively. But perhaps an equally important factor in the Jangali movement's defeat was the role of the young Soviet Union as it withdrew its support for the Gilan revolutionaries upon making concessions with the British and Iranians (SURMJ vi–vii). This latter point—what Sho'aiyan called the 'betrayal' of Lenin and the revolutionary Soviet Union— became a key factor in Sho'aiyan's analysis, appropriately captured by the book's title, *A Review of the Relations Between the Soviet Union and the Revolutionary Movement of Jungle*. The book was printed in 1968 but SAVAK agents seized and destroyed all copies. A few surviving unbound copies, however, allowed for the book's publication some years later by Edition Mazdak, and a pirated edition was also published in Tehran after 1979. In the context of Sho'aiyan's preparation for militant action and his association with the intellectual magazines of the time, this research turned out to have contained a formative theoretical epiphany for Mostafa, as he clearly points out that the roots of his ground-breaking treatise, *Rebellion* (*Shuresh*)—later renamed *Revolution* (*Enqelab*) after the author's third revision—go back to *A Review*. 'Before writing [my] *Jungle and the Soviet [Union]* what appears in *Revolution* was only a faint and scattered cloud of the disorganised and crude ideas in this author's mind,' Sho'aiyan reflects. 'Alongside *Jungle and the Soviet [Union]*, the scattered cloud of these inceptive ideas slowly became condensed. And after the conclusion of the *Jungle* story, these clouds began precipitating' (Rev 9).

It is important to heed the fact that Sho'aiyan did indeed regard himself as a writer of the Left and missed no safe chance to propagate his ideas—those that were banned. He notes that in the late 1960s he secretly sent two of his articles to Hassan

Habibi, the National Front Director in Europe for publication. These articles were delivered to Europe by his friend Mr Mofidian, who was terminally ill, on his way to London for cancer treatment. Upon returning to Iran, Mofidian passed away, leaving no trace of anything ever having been sent. But instead of publishing the articles, Sho'aiyan observes, the National Front began probing the identity of its author, and allegedly it eventually exposed Sho'aiyan ('Exposing' in SW i).[71] This claim cannot be substantiated.

At home, while emerging onto the public scene as an analyst and writer, however marginally, Sho'aiyan remained steadfast to his earlier vision of fighting against the regime. He refused, in other words, to remain either a professional theoretician or a pure practitioner. Thus, he began a dual life: one of public presence and enjoying his contacts with personal friends and acquaintances from different backgrounds and ideological inclinations (and thus to some extent under the surveillance of SAVAK), the other of the secret organiser of a clandestine group. Security reports from 1969 and 1970 indicate him attending the meetings of the Socialist League of the Nationalist Movement of Iran, about which SAVAK was very sensitive.[72] In fact, Sho'aiyan's close friend Monajemi provided him with many opportunities to meet in person with some of the prominent (dissident) intellectuals of the country in 1968 and 1969. Through Monajemi, Sho'aiyan met Maleki, Al Ahmad, Gholam Hossein Sa'edi, Manouchehr Hezarkhani, and Dariush Ashuri. Mostafa attended Maleki's funeral and memorial in July 1969, exposing himself once again to SAVAK. Also important was Sho'aiyan's trip to Asalem in Gilan, along with Monajemi, to meet Al Ahmad, a visit that likewise did not escape security surveillance.[73] This is where Sho'aiyan's famous picture with Al Ahmad was taken by Monajemi. One of Iran's most outstanding dissidents, an essayist and author, Al Ahmad died shortly after this meeting. He was forty-six.

From this point onwards, circa 1969, Sho'aiyan's life enters a period of intense activity. His joint endeavor with Sadri to produce hundreds of grenade shells as a part of their logistics for long-term urban guerrilla warfare qualifies Sho'aiyan and Sadri, by 1967, as pioneers of the armed struggle in Iran. Their attempt is obviously independent and different from Jazani's well-organised and strategic plan for mountain and urban guerrilla teams since 1965, a careful plan suspended temporarily but not fully exposed upon the arrest of Jazani and several of his comrades in January 1967. In 1968, though, Sho'aiyan and his comrades Sadri and Nabavi formed an underground cell with the clear intention of challenging the regime militantly; it was based on the principle of partitioned units, with each of the three leading their own sous-cells independently.[74] I mentioned 1968 as the year of 'foundation' of the group, but attaching a date to the group's formation is somewhat illusive: we must think of the group's foundation as a process, both intellectually and activity-wise, undertaken by close friends who had experienced the turbulent trials of the 1960s. In any case, what is unique about this group is that, unlike the political groups before and after it, this cell was *not* ideologically homogeneous. Sho'aiyan and Sadri were self-declared Marxists while Nabavi was a devout Muslim. The group's composition reveals Sho'aiyan's 'frontal thinking,' a theoretical legacy he had brought with him from his memory and experience of Dr Mosaddeq's National Front, except this time the unifying factor was the *praxis* of armed struggle against the regime. While a Marxist, Sho'aiyan was on good terms with the Muslim militants from the early 1960s who later became the cadres of OIPM.[75] Until 1970, Sho'aiyan, Sadri, and Nabavi still held paid jobs and were engaged in open activities—in Sho'aiyan's case, publishing articles and attending academic and public lectures, aside from his teaching position at Naziabad Technical Secondary School[76] and the research he conducted mostly at the Social Studies and Research Institute. Nabavi reminisces that the group was called the National Democratic Front (*Jebheh-ye Demokratik-e Melli*), but this claim is not correct.[77] In his writings Sho'aiyan never gives any designation for this group, and nor does he mention the name of his subsequent group. What is known of this group's activities is that Sadri had made efforts to recruit high school students,[78] as the group had resolved to recruit young activists unknown to the police (unlike the three of them) to protect its security. Nabavi had recruited a cell consisting of three individuals from Isfahan headed by Reza Asgariyeh (also a Muslim). Sho'aiyan made many contacts with the young activists, the most notable one being the young Karamat Daneshian who later made national headlines in 1973–4 when he was sentenced to death by the military court for allegedly planning to kidnap the royal family. It is not known if Daneshian was involved in any of Mostafa's plans, particularly his idea to sabotage oil plants in Khuzestan Province, where Daneshian spent some time as a teacher (see Chapter 3). In any case, film-maker and director Reza Allamehzadeh, who was also charged in this case, rejects the kidnapping plan.[79] The whole case, of course, was an elaborate SAVAK sting, aimed at the liberal reformers headed by Reza Qotbi, supported by Empress Farah and intended to expose and discredit the intellectuals for having subversive ideas. Qotbi and the Empress (they are cousins) had tried to accommodate the dissident intellectuals through various grants and publication and employment opportunities in order to keep them away from radical activities. SAVAK, on the other hand, engaged in a powerplay against the liberal-minded reformists within the ruling elite, headed by Qotbi, to prove, primarily to the Shah, that dissident intellectuals were not to

34

be trusted. SAVAK had rounded up twelve poets, intellectuals, and film-makers, some entirely unrelated to each other, and charged them with the kidnapping of the royal family. In any case, the courageous defense statements of Daneshian and the poet Khosrow Golesorkhi who attacked the regime on the only televised military court proceedings at the time, brought them death sentences and turned them into the martyrs of the new generation of activists (see Rev 199–200).[80]

On 8 February 1971, five armed militants attacked the Siahkal gendarmerie post in the Caspian province of Gilan. Calling their group the 'Armed Revolutionary Movement of Iran'[81] in their tract, they were members of a nine-man guerrilla 'Mountain Team' (*tim-e kuh*) stationed in the mountainous jungles of Gilan and a support network known as the 'Urban Team' (*tim-e shahr*)— mostly survivors of the militant network that Jazani and Zia Zarifi had founded before their arrest in 1968. In response, the state militarised the entire region and deployed the Gilan Gendarmerie Regiment, along with police forces and helicopters, to suppress just a handful of militants. The Commander of National Gendarmerie, Lieutenant General Oveysi, was placed in charge of the operation and the Shah's brother, Gholam Reza Pahlavi, supervised the counter-insurgency operation. Within days two militants had been killed, and others and their comrades from the Urban Team arrested and put through an expedited military trial that sentenced them to death; thirteen guerrillas were shot on 16 March 1971 (one received a life sentence). The 'Siahkal Resurrection' (*Rastakhiz-e Siahkal*), as the activists soon named the brazen attack, immediately emerged as the foundational moment for the guerrilla movement in Iran.[82] The Siahkal attack catalysed the formation of urban guerrilla cells that fashioned themselves after the Fadai Guerrillas' appealing melange of selflessness, elusiveness, and resoluteness—qualities that galvanised an entire generation of student activists into forming militant groups as a generational response to the authoritarian state.

Sho'aiyan's group, already set upon this path, was no exception. By 1972, Mostafa had left his teaching position to dedicate himself to his group (SOLI 14). He left his family home and moved into a residence provided by Asghar Monajemi, living a semi-clandestine life.[83] Sho'aiyan's group reached a turning point when Reza Asgariyeh proposed an ambitious plan for sabotaging the state-owned Isfahan steel plant—built by the Soviet Union (at the time fully operational but not yet finished). Asgariyeh was an engineer with the rank of lieutenant who worked at the plant as a part of his military service and lived in Isfahan where he was in charge of a partitioned cell under Nabavi, containing two other individuals known as Marami and Davudi. As incredibly naive as it sounds, the group decided to proceed with this fanciful plan. According to Asgariyeh, the idea was fed to him unknowingly by SAVAK through Davudi, and neither was he in it, nor did he believe it was practical. Reportedly, Sho'aiyan became very enthusiastic about the plan and apparently pushed it through.[84] In retrospect, Sho'aiyan scorns the plan, calling it a 'quasi-coup': to disable the major infrastructure of the country as a substitute for the armed struggle the Fadai Guerrillas had founded. The plan was to blow up the water coolants for the furnaces so that the smelters would melt as a result of overheating (Rev 209 n. 3; 211–12, n. 4). But shortly after, Asgariyeh fled to Tehran, reporting that the plan had been exposed (Rev 211–12, n. 4).[85] This caused an infuriated Sho'aiyan to go into hiding (SOLI 14; SOLF 34) after Nabavi was arrested on 24 July 1972. Sadri, who already had gone into hiding by the winter of 1971 (through another incident that had exposed him), was no longer in sight.[86] The affair blew four years of clandestine preparations and outraged Mostafa. Sho'aiyan accused Asgariyeh, who surrendered himself to the authorities, of exposing the group, calling him a 'masterpiece of betrayal' (Rev 10). Decades later, however, Asgariyeh claimed that his turning himself in was out of desperation and lack of support, and SAVAK had known everything about the plan already.[87] In any case, the plan exposed members of the group, and, as a point of no return, it pushed Sho'aiyan's life in new directions. He was soon to become one of Iran's most wanted men.[88]

THE DECISIVE YEARS

In retrospect, Sho'aiyan's group in the early 1970s was a dress rehearsal for his later activities. While his earliest attempt—producing grenade shells along with Sadri—may be deemed as a logistical-preparatory step for armed struggle, his ideologically eclectic 'front' (1968–72) containing activists from the early 1960s shows an attempt at launching armed operations. Yet attested to by the fact that the group did not carry out any operations during its existence and instead focused on recruiting clearly shows that it lacked the necessary dynamic for such a demanding feat as armed struggle.

While increasingly engaged in the all-consuming life of an underground activist, Sho'aiyan nonetheless remained steadfast with his research and writing. How he managed to reconcile the two—living a clandestine life and becoming arguably Iran's most prolific writer of the Left—remains baffling. It suggests an untameable intellect, infinitely curious and unwaveringly committed. As we shall see in subsequent chapters, the reception of his ideas was precarious at best due to his maverick theoretical positions, complex prose, and strange political alliances with the militant Muslims. As such, just as he had tried to have his writings published in Europe in the late 1960s, so in 1972 he sent a copy of *A Review* and the first version of *Shuresh* to the Socialist League in Europe, through Asghar Monajemi, 'a friend who was very kind to this author' (Rev 10; see also OLM 51).[89] According to Monajemi, what he delivered to Dr Amir Pishdad, Director of the Socialist League in Europe, was a copy of the Jangali book that was printed but not bound, and a typed copy of *Shuresh* that only contained an annotated table of contents and some introductory remarks—nothing publishable at all.[90] This first attempt soon brought him into contact, via a third party, with Chaqueri who published, through Edition Mazdak, Mostafa's writings anonymously until his death, when Chaqueri published (in 1975 and 1976) all of Sho'aiyan's writings he had received, this time with his name indicated. Although Mostafa's loyal comrades published a number of his writings after the 1979 Revolution, it was the publication of Sho'aiyan's works in the mid-1970s that rescued Sho'aiyan from total oblivion and saved his works for posterity.

After the failure of the Isfahan operation in 1972, Sho'aiyan was sheltered by Mojahedin. According to one of Mostafa's comrades, he was very close to Mojahedin, to the extent that he had detailed knowledge about their activities.[91] While in the company of *Mojahedin-e Khalq*, he masterminded the prison escape of Reza Reza`i, the group's leader at the time (SOLI 23, n. 2).[92] The plan was successful, and a key player in it was the very young brother of his comrade Nader Shayegan (see below).[93] After Reza`i's escape, Sho'aiyan assisted him in rebuilding the OIPM network that was severely damaged following the August 1971 security raids through which some seventy members or supporters of the OIPM were captured. Sho'aiyan also wrote articles for Mojahedin's radio program broadcast from Iraq ('Some Hasty Glances' in SW 1). Sho'aiyan was so close to Mojahedin that, while the group was engaged in a life-or-death battle with the security forces, he is said to have written the introduction to the OIPM's *An Analysis of Hossein's Movement* (circa 1971) and a (June 1973) communiqué.[94] He also supplied Mojahedin with the grenade shells and some funds from his group that were buried on the outskirts of Tehran.[95] This attitude—cooperating with a Muslim group—indicates Sho'aiyan's advocacy for creating a unified front of revolutionary militants that included Mojahedin, Fadaiyan, and other militant groups regardless of their ideological positions. As we shall see later, his 'frontal thinking,' while pragmatic and organisational, is indeed based on his specific conception of politics, which is not without its problems.

Sho'aiyan's presence within Mojahedin, as it turned out some years later, was not without controversy. In 1975, a faction within the OIPM whose members had secretly developed Marxist ideas since the early 1970s staged a 'coup' within the organisation. Led by Taqi Shahram, Bahram Aram, and Vahid Afrakhteh, they killed their comrade and one of the leaders of the group, Majid Sharif Vaqefi, a devout Muslim who was resisting the Marxist takeover, and tried to assassinate Morteza Samadiyeh Labbaf (escaping the assassination attempt, he was injured, captured, and later executed by the regime).[96] Not surprisingly, the incident had an enormous, negative impact on militant Muslims such as Nabavi who had believed that collaboration between Muslims and Marxists was a viable proposition. After the bloody Marxist takeover of the OIPM, Nabavi and many others like him were radicalised, now strictly adhering to the principle of working with Muslim activists only. Notably radicalised was Mohammad Ali Raja'i (1933–81), a key OIPM member, who leaned toward traditional Islam in prison and became a follower of Ayatollah Khomeini after the Marxist takeover.[97] A former member of the Liberation Movement of Iran in the 1960s who had served a prison term, Raja'i had joined the OIPM in the late 1960s. He was arrested in 1974 and remained in prison until the 1979

Revolution. After the Revolution, he assumed many official positions including member of the Cultural Revolution Council (tasked with 'cleansing' Iranian universities from western influence and purging dissident students and professors), Member of Parliament, Prime Minister, Minister of Foreign Affairs, Minister of Education, and Second President of Iran (2–30 August 1981). Having replaced the deposed President Abolhassan Banisadr, Raja`i was assassinated in his office, along with Prime Minister Mohammad Javad Bahonar and other officials, by his former Mojahedin comrades as they staged an armed uprising against the state in June 1981. Back to our story: in the interrogation records of a captured OIPM member Sho'aiyan is mentioned as one of the individuals who, while working with Reza`i to rebuild the OIPM network, had met with, influenced, and accelerated Shahram's turn to Marxism, and thus Sho'aiyan was implicated in the horrendous actions of Shahram and his comrades, actions for which he was clearly not responsible.[98] Sho'aiyan's encounter with Shahram was by chance and took place under difficult conditions, and in any case his 'frontal thinking' would not support such activity and intrigue. Nabavi, his long-time comrade, also denies any such association, and asserts that Sho'aiyan was not some kind of ideologue who would try and 'convert' others to Marxism; in fact, during his long association with Sho'aiyan, Nabavi recalls that Sho'aiyan was never interested in ideological debates with his Muslim comrades.[99]

Sho'a'iyan had probably met Nader Shayegan Shamasbi (1945–73; henceforth Shayegan) by the winter of 1973. Shayegan was a student activist in the 1960s who had formed a circle with his friends from their military service. His father, a Tudeh sympathiser, had divorced his mother and married Fatemeh Sa'idi, Shayegan's stepmother, but had subsequently divorced her, too. Shayegan had chosen to live with his stepmother and his young stepbrothers (Abolhassan, Arzhang, and Nasser, at this time thirteen, ten, and seven years old respectively). The middle-aged mother and her three youngsters were destined to be involved in Iran's most celebrated and prosecuted armed group, the PFG (see Chapter 3). Bizhan Farhang Azad, Abdollah Anduri, and Hassan Rumina were the other members of Shayegan's circle. Shayegan had visited Germany in 1969 and contacted the directors of the Confederation of the Iranian Students-National Union (CISNU), but returned to Iran upon his friends' suggestion to avoid being identified by SAVAK agents among student activists. It was in early 1973 that, after his former group's disintegration in the summer of 1972, Sho'aiyan and Shayegan began organising a new underground group. It was called the People's Democratic Front (*Jebheh-ye Demokratik-e Khalq*, or PDF) and based on the two partitioned teams that they each individually commanded.[100] Although the group did not externally use this designation in its brief presence, the group's designation has been selected to reflect its 'frontal' character.[101] The first team was mostly made of Shayegan's comrades, while the second team consisted of Sho'aiyan's recruits from the Literary Corps Institute at Mamazan (30 km outside Tehran). These included three women, Sediqeh Serafat, Marzieh Ahmadi Oskui, and Saba Bizhanzadeh. In Serafat's recollection, 'In our relationships, Mostafa occupied the role of our leader and commander and we were the soldiers and apprentices. He was underground and armed, a writer and a theoretician. We were university students who lived a normal life.'[102] The PDF soon engaged in logistical activities, setting up a chemical lab in which they produced picric acid, an explosive used to fill the grenade shells.[103] Unlike Sho'aiyan's former group with his old comrades, the People's Democratic Front was an unmistakably militant group fashioned after the Fadai Guerrillas but with one major difference: Sho'aiyan was the theoretical mind behind the group, and his theory was notice-ably anti-Leninist—a sacrilegious stance in the eyes of Marxist militants of this time—although this feature had no impact on the group's planned activities. Also, contrary to its designation as a 'front,' the group's members identified themselves as Marxists. Moreover, the stamp of the Cuban-style Tricontinentalism on the thoughts of Sho'aiyan and Shayegan was clear: in his book *Shuresh* (*Rebellion*), which he regarded as the guiding theory of the PDF, Sho'aiyan had advocated an internationalist liberation movement with Iran being its first trench to capture. Shayegan, too, had reportedly stated, 'After the revolution in Iran, we will stage revolutions in other countries.'[104] For Sho'aiyan, this was the time of heightened theoretical elaboration on his concept of the front. His essays, 'A New Threshold' (January 1973; in SW) and 'Half-a-Step on the Way: The People's Liberation Front' (March 1973; HSW) indicate his hopes for the formation of a militant front against the regime.

The group's inner life, however, was permeated by expectations and discontent. Most notable was Oskui's constant critique posed against Mostafa about the PDF's lack of engagement in action. Her dissatisfaction with the group's progress, in the aftermath of the security raids against the group in the spring of 1973, paved the way for the survivors of the group to join the Fadai Guerrillas (see below and Chapter 3).[105]

Security surveillance on one of the group's side-cells led the police to Shayegan (SOLF 43–4). Unbeknownst to PDF mem-bers, SAVAK had identified those associated with Nader and his team (namely, Farhang Azad, Serafat, Rumina, and Anduri). In May 1973, following Anduri's arrest, the PDF's 'chemical lab' was raided by Iranian security. In the shootouts that ensued around this time, Shayegan, Rumina, and Nader Ata'i were killed and ten members arrested. Once again, Sho'aiyan just managed to escape and his team (Sa'idi, her three children, Oskui, and Bizhanzadeh), as well as its adjacent team, remained intact.[106] But, once again, Sho'aiyan's group was exposed and broken up before it could carry out any operation, and with it Sho'aiyan's dream of creating a militant 'front' was lost. In his reflections, Sho'aiyan attributes the raid to Anduri's weakness under police interrogation; in fact, he attributes Shayegan's death to Anduri's revealing his rendezvous with him (Rev 212, n. 5).[107] After the Revolution, a letter from 'the comrades of Mostafa Sho'aiyan' was sent to Chaqueri, stating that Sho'aiyan had made an error of judgment about Anduri's role in exposing the group, and that Shayegan was identified to the security forces by another person.[108]

The life of an underground militant living and acting in a police state reveals that indeed, in the cogent words of Serafat, 'the distance between a martyr and a traitor is thinner than a strand of hair.'[109]

In the security raids on the secret base of the PDF the police found Marxist literature along with the publications of Mojahedin. This is where the term 'Islamic Marxists' (*Marksist-e Eslami*) originated[110]—one that was invented by SAVAK and through state propaganda became a key phrase in the political terminology of the decade.

Meanwhile, Sho'aiyan kept writing. He worked on revisions to *Rebellion*, which by this time he had renamed *Revolution*. Oskui was a poet and writer of fiction. Her posthumous book, *Memoirs of a Comrade*, contains her careful observations, seasoned with the prose of fiction, about the dire conditions of the working poor in Iran.[111] Unpublished exchanges at this time, and following the group's collapse (acquired by this author), include Sho'aiyan's reflections on Oskui's short story as well as his writing on his own poem and those of his comrades Oskui and Gh. Farhang Forutan (Abbas) in the manner of literary criticism.[112]

With the surviving teams in desperate need of cover, the remaining individuals from the PDF joined the PFG in June 1973. According to Sho'aiyan, the decision had already been made when Shayegan was still alive and Oskui was instrumental in arriving at it. Sho'aiyan reports that Shayegan did not believe in unification with Fadaiyan (SOLI 40–1). The PFG's expedited sheltering of the PDF members indicates that they had been aware of the PDF's decision to join. According to Sho'aiyan, he had proposed a condition for his joining: that he would be able to circulate his *Revolution* and frontal ideas in the Fadaiyan's ranks, which, he states, the PFG leadership had already accepted (SOLI 42). But the circumstances imposed its own logic and Sho'aiyan's condition was practically suspended (SOLI 42). If such was indeed the case, it sounds rather strange, or opportunistic for that matter, since the PFG clearly identified themselves as a Marxist-Leninist organisation and thus unreceptive to Sho'aiyan's devastating critique of Leninism. In fact, (nominal) adherence to Marxism-Leninism was a requirement for joining Fadaiyan. Obviously, there are no Fadai documents to corroborate the above observation. We only have certain facts to decipher in this case.

Sho'aiyan was no stranger to the Fadai Guerrillas. He personally knew the PFG co-founder, Amir Parviz Puyan, and had conversations with him about his critique of the Soviet Union even before the foundation of the PFG (OLM 85–6, n. 13). Puyan was associated with Social Studies and Research Institute.[113] Hossein Sadri reports his conversation with Sho'aiyan, circa June 1971, in which Mostafa reported his meeting with Puyan and the latter's asking him to join his group, the PFG.[114] A veteran activist with a finger on the pulse of a generation's rebellion against its authoritarian rulers, Sho'aiyan closely followed the works that later grew into the theoretical pillars of the PFG. He had defended Puyan's famous pamphlet, *The Necessity of Armed Struggle and the*

Refutation of the Theory of Survival—a pamphlet credited with attracting a new generation of student activists to armed struggle—against its critics, even before he discovered the identity of its author.[115] He also wrote a critique of Ahmadzadeh's *Armed Struggle: Both Strategy and Tactic* (1970) when he received it as a manuscript, not yet distributed, and without knowing the identity of its author. Dated June 1971, Sho'aiyan's critique reproaches the treatise for its 'sloppy' (*nadarchideh*) defense of armed struggle— a new path opened by the militants of 'Siahkal-Tehran.'[116]

While Sho'aiyan joined Fadaiyan on the (loosely agreed) condition that his *Revolution* would be debated by Fadai members, the PFG under the leadership of Hamid Ashraf (1946–76), Iran's most wanted man, intended to absorb the competent militants of the PDF. From the start it became clear to Sho'aiyan that Fadaiyan would not entertain his anti-Leninist treatise, although they did indeed honor their loose agreement with Mostafa by assigning Hamid Momeni (1952–76) to debate him (see Chapters 3, 4, and 6). In any case, Sho'aiyan, Fatemeh Sa'idi, and her two younger children, Nasser and Arzhang, were assigned to Ali Akbar Ja'fari, the PFG's second-in-command and the commander of the Mashhad branch (SOLI 15). While they were deployed to Mashhad, Abolhassan, the eldest son of Sa'idi, along with Oskui and Bizhanzadeh stayed in Tehran. While in Mashhad, Sho'aiyan kept working on his writing. He engaged in a sharp, at times bitter, exchange with Momeni, Fadaiyan's mid-career theorist. Mostafa's association with Fadaiyan convinced him about the Stalinist tendencies within the Fadai organisation (see Chapters 3 and 4). The eight letters he wrote (and preserved) to Fadaiyan (SOLI, SOLF)[117] about the way he was treated by them and his position regarding such treatment left no doubt that his being sheltered by the PFG would be only short-lived. Nevertheless, Sho'aiyan had a specific impact on Fadaiyan in more than one way: for one thing, the first issue of PFG journal *Nabard-e Khalq* (The People's Combat) was published in the winter of 1973, although Sho'aiyan expressly states that he was not tasked with publishing it. At this time, though, two Fadai members were assigned to produce grenade shells under the cover of a household appliances repair shop, a plan that must have come from Sho'aiyan's past experiments. After a copy of *Nabard-e Khalq* went missing, Ja'fari ordered the shop to be evacuated. While transporting the shells to the outskirts of the city (where they would be buried for future use), the two members were arrested.[118]

In the chain of events following their arrest, Sa'idi was arrested on 14 February 1974 (SOLI 119) in Mashhad during a risky and badly managed retrieval task assigned to her by Ja'fari. Her arrest infuriated Sho'aiyan who interpreted the whole affair as an indication of Fadaiyan's discriminatory treatment against him and those associated with him. At this time, Sho'aiyan was working on the last version of *Revolution*, but with her arrest he quickly had to retrieve his notes and leave the secret base (OLM 82, n. 6). Following a few meetings with Ashraf and Ja'fari, Sho'aiyan sensed a mendacious attitude on the part of the Fadai leaders. Their relationship quickly turned sour. In fact, it became so hostile that rumours of a Fadaiyan plan to assassinate Sho'aiyan, although completely baseless, began to circulate among some activists at the time.[119] Having been asked to leave the sons of Sa'idi in Fadaiyan custody, Sho'aiyan left Fadaiyan on 7 March 1974, after Ashraf failed to show up for their rendezvous (SOLI 119).

THE LONESOME GUERRILLA

This was the end of organised, collective activism for Sho'aiyan. From this point on there began the arduous life of a lonesome guerrilla, one of Iran's most wanted men. Having lost organisational cover and resources, from now on he had to rely on the support of his many friends and comrades—friends whose love and dedication for him remain legendary, if quiet and unassuming. These friends put themselves at great risk to shelter him, assist with his research and writing, and smuggle his writings to Europe. His poems from this period clearly reflect the depth of isolation he experienced:

> Look now,
> the desert of my heart is the garden of life!
> (PFB 15; poem dated 1974)

After his departure from Fadaiyan, he had one last meeting with Ashraf in September 1974, a meeting arranged by Mojahedin, which he reluctantly attended, but this shows he was still in touch with OIPM and possibly supported by them, to some extent at least. The bitter conversation between the two, as he reports, brought him to the point of no return (SOLF 3–5). For almost the next two years, Sho'aiyan mostly stayed in the apartment provided by his friend Azam Heydarian and her husband Turaj who took some of his writings to Edition Mazdak in Europe. Most of his time was spent rewriting and editing his works, especially *Revolution*. In Europe, Heydarian typed up Mostafa's manuscripts that she had smuggled out of the country, while Sho'aiyan took refuge in her home in Tehran.[120] Most of these works were published by Mazdak. Worthy of particular mention is *Revolution*, which Mazdak published in the summer of 1976. This period proved to be a productive time in Mostafa's political career. While focusing rigorously on his writings, he did not hesitate to pay surprise visits to old friends and acquaintances.[121] At this time, thanks to the efforts of his dedicated friends, he had established two-way communication with Edition Mazdak in

Florence, sending it his writings and receiving some publications from Mazdak that were necessary for his research. He also wrote several short critical reflections on Fadaiyan (TCE) and further elaborated on his theory of the 'front' in subsequent writings. As usual, he lived meagerly and hermetically, a legacy of his harsh youth. When not sheltered in Heydarian's apartment (she had returned to Iran in October 1974), Sho'aiyan stayed in the home of Azam Vafai. She was a Fadai member who lived in a Fadaiyan secret base; this was apparently an unusual base frequented by others, including Sho'aiyan and Ashraf.[122] Obviously, though, this does not mean that Mostafa was once again in contact with the PFG.

Returning from Vafai's house to Heydarian's, at 7.40 a.m. on Thursday, 5 February 1976, Sho'aiyan was ordered to stop by a patrol officer, Constable Yunesi, in Estakhr Street in central Tehran. A single shot was fired but it is not clear who fired it: security documents report that it was Sho'aiyan who took a shot at the officer, while eyewitness accounts mention that the officer had taken a shot at him (and missed!).[123] The picture of his dead body, acquired after the Revolution, does not show a wound, and an eyewitness account reports no blood on his clothing.[124] What is clear is that Sho'aiyan's revolver had jammed and he committed suicide by swallowing his cyanide capsule. Although he was also armed with a grenade, it seems he refused to discharge it in this busy pedestrian area, and preferred to die without causing collateral damage.[125] His lifeless body was yanked away from the scene by frightened police officers, first taken to Sina (Avicenna) Hospital were Sho'aiyan was declared dead, and from there delivered to the Anti-Terrorism Joint Task Force prison in central Tehran and shown to his imprisoned comrades, including Nabavi, for identification.[126]

In its 7 February 1976 issue (p. 4), the daily newspaper *Ittila'at* headlined 'In a Shootout a Terrorist Was Killed' and stated in a two-sentence report: 'In the morning of the day before yesterday, police officers who intended to arrest a terrorist named Mostafa Sho'aiyan were shot at by him and the officers inevitably shot back at him. He subsequently was shot and taken to hospital but the doctors' efforts were fruitless and he passed away.' Mostafa was buried in Section 35 of Behesht-e Zahra Cemetery in the south of Tehran. When Sho'aiyan's mother passed away in 2004, she, too, was laid to rest in Mostafa's tomb, as her will had stipulated, reuniting her with her beloved son. This ultimately led to the revelation of a most curious phenomenon: Mr Monajemi reports from his conversation with Parvin, Mostafa's sister, that when they opened Mostafa's grave to place his mother's body with his, they found no human remains in it.[127]

This is how the country recorded the death of one of Iran's most wanted men and most prolific and original revolutionaries, the man who had once declared, 'Love perpetual becoming' (PFB 24), a motto by which he lived.

*

On 5 February 1980, four years after Sho'aiyan's death, the first public commemoration of Sho'aiyan was held at this gravesite in Section 35 of Behesht-e Zahra Cemetery. Tracts have been distributed about the event. Some of his closest comrades did not participate because of concerns about possible reprisal by other leftist groups.[128] In the end, however, about a dozen devoted comrades showed up. This is how Iran remembered one of its most original and maverick thinkers.

2

EXPERIENCES AND
EXPERIMENTS IN THE 1960S

Before our people Mosaddeq opened a path that
they will never forget.

Sho'aiyan, YGNF 29

Sho'aiyan's experiences and experiments in the 1960s
nourished his maverick theory of the *revolutionary front.*
Clearly, a key element in his formative experience was
the 1953 coup—a major setback imposed by American and
British imperialisms on the democratic aspirations of Iranians.
The slightly more relaxed political climate of 1960–3 cautiously
revived the Iranians' hope for the possibility of democratic
change through constitutional means. As a young Marxist
deeply influenced by the experience of the democratic-liber-
atory essence of the movement led by Dr Mosaddeq—crystallised, respectively, by Mosaddeq's demand that 'the Shah
must reign not rule' and the oil nationalisation movement—
Sho'aiyan hoped the relaxed political conditions of 1960 would
allow for the resurgence of that spirit through mobilisation

of the nation into resuming the drive toward liberation interrupted in 1953.

That hope, however, conclusively dissipated following the 1963 crackdown. Not surprisingly, like two other activists of his generation, namely Jazani and Zia Zarifi, the two major setbacks within a decade influenced Sho'aiyan's thought in myriad ways. His complex theories of the front and revolution originate with the life-altering decade of the 1960s—a decade of rapid modernisation, intellectual thriving, the advent of women and university students as growing forces in society, and the turn to armed struggle. It was in the 1960s, as Hamid Dabashi explains, that Iran's quintessential cosmopolitan intellectual and cultural life shone most brilliantly.[1] Sho'aiyan is the unconventional intellectual progeny of this time. He *belonged* to this time. In the revolutionary 1960s, to quote Fredric Jameson, 'for a time, everything was possible;... this period, in other words, was a moment of a universal liberation, a global unbinding of energy.'[2] Sho'aiyan's entire intellectual legacy—frontal thinking, revolutionary spirit, Tricontinentalism and internationalism, and ruthless but principled criticisms—sums up the gestalt of this decade, a revolution indeed in the world-system, as Immanuel Wallerstein argues.[3]

As an intellectual biography, this chapter analyses the *key, formative moments* in the 1960s that anticipated the internationalist revolutionary thinker Sho'aiyan became in the 1970s. Given the limitations of a book-length study of the writer of thousands of pages, I am forced to be selective, but I shall try to incorporate the necessary contexts of his works. It is important to register the intertextual connections between Sho'aiyan's thought within a specific turning point in Iranian modernity and the cosmopolitan character of modern Iranian thought at this time: this intertextuality reveals itself most vividly when the modern intellectuals insist on the moment of liberation.

DISOWNING THE TUDEH LEGACY

Given the historical background of the Tudeh Party's indecisiveness and thus inaction against the 1953 coup, it is not surprising that the revolutionary 1960s dawned on young Iranian communists through vivid and accentuated abandonment of Tudeh legacy. The Maoist ROTPI (a splinter from the Tudeh Party) as well as the Jazani–Zarifi group and later the Fadai Guerrillas stand out in the 1960s/1970s as militants who tried to redeem Iranian communism by disowning the Tudeh failure, thus surpassing it. They were more than willing to overlook the various contributions of the Tudeh to social and political organisation and discourses and focus on the Party's failure to stand up to the coup. Sho'aiyan was no exception. The detached armchair historian who supposedly views history 'objectively' may call this approach unscientific, irrational, and emotional, but history is actually nothing but layers of interpretation. Disowning the Tudeh legacy was thus the rite of passage for the generation of Fadaiyan that founded Iran's 'New Communist Movement'.

In his mid-twenties and impressed by Tavakkoli's criticism of the Tudeh Party, Sho'aiyan joined a circle named Jaryan in the late 1950s. But Tavakkoli was not the only self-declared Marxist to resist the Tudeh's ideological domination over the Iranian Left. Enjoying popular support, however, Tudeh leaders utilised every opportunity to advance their pro-Soviet agendas, using tabloid-style smear attacks against their critics and political rivals, including Premier Mosaddeq. There are many examples of this. Maleki and his comrades and supporters, although small in number and thus limited in their public reach, had also tasted generous doses of Tudeh smear campaigns when they split from the Party in 1946 after the Autonomous Azerbaijan Government fiasco.[4]

Mostafa's disavowal of his youthful Pan-Iranism and turn to Marxism by the mid-1950s took place in the context of a failed socialist party whose leadership, having fled to the bosom of the socialist fatherland, had deserted its massive following and left it to the mercy of the regime, having created a disheartening intellectual vacuum. In these unkindest of times, *two distinguishable attempts* were made to keep Iranian socialism afloat and retain its emancipatory edge: in embryonic ways, *older activists* like Maleki (and his followers) and Tavakkoli (and Jaryan) launched critical engagements with their Tudeh past to find a way out and forward, while the *younger activists* from the (Tudeh) Democrat Youth Organisation such as Jazani and his future comrade Abbas Surki (d. 1975) refuted the tradition to which they had once belonged and began, in rudimentary ways, to prepare, by the mid-1960s, for the armed struggle that launched Iran's New Communist Movement (*Jonbesh-e Novin-e Komonisti*; aka *khatt-e do*, the Second Line). This *generational gap* is important to note, for it registers the *changing modus operandi of Iranian socialists* in the aftermath of the most devastating defeat of the Iranian Left in the 1950s. In his early twenties, *Sho'aiyan joined the first stream* (Jaryan), *only to end up in the second*, and thus he intellectually bridged two increasingly alienated generations, showing that the two aforesaid attempts (as mentioned above, by older and younger activists) did not need to be mutually exclusive. He held the two diverging generational horizons together. History showed that as the older generation dissipated for one reason or another by the late 1960s, so the new generation embarked on its perilous journey toward the ultimate expression of liberation: armed struggle.

Disavowing the Tudeh legacy is originally traceable to Maleki and the Third Force (and the Socialist League later), as we already have seen (Chapter 1). Through the split from the Tudeh, Maleki emerged to resuscitate Iranian socialism in the form of a 'democratic socialism,' poised against 'totalitarian socialism' or Russian communism and its satellite parties.[5] From liberalism, Maleki extracts a certain democratic self-organisation.[6] Maleki dedicated his life to ascertain that a 'third way' between capitalist liberalism and Soviet communism was possible, and although he stands out for this approach, he produces an impasse. In posing socialism against communism in the post-World War Two context, Maleki surprisingly finds himself on a slippery slope: 'the conflict (*ekhtelaf*) between capitalism and Moscow communism is not as intense as the conflict between socialism and communism.'[7] This is why in 1956 he wishes in retrospect that Mosaddeq had done what Gamal Abdel Nasser had done in Egypt: abandoned 'wayward (*bibandobar*) liberal policies' and imposed 'discipline' by suppressing Egyptian communists.[8] Maleki wished Mosaddeq had suppressed Tudeh. This position is clearly unprincipled and shows that Maleki reads history backwards.

His version of democratic socialism—the Third Force—entailed a liberation trajectory that rendered his views postcolonial.[9] Maleki asserts in 1952 that the Tudeh Party stands as a docile puppet of the Soviet Union foreign policy in a bipolar world divided between Moscow and Washington and therefore is incapable of understanding the inner dynamics of *nehzat-e melli*—the nationalist movement.[10] Recall Stalin's initiative in 1947 to create Cominform, a pact between the socialist states in Eastern Europe to bring them under Soviet tutelage and push them into adopting domestic and foreign policies that would augment the international position of the socialist fatherland. Cominform was dissolved in 1956 after the de-Stalinisation process began under the leadership of Nikita Khrushchev. One should understand Tudeh's internal policies in this light: Tudeh had no intention of supporting the struggles of the Iranian people for self-assertion in the manner intended by Mosaddeq; rather, Tudeh primarily pushed Iranian politics against American imperialism such that it would sway Iran toward the Soviet Union. As early as February 1953—before the coup and after Tudeh's policy about-turn (now 'supporting' Mosaddeq)—Maleki blames Tudeh for neglecting its 'social responsibility' in promoting the nationalist movement. Had Tudeh performed, Maleki speculates, as a true agent of Iran's liberation movement, it would have been able to defeat the ruling class and render the liberal-nationalist leadership of Mosaddeq unnecessary, as Mao did in China.[11] While it is 'fortunate' that this did not happen,[12] Maleki still implicitly believes the Tudeh Party could have led the movement. This is a contradiction. Maleki regards Leninism—with which Iranians are (were) familiar—as 'Stalin's Leninism.'[13] In any case, even in finally supporting the nationalist movement, the Tudeh had ulterior motives: it regarded the movement as a strategic reservoir for the Soviet foothold in Iran.[14]

And yet, during the oil nationalisation movement, Maleki argues, the Tudeh policy was actually aligned with that of Britain. British imperialism insisted on identifying the National Front with Tudeh in order to persuade the United States to overthrow Mosaddeq, which is exactly what happened in 1953: after Tudeh's U-turn in supporting Mosaddeq by mid-1952, the United States was convinced about the danger of communism in Iran. All the while, Maleki charges, Tudeh was played by Britain in opposing the oil nationalisation movement and creating multiple crises for the Mosaddeq government.[15] In fact, according to Maleki, the greatest factor in the failure of the National Front was the Tudeh Party.[16]

Although Tavakkoli's criticism of the Tudeh Party was more or less contemporaneous with Maleki's, it was not until a decade later when Tavakkoli's engagements appeared on the Iranian intellectual scene, however marginally. His book *An Analysis of the Political Directions of the Tudeh Party of Iran* (1959) contains a long, polemical and unforgiving indictment of the Tudeh leaders, in particular a rejoinder to the Tudeh's analysis of its performance during the oil nationalisation movement. The book was never published in Iran, and although typed mimeographed copies of it circulated among the activists, it was only in 1975 that the original typeset book was published by Mazdak in Florence.[17] Calling Tudeh leadership 'stupid' and their actions 'criminal,'[18] Tavakkoli wishes to reintroduce Iranian Marxism to the national self-assertion movement—a task Tudeh had failed to recognise, let alone implement. Because of Tudeh's docility toward Soviet foreign policy, the party had led the Iranian workers' movement toward opposing the national liberation movement. Unlike Maleki, who sought an Iranian 'democratic socialism'—quite a refreshing approach regardless of its possible theoretical issues—Tavakkoli does not abandon Marxism; on the contrary, he wants the Marxists to join forces with the progressive elements of the national self-assertion movement.[19] From a historical point of view, Tavakkoli's proposed strategy involved *returning* to the experience of the Constitutional Revolution in which social democratic and workers' movements (in the Caucasus) played an important role in advancing constitutionalism and radicalising its objectives.[20] 'From its inception, Iran's workers' movement has always been the powerful and valuable friend and ally of our national-democratic movement.'[21] Therefore, 'We must disregard the Tudeh Party of Iran as an organisation corrupt and in decline.'[22] The Party has proved itself to be a petite bourgeois party without a working-class character and always looking toward a saviour.[23] Jaryan believed that Tudeh was not a 'true' Marxist party, despite its unwavering adherence to Marxism (albeit the Soviet version of it), and thus it diverted the working-class movement away from its true path.[24] The Tudeh Party was 'not a genuine workers' party, and 'it could not even function as a genuine national-democratic party within the revolutionary movement.'[25] In fact, Tudeh is Marxist only in its rhetoric, lacking the 'revolutionary essence of Marxism,' and definitely not a communist party.[26] Since Tudeh cannot be reformed, it is useless to embark on 'ideological struggle' against it.[27] Tavakkoli debunks Tudeh's call to Iranian activists to organise.[28] The struggle against colonialism and domestic reactionary classes will involve the strategic unity of proletarian and nationalist bourgeoisie forces, just as was the case with the Constitutional Revolution.[29] It is in this book that Tavakkoli frequently uses the word 'Tudehist,'[30] a term adopted by Sho'aiyan in his later writings.

In short, the task of the post-1953 Marxists was to complete the suspended project of decolonisation and national liberation in Iran. Naturally, I am speaking specifically of the Iranian case here, but the erudite reader is aware that since the 1960s there has been an increasing disavowal of older (Soviet-style) Marxism by younger activists around the world. To these activists, the communist parties of their respective countries had become too sedentary in their ideology and social reach: they had lost the emancipatory character of Marxism (and Leninism). Just to point out a few highlights, recall that the Cuban revolutionaries, led by Fidel Castro, launched their movement when they reached the conclusion that they needed to take actions that did not conform to the then policies of the Cuban Popular Socialist Party (PSP). It was not until 1957, when the revolutionary movement was solidly established and the defeat of the American-backed Cuban regime was in sight, that Castro and the PSP reached an agreement about the movement's strategy which necessitated new organisational turns by the PSP. This example should epitomise the approach of the 'new communists' in the 1960s toward their traditional communist parties. As Héctor Béjar, a founding member of Peruvian ELN in 1962, reflects, 'the guerrillas carried within themselves, from the beginning, a great many of the historical defects of the Peruvian Left political parties.'[31]

This is precisely how the PFG founders perceived their struggle. Jazani, who coined the derogatory term 'American Marxists' to humiliate Jaryan (Tavakkoli and Sho'aiyan), had written his honor's thesis in 1962, *The Iranian Constitutional Revolution: Forces and Objectives*, which had won him an academic award from University of Tehran.[32] Jazani asserts that the Constitutional Revolution marks the Iranians' uprising against the colonial powers of Russia and Britain, thus identifying it as a bourgeois-democratic revolution.[33] He traces the liberation movement to the Constitutional Revolution.[34] Therefore, it is indeed Fadaiyan who tried to complete the unfinished project of national self-assertion, although they conceptually transformed it into a national liberation movement led by militant Marxists.[35] Sho'aiyan joined this last approach by the late 1960s but through his own path.

As early as the 1960s Sho'aiyan expressed his defiance in recognising the Tudeh legacy. In an unpublished piece, 'Betrayal' (signed by Yoldash; dated 11 May 1960), Sho'aiyan tells of a gathering of old comrades to celebrate the release of a Tudeh member after seven years of imprisonment. Elements of fiction in the author's depiction of the ambiance leads Sho'aiyan to dwell in this former prisoner's reporting of the unbridgeable chasm between the Party leaders and its rank-and-file members who bore the brunt of harsh consequences for the leaders they once cherished. This comrade's disillusionment allows Sho'aiyan to confirm 'so much weakness and betrayal' on the part of Tudeh leadership, and yet he closes this piece with the former prisoner's declaration that he would join a new struggle but not 'with that leadership or that Party.'[36]

While 'Betrayal' registers Sho'aiyan's resentment and refusal to acknowledge the Tudeh as the bearer of the Marxist legacy in Iran, his future work actually theorises his stance. His position regarding Tudeh prepares Sho'aiyan to critically engage with Fadaiyan in 1973 (Chapter 3). Sho'aiyan follows the ruthless criticism of the Tudeh launched by Maleki and Tavakkoli. But Maleki had abandoned Iranian Marxism in the interests of his Third Force-style democratic socialism, which in the end remained within the constitutionalist opposition. Maleki's position, therefore, increasingly diverged from the national liberation trajectory of the post-coup generation. No wonder Sho'aiyan and the PFG founders distanced themselves from Maleki's Socialist League. For them, Maleki's rhetoric did not yield a new, let alone a path-breaking, struggle. Maleki became the very thing he criticised. In Sho'aiyan's accurate verdict, 'The Tudeh Party "splinters" [Maleki and company] were Tudeh-ish [*Tudehi*] with certain characteristics... They were Tudeh-ish against the Tudeh Party' ('Some Hasty Glances' in SW 13). Tavakkoli still hoped to resuscitate liberationist Marxism, avers Sho'aiyan, but he, too, had failed to recognise that the old tools—party politics—were obsolete under the iron grip of the Shah. 'The "Marxist" [Jaryan] circle, just like the Third Force and others, was the Tudeh Party opposing the Tudeh Party' ('Some Hasty Glances' in SW 31), Mostafa declared, because it lacked revolutionary essence. Tavakkoli's strategy to utilise the conflict between the UK and the US was not only unoriginal, it amounted to politicking (*siyasat bazaneh*). Jaryan erred in regarding the somewhat relaxed period of 1960–3 as having resulted from conflict between the UK and the US ('Some Hasty Glances' in SW 31). As such, Sho'aiyan followed Jaryan to the point when Tavakkoli's analyses had been exhausted: he was more original than Jaryan would have allowed. Sho'aiyan's project was far more radical, too: like Jazani, he wanted to rescue Iranian Marxism—as a master signifier—from the parasitical referential anchorage to Tudeh's history with which the younger Iranian Marxists were unwillingly identified.

It is true that despite many other militant attempts in the 1960s, Jazani, Zia Zarifi, and their comrades stand out as the originators of Iran's New Communist Movement and urban guerrilla warfare. Curiously, though, they still insisted that Tudeh was the working-class party up until its 1953 fiasco. The original, key document of the Jazani–Zarifi group (Group One) (dated Fall 1967 but actually written between 1965 and 1967) holds that although a non-communist will hold all the forces (nationalists, etc.) responsible for the defeat of the movement, '*we who believe in the vanguard party of the working class hold the leadership of the Tudeh Party of Iran fully accountable for not counteracting the 19 August [1953] coup.*'[37] Furthermore, the treatise states: 'In our opinion, the root cause of the failure of the movement on 19 August [1953 coup] was not the lack of unity among anti-colonial forces; it was the lack of mobility of the leadership of the anti-colonial forces and above all the leadership of the Tudeh

Party of Iran.'[38] Clearly, these statements recognise Tudeh as the working-class party and count it among the anti-colonial forces. Indeed, the Jazani–Zarifi assessment still believes the Tudeh's proposed coalition after its policy U-turn in June 1952 as evidence of the Party's 'legitimacy' (*haqqaniyyat*).[39] Sho'aiyan expressly rejects these claims. Some years later, Zia Zarifi still notes, 'If, *as the political organization of the working class*, the Tudeh Party had carried out its revolutionary duties and led the action against the counter-revolutionary forces, it would have inevitably maintained the leadership of the [Tudeh] Party over the entire movement.'[40] Reportedly, Zia Zarifi repeats this position in a debate from the early 1960s with Sho'aiyan ('Let Us Not Kill Marxist Criticism' in TCE 27, n. 5). Still, the Jazani–Zarifi appraisal points out that Tudeh's defeat in 1953 was not 'a defeat in the battlefield and while resisting but [a defeat] while retreating without any program and plans.'[41] In his 1973 preface to Arsalan Puriya's *The Record of Mosaddeq*, which he had retrieved from his hidden resources around this time, Sho'aiyan contends,

> We do *not* believe in [Puriya's] verdict that the Tudeh Party of Iran was a part of the 'national forces.' The fact that the Tudeh Party had strung certain sectors of the people's forces (*niruha-ye khalq*) to itself does not mean the Tudeh Party belonged to the people's forces (*niruha-ye tudehi*). The party that does not depend on the masses and is totally submissive to the governments that not only are clearly opportunistic and unproletarian (*nakargari*) but actually anti-proletarian and alien [USSR] is not the party to be credited as a part of the 'national forces.'[42]

In short, the Tudeh Party has never been the working-class party, not even before the 1953 coup (SOLF 13; TCE). Sho'aiyan dedicates his very last work (February 1976; published post-humously as *Two Critical Essays on the People's Fadai Guerrillas* [1976]) to questioning Fadaiyan's latest commentary on the Tudeh—a reiteration of the positions of Jazani and Zia Zarifi.[43] For Sho'aiyan, this claim is as factually incorrect as it is logically flawed ('Let Us Not Kill Marxist Criticism' in TCE 3). Sho'aiyan's position is more radical than that of the originators of armed struggle and is closer to the younger generation of activists-turned-militants. For instance, Amir Parviz Puyan, a co-founder of Group Two and PFG, argues that if Tudeh had been the working-class party, it would have fought for the emancipation of the working class. This is why Puyan contends that revolutionary action is 'to pave the way for the institution of the Communist Party and achieving a revolutionary theory.'[44] Ahmadzadeh also echoes this view.[45] Sho'aiyan's position on Tudeh remains uncompromising but controversial and to some extent unsustainable: reflecting on the excerpted commentary on Purya's work, we can see how he achieves that. We may agree with Sho'aiyan, Puyan, and Ahmadzadeh, as well as Jazani and Zia Zarifi (their differences notwithstanding), that Tudeh's failure disqualifies it as a communist party because due to the Party's clear lack of emancipatory project it delayed the national liberation movement of Iranian people significantly, but disqualifying Tudeh as one of the popular forces (*niruha-ye tudehi*) is unwarranted and cannot be defended. This judgment indicates Sho'aiyan's parallactic view that collapses the distinction between the Party leadership and the movement attached to the Party.

Over a decade later, while (briefly) in the PFG ranks, Sho'aiyan was assigned to write a rejoinder to the Tudeh Party's pamphlet, *What Do the People's Guerrillas Say?*—written by Tudeh Central Committee (CC) member Farajollah Mizani

(Javanshir), a pamphlet that reports that the self-exiled Party leaders did not have the slightest idea about the generational aspirations of the younger militants.[46] Armed struggle had confused the Tudeh leaders, as they disregarded the Siahkal operation and subsequent PFG operations in the same manner as they had treated the ROTPI operations in the mid-1960s: as pointless and fleeting. But then the leaders had woken up to the reality of the New Communist Movement. The pamphlet basically contains 'fatherly' advice from aging Tudeh leaders to the 'youthful' guerrillas on how to carry out their propaganda and how to secretly organise instead of engaging in armed action, as if these leaders did not know that the new generation had already disowned Tudeh. In his rejoinder, 'The Instruments of Logic' (September 1973), Sho'aiyan shows why the proletarian culture involves 'interpreting the world' (following Marx's famous Thesis Eleven) by transforming itself and transforming other classes through the revolutionary party—that is, to change it. The proletarian logic therefore entails a devastating critique of opportunistic tendencies—here signified by Tudeh—that prevent the proletariat and its militant vanguards from partaking in their unifying task of staging the revolution ('The Instruments of Logic' in SW). Avoiding cheap polemic, Sho'aiyan advances a defense of armed struggle. This is precisely the position from which he had concluded his fictionalised memoir in 'Betrayal' some fourteen years earlier: if there was a new beginning, Tudeh would not be a part of it.[47]

Let us emphasise here that the Tudeh Party that Sho'aiyan attacks is not the party that introduced to Iranian society partisan politics, public discourse, political literature and terminology, popular labor unions, advocacy of the rights of women and national minorities, and its steadfast promotion and support of modern Persian poetry and fiction. Its disastrous policies aside, the Tudeh Party must be credited for bringing these important components of democratic life to the Iranian public. These contributions cannot be separated entirely from the Party's ideological inclinations, nor from its docile attitude toward the Soviet Union's foreign policy. History does not work logically and connections between social forces are never straightforward. What Sho'aiyan attacks is the Party that, due to its abject submission to the foreign policy of the Soviet Union, had failed, for its part, the national liberation movement, and had thus inadvertently thrown Iran back into the grip of imperialism and dictatorship. We are facing *two* Tudeh parties here, and an honest assessment of the Tudeh performance in relation to the national-democratic movement under the National Front and Mosaddeq shows that Sho'aiyan's observation is *principled*: Tudeh had deviated from the national liberation movement of Iran from the very start, and, for all the worth of its contributions, had broken away from the '*liberation front*' of the people against British and American imperialisms. Even its paralysis in the face of the coup was consistent with its previous positions. For this view to shine, however, the social, cultural, and political contributions of the Tudeh Party had to be dimmed, even committed to oblivion. It is true that since no one enters history with a clean slate, the revolutionary generation of the 1960s inevitably owed many of its aspects, above all its Marxist discourse, to its predecessor. And yet, disowning the Tudeh legacy is a key moment in this revolutionary generation's emerging gestalt. The verdict of Sho'aiyan, and in fact that of the Fadaiyan's generation, was that because of its detachment from national self-assertion movement, Tudeh had functioned *not* as a communist party or a working-class movement. Thus, the task of building a new Iranian communist movement fell to the post-coup generation.

Like the Sphinx, the Iranian Left must have re-emerged from its own ashes.

THE YOUNGER GENERATION AND
THE NATIONAL FRONT

We have already seen that, despite the efforts of the leadership of the Second National Front to ban student representatives to its First Congress (25 December 1962–1 January 1963), Sho'aiyan managed to attend the Congress, not as a student representative, which would have disqualified him (as was Jazani), but as an independent. He submitted the 100-page treatise, *Nasl-e Javan va Jebheh-ye Melli* (*The Younger Generation and the National Front*), dedicated to the Congress and signed by his pen-name: *Sarbaz* (soldier).[48] The Congress did not allow a reading of this treatise for fear of its radical ideas. Copies of the treatise, however, were distributed among students and some leaders of the Second National Front.[49] It was written in the summer of 1962. Sho'aiyan sent a copy to Dr Mosaddeq, at this time under house arrest on his family estate in Ahmadabad, along with a letter in August 1962, to which Mosaddeq replied in a letter dated 23 September 1962, in which he addressed Sho'aiyan by his real name, stating: 'Your letter dated August 1962 and the essay "The Younger Generation and the National Front" pleasantly arrived a few days ago and I enjoyed reading it very much and I am thankful that our dear homeland has men who can analyse the circumstances so well and enlighten the public opinion, and this creates hopes that in the near future Iran will regain its lost independence.'[50]

The treatise intends to offer concrete recommendations for the reconstruction of the nationalist movement through the Second National Front (YGNF 99). Sho'aiyan offers a study of the movement's past for its future (YGNF 9–11). Iran had fought British colonialism in the past and is now confronted with the growing hegemony of American imperialism, which had risen as a superpower by encroaching upon the territories previously colonised by British or other European imperialisms (YGNF 16–17). The British challenged Iran's nationalist movement and were aided by Tudeh whose strategy in undermining Mosaddeq overlapped considerably with the British policy. Evidenced by its opposition to oil nationalisation, the Tudeh Party in fact pushed the British agenda ahead (YGNF 18, 22, 31). On the other hand, Mosaddeq directly challenged the British but he rightly and strategically did not antagonise the United States, and for that the Soviet Union and Tudeh called him an American puppet (YGNF 30). According to Sho'aiyan, Mosaddeq was alone: 'Mosaddeq's colleagues were mostly honest and respectable individuals but they were not capable of taking some of Mosaddeq's responsibilities off his shoulders' (YGNF 25). 'Mosaddeq's character stood out so highly compared to those of his colleagues that even today our [National] Front cannot name anyone to replace him' (YGNF 26). What is more, the National Front lacked organisation (*tashkilat*) and Mosaddeq's liberal views did not allow him to repress the movement's opponents. Mosaddeq should have dissolved the army or replaced its command structure but was unable to do so due to *qaht ol-rejal*—lack of reliable personnel. In short, Mosaddeq assumed a passive, non-violent politics, which he should have relinquished after the peak of his popularity in 1952 (YGNF 26–8). Interestingly, in his short reply to Sho'aiyan, Mosaddeq agrees with *qaht ol-rejal* and implicitly suggests that he might have used force: 'That I preferred silence between the 16 [August] [failed coup attempt] and 19 August [the coup],' declares Mosaddeq, 'was because I did not have any troops. The two officers who were my relatives and guarded my residence were later tried and sentenced.'[51] Sho'aiyan also criticises Mosaddeq for not mobilising the peasants by implementing land reform (YGNF 48–50). In the end, Sho'aiyan avers, the two major political forces, the National Front and the Tudeh Party, reaped what each had sown: 'All the blood shed by the many martyrs of the Tudeh Party in the [army] shooting ranges could not buy the slightest honor for the [Tudeh] Party while the one prominent martyr of the National Front, Hossein Fatemi, became a precious [moral] weight for the National Front' (YGNF 34). Due to these positions, Mosaddeq stands on the Left and Tudeh on the Right side of the political spectrum (OLM 54). 'In short, the coup... brought the Tudeh Party dishonor and the National Front defeat' (YGNF 34).

Attempts at continuing the National Front through the short-lived *Nehzat-e Moqavemat-e Melli* (the National Resistance Movement) as well as the pro-Mosaddeq circles were unsuccessful and suppressed by 1955 (YGNF 37–8). The Second National Front emerged in 1960 under different international conditions: now there was a strong Non-Aligned Movement (est. 1961); Stalinism was long gone; and the Dulles Containment Policy in USA had disappeared (YGNF 40). Under these circumstances, the regime allowed the Second National Front to open activities so that it would show the National Front's incompetence and disappoint its young supporters (YGNF 43). Sho'aiyan insists, somewhat counter-factually, that Premier Amini was a British agent (YGNF 58, 63–4) and the Second National Front was rather passive with regard to Amini's government.

Instead of mobilising its young supporters, the Front leaders have started negotiating with the government, thereby committing a 'dangerous distancing' of the younger generation from the older generation (YGNF 66) and letting the movement die away gradually (YGNF 49–50). Here, in 1962, Sho'aiyan anticipates that the younger generation gathered around the National Front will turn away from it, but he prophecises that this generation will choose a different path when he defiantly insists that confessing to the power of the regime only means we have accepted defeat (YGNF 44).

Sho'aiyan's concrete proposals to rebuild the National Front in this document resemble the positions advanced by the Socialist League (YGNF 87). He advocates the installment of an assertive leadership that includes leading figures from among university students. He also advocates the training of cadres, choosing a general secretary, recruiting according to principles, and promoting the National Front's student organisation (YGNF 71–4).

One can observe that Sho'aiyan wrote this document under the influence of Tavakkoli's proposition in *What Is To Be Done?* (1961) that the liberation movement in Iran must exploit the antagonism between British and American imperialisms in Iran to advance the movement's objectives. This is the analysis that had won Jaryan and thus Sho'aiyan—through guilt by association—the unfortunate designation 'American Marxists'—propagated by Jazani.[52] But in 1961, long before Jazani relegated this derogatory designation to collective memory by writing it in his *The Thirty-Year Political History* (circa 1973), Tavakkoli had stated that the label 'American communists' came from the Tudeh Party.[53] Tavakkoli believed that the British were the deep-rooted colonial force in Iran, connected to Iranian politics through the land-owning (feudal) class. America was a newcomer and thus loosely tied to the nascent and ineffective industrial class—the bourgeois class that is the key to Iran's future development. According to Tavakkoli,

Compared to American imperialism, British imperialism is the dominant and primary colonizer [in Iran]. The parties or individuals that in the struggles for liberation, without taking note of the aforesaid objective reality, pointedly attack America instead of Britain are either naive or insincere. In the first case [naivety] one must make them see their error so that they would reconsider their political tactics, and in the second case, that of insincerity and persistence, one must challenge them mercilessly as the cronies of Britain.[54]

This excerpt says it all: falling back on Mosaddeq's tactic of antago-nising British imperialism while keeping the Americans at a safe distance, Tavakkoli theorises a tactic for the post-coup era. The idea, of course, precedes him: as early as 1956, Maleki had offered similar analyses,[55] and the Statement of the Socialist League (1960) also contained the analysis[56] but it did not quite advocate Tavakkoli's position. Jazani, too, observes that Tavakkoli's pro-posal is only a reproduction of Maleki's idea—a half-true claim.[57] Clearly, however, Tavakkoli's analysis suffers from a time lag: the coup had shifted the position of the competing imperialists, but Sho'aiyan dogmatically insists on the conflict of two imperialists (YGNF 61), calling Britain the primary enemy of the movement (YGNF 76), thus exposing a parallactic view. That said, we must note that this treatise was written prior to the Shah's land reform and while the land reform bill was being debated in the Majles. Thus, there was still a viable position for the Second National Front to demand the elimination of 'feudalism' (through land reform) and support domestic resources and foreign investments to mobilise workers and national investors in industry and have the bazaaris support the trade (YGNF 81). This latter position, however, contains the core of Sho'aiyan's future frontal thinking: he wishes to mobilise *relations of equivalence* between heterogene-ous social forces through an economically motivated program that can eventually lead to the forging of a liberational front. The idea is scattered at this point but one can glean its intimations from his defending the internal diversity of the National Front and the existence of multiple parties (*tahazzob*) (YGNF 94–5) and from his advocacy of an unspecified anti-colonial regime instead of a parliamentary democracy of which he is highly suspicious. He regards participating in parliamentary elections as merely tactical (YGNF 88–9; 91).[58] Since this book is primarily an intellectual biography, it is important to register what Antonio Gramsci would call, in a different context, the 'molecular phase'[59] of the formation of Mostafa's soon-to-be theoretical pillars—a gradual, organic, and subterranean conceptual process. This idea returns in a further attempt within a few months (see below).

The Younger Generation and the National Front encapsulates the deep rift between, on the one hand, a legalist 'old guard' politicking around vague demands with a regime that practically scorned them, and on the other hand, a younger generation bursting out of its proverbial skin to bring about liberation and change. Those days are long gone, and history has already played its hand: as Sho'aiyan had anticipated, the land reform impoverished the Second National Front policy-wise and the regime conclusively suppressed the Second and Third National Fronts by the mid-1960s.

A THESIS FOR MOBILISATION

Sho'aiyan did not expect any concrete outcome from his recommendations for the Second National Front: he had already lost faith in its leadership. In any case, he was to leave Tehran for Kashan upon graduation, a departure he had delayed until November 1962.[60] In the meantime, though, he contemplated his first serious attempt at forging frontal politics outside of the National Front. It was a genuine political *experiment*. After his dismay with the National Front as the political representation of a wide range of mainly secular tendencies, this experiment would gauge the capacity of the Shi'i clerics for popular passive resistance. The experiment must have been made and concluded during the more relaxed political atmosphere in 1962–3 and prior to 5 June 1963 when the Shah ordered a heavy-handed crackdown of clerical opposition. Thereafter Ayatollah Khomeini was arrested and then exiled. The idea was not Mostafa's alone: Parviz Sadri had also contributed to the idea of economic struggle,[61] and the original idea dawned on Sho'aiyan through his conversation with a Liberation Movement member who had complained about the people's despair and the lack of impetus ('Today's Jihad' in SW 1).

The report titled 'Today's Jihad or A Thesis for Mobilization' ('*Jahad-e emruz ya tezi barayeh tahharok*') is dated 21 March 1964 and signed with his full name. He also offers a synopsis of this report in a later article ('Some Hasty Glances' in SW 16–20). He sent a copy of it to Mosaddeq along with a letter dated 24 May 1964, and he reports that in his response Mosaddeq had expressed his doubts about the outcome of this project in his idiosyncratic, subtle way ('Today's Jihad' in SW 1). The report on the experiment was lost, only to be retrieved in 1973. Then, he duplicated the entire record—including Mosaddeq's letter, his letter to Mosaddeq on behalf of Mehdi Bazargan, and his analysis of the 5 June 1963 crackdown—in a few copies and handed to Fadaiyan, which they neither redistributed nor returned to him. As such, this record was lost, and the published version available to us is only a version, written later, close to the original pamphlet ('Today's Jihad' in SW 3).

This experiment stands out as an attempt at frontal politics with the lost pamphlet functioning as its platform. The 'thesis for mobilisation' begins by stating that a century of setbacks and defeats has created a deep mistrust of politics among the people; to overcome this, new tactics are needed. Although political struggles are necessary, they have proved insufficient. We therefore need to abandon the classical forms of struggle. Sho'aiyan is not dismissive of political struggles, but at this point he does not assume politics as the basis of other forms of struggle either. 'Unfortunately in our country those who speak of leading political struggles do not know that *in many occasions utilising small and negligible possibilities at the proper moment, insofar as they conform to the objective conditions of the struggle, can mobilise the populace and attract increasing numbers of people to the most active [fa'alanehtarin] and decisive [ta'inkonandeh] struggles*' ('Today's Jihad' in SW 9; emphasis in the original). He dwells on 'discontent' as a frontal *nodal point* and a new basis for mobilisation ('Today's Jihad' in SW 8), but since discontent does not automatically lead to struggle, with emphasis, discontent should be interpreted and rearticulated. The 'passive and cursed discontent' of the people, in other words, should be transformed into *active discontent* through what we might today call the *articulatory practices* of the emerging front. Therefore, the new tactics should not impose personal risks on potential participants; rather, they should exploit the regime's weaknesses. Consequently, a frontal struggle that would hinge on a passive but united 'economic assault' (*tahajom-e eqtesadi*) against the regime could end the despair of the people ('Today's Jihad' in SW 5, 7–8, 9).

Since colonialism (*este'mar*) in Iran has historically been indirect (unlike colonised India, for example), the people's enemy never stands out clearly within society. There has *never* been an 'open presence' of colonisers or the 'exercise of force and oppression against people by the foreign colonial power in Iran' ('Today's Jihad' in SW 9)—well, to correct Sho'aiyan, I should say, at least not steadily. Neo-colonialism functions through the dominant class (the state), and therefore, '*showing the catastrophes [caused by] colonialism in this country is far more difficult than in countries where colonialism manifestly stands on its own feet*. In the words of Jean-Paul Sartre, semi-colony is the same as a colony plus deceitfulness and forgery' ('Today's Jihad' in SW 10; emphasis in the original). Accordingly, to end colonialism in Iran inexorably signifies terminating the dominant class: '*If we intend to crush the enemies of [our] nation, we should primarily force the dominant class down on its knees*' ('Today's Jihad' in SW 10; emphasis in the original).

The regime relies heavily on four main apparatuses (*dastgah*) of domination: (a) a sizable military machine; (b) SAVAK; (c) the systematic undermining of the citizens' constitutional rights; and, finally, (d) the state propaganda ('Today's Jihad' in SW 10–12). In analysing power in Iran, he argues, we must be cognisant of the conflict (*tazadd*) between British and American imperialisms (here Tavakkoli's thesis resurfaces): '*Insofar as the conflict between the two imperialisms allows, [we] must utilize this conflict as a possibility*—as did Mosaddeq who, unfortunately, did not conclude it successfully [*beh salamati*]. Nevertheless, in Egypt Nasser concluded it well' ('Today's Jihad' in SW 14; emphasis in the original). But at this point, 'the movement's leadership can skillfully utilise this conflict *not by relying on it, but by relying on the Iranian nation*' ('Today's Jihad' in SW 15). Note how this statement is simultaneously an advancement of Tavakkoli's idea and its annulment: the so-called conflict does not inform his tactic at all. In the face of regime's repressive measures, he proposes an 'economic campaign' 'for it is here that, contrary to other loci, the government is forced to stretch its hand out to the people.' The economic campaign is individual-oriented and should not cause potential danger to the people ('Today's Jihad' in SW 17–18).

The tactics for a passive but united economic offensive against the regime include: withdrawing funds from banks; boycotting the national railways; boycotting tobacco products (state monopoly); refraining from using imported goods so as to diminish customs revenue; boycotting newspapers; defaulting on bank loan payments by peasants; and boycotting lottery and sugar (state monopolies) ('Today's Jihad' in SW 18–22). Evidently this kind of extended economic boycott is reminiscent of the spirit of the historic experience of the Tobacco Movement (1891–2), reportedly led by Shi'i cleric Hajj Mirza Hassan Shirazi,[62] from which Sho'aiyan must have received some inspiration.

This is why Sho'aiyan approaches the clerics: he postulates that within the 'people's forces' the clerics enjoy the strongest popular network, and proposing the platform (pamphlet) to them would hopefully amount to the mobilisation of this network. However, he is quick to remind us that the clerics, led by Ayatollah Borujerdi, had betrayed Mosaddeq. I must point out that we do know how Ayatollah Kashani in particular conspired against Mosaddeq, and we have recently released documents that prove it. Ayatollah Borujerdi was probably not complicit in this conspiracy. In addition, continues Sho'aiyan, Shi'i clerics have a tendency to divert the blame from Iran's principal colonial enemy (British imperialism) by attacking Israel, which is not the immediate enemy of Iranians. Nonetheless, Sho'aiyan believes that the new generation of clerics, including Ayatollahs Milani and Taleqani, are different from their predecessors ('Today's Jihad' in SW 23–5).

Sometime in 1962, the pamphlet was taken to the country's three leading Ayatollahs—Khomeini, Milani, and Shari'atmadari. Initially, Sho'aiyan wanted to present the pamphlet to the clerics and publish it simultaneously, but he abandoned the idea for fear of causing suspicion among the Ayatollahs. He presented it to the clerics secretly and through intermediaries (facilitated by the Liberation Movement personalities since its leaders had approved of the pamphlet). The pamphlet was first presented to Ayatollah Hadi Milani (1892–1975) in Mashhad. Reportedly, he received it eagerly and asked for three days to study and approve it, but then he refused to sign it, announcing that the content was objectionable. The pamphlet was then taken to Ayatollah Ruhollah Khomeini (1902–89) in Qom who was reportedly 'thrilled' (*beh vajd amad*) about it. Purportedly, though, Khomeini had asked that the pamphlet be viewed by Ayatollah Kazem Shari'atmadari (1905–86) first, while also delaying his own approval for three days, at which time he also refused to endorse it on the grounds of its implausibility. Shari'atmadari, likewise, declined to support the pamphlet after three days. In short, the pamphlet failed to secure clerical approval and become the platform for a new united front against the regime.

Frustrated and disappointed by the top clerics' reaction, which confirmed Mosaddeq's suspicions, Sho'aiyan originally decided to publish the pamphlet along with a report on the clerics' reactions, but this was simply not an option. Later, he gave a copy to the Third National Front (led by Allahyar Saleh) where the pamphlet allegedly remained unread until the Front's disintegration nine months after its foundation. The police soon discovered the pamphlet in a Liberation Movement leader's residence. Soon afterwards, Sho'aiyan claims, the government introduced payroll reform for state employees by shifting to a direct deposit system

('Today's Jihad' in SW 1–3), thus effectively blocking any future bank boycotting tactics.

These two attempts in the early 1960s—new measures for rebuilding the National Front and an economic boycott—wrapped up Sho'aiyan's direct involvement in the politics of the days. He sought to unify both Shi'i and secular-nationalist oppositions, and through them provide an opportunity for the leftist opposition to re-emerge. The National Front was certainly not up to the task, and the clerics' cunning deflection caused him to lose faith in the religious establishment. Both cases were intended to examine the revolutionary potential of hitherto existing political tendencies. After 1963, and like so many of his generation including Jazani and Zia Zarifi, Sho'aiyan reached the conclusion that a brand-new generation should forge their brand-new politics and that the presence of the Left was indispensable. Rejecting Tudehism, being critical of the Socialist League, and phasing out of Jaryan's ultimately unworkable theorisations, Sho'aiyan was convinced that an altogether *new Left* should be founded.

In these two experiments Sho'aiyan was certainly inspired by the experience of Indian independence and Gandhi's philosophy of non-violence. He even states that his article was soon called 'passive resistance' (*mobarezeh-ye manfi*) ('Some Hasty Glances' in SW 16). But non-violence certainly has its limits, and it turned out to be ineffective in the liberation of the Iranian people. In fact, Sho'aiyan explicitly admits that this experience led him to the only possible conclusion:

> The defeat of various organisations in the late era [1960–3] was not simply their defeat; it was the defeat of their policy (*khatt-e mashy*) and essence (*seresht*)... The movement stepped in a new and foundational path: revolution!... Only one road is left for us: violence (*qahr*)! Revolutionary

violence. One must be armed. One must stage a revolution.
('Some Hasty Glances' in SW 20)

The global wind blowing through the 1960s from Algeria,
Vietnam, and Peru, where revolutionary movements *directly*
challenged colonial occupiers, imperialist invasion, and repressive states, had already sketched new horizons for Mostafa's
generation.

The Promethean generation's years of blood and steel were
still ahead.

THE PUBLIC INTELLECTUAL

Following his experiments with the National Front and the clerics
and while 'kept away' in Kashan (likely sanctioned by SAVAK[63]),
and thus unwillingly sheltered from the extensive police raids and
arrests of post-1963 period, Sho'aiyan had some years to contemplate, along with his closest comrade Sadri, the steps to be taken.
He wrote some material which could not be published that he
distributed anonymously or signed by one of his aliases among
trusted activists. Evidently, by 1967–8 he had already arrived
at the conclusion that armed resistance against the state—à la
Algerian and Peruvian experiences—had become inevitable. But
at the same time, he wanted to divert the security surveillance
from his impending clandestine activities and create the public
persona of a (legal) dissident writer. He wanted to publish his
ideas on various subjects, just as he believed that many issues
pertaining to anti-colonial efforts could and should be presented
in the public arena, however restricted the latter might have been
because of censorship. His public appearance, however, should
not be interpreted simply as a ploy: through it he also intended

to recruit university students for his future People's Democratic Front (Chapter 3) (SOLF 44, n. 18).[64]

So, in 1968 and 1969 he published several pieces, namely a poem titled '*Bazjui*' ('Interrogation') (later republished in PFB 8) and two articles, '*Vazhehha*' ('The Words') and '*Sargozasht va Dafn-e Yek Te'ori*' ('The Life and Burial of a Theory'), all published in *Jahan-e Naw*. He also wrote '*Negahi beh Towte'eh-ye Khal'-e Selah-e Omumi*' ('A Glance at the General Disarmament Conspiracy') intended for *Fasl-ha-ye Sabz* but the magazine was shut down before it could be published. Lastly, he wrote '*Khordehgiri-hai az Amuzgaran*' ('Review of *The Teachers*'), a review of a play written and directed by Mohsen Yalfani.[65] These articles have been reprinted in *Selected Writings* (1976).

A key theme runs through three of these published articles: that the interests of the socialist bloc, despite its revolutionary rhetoric, are factually in conflict with the decolonisation of nations on capitalist periphery. These three pieces showcase his ideas in relation to his critique of the Soviet Union and Leninism in nascent shape, ideas that inform his future writings. 'The Life and Burial of a Theory' addresses the 'peaceful coexistence' policy of the Soviet Union. In his Speech to the Twentieth Congress of the Communist Party of the Soviet Union (24–5 February 1956), First Secretary Nikita Khrushchev denounced the cult of personality of Stalin and his crimes, and announced the process of de-Stalinisation, rapprochement with Yugoslavia, and the Soviet 'interest of strengthening peace in the whole world.'[66] He later developed the latter idea in the Soviet policy of 'peaceful coexistence' with the capitalist world. Particularly irritating for Sho'aiyan is Khrushchev's claim about the policy's proletarian character. 'Our desire for peace and peaceful coexistence is not conditioned by any time-serving or tactical considerations,' Khrushchev asserts. 'It springs from the very nature of socialist society in which there are no classes or social groups interested in profiting by war or seizing and enslaving other people's territories.' The reason is because the socialist system has now become economically self-sufficient. 'The Soviet Union and the other socialist countries, thanks to their socialist system, have an unlimited home market and for this reason they have no need to pursue an expansionist policy of conquest and an effort to subordinate other countries to their influence.'[67] To Sho'aiyan, this position represents an unprincipled compromise to the detriment of liberation movements. He was not wrong. Already, the concern had been echoed by Ernesto Che Guevara, whom Sho'aiyan admired as 'the internationalist guerrilla of the proletariat' (Rev 276, n. 204): in his 26 February 1965 speech in Algeria, while expressing appreciation of the Soviet aid to Cuba, Che criticised the Soviet Union's approach to national liberation movements in Asia and Africa, stating that 'the socialist countries are, in a certain way, accomplices of imperialist exploitation. It can be argued that the amount of exchange with the underdeveloped countries is an insignificant part of the foreign trade of the socialist countries. That is very true, but it does not eliminate the immoral character of that exchange.'[68]

In a short preface (dated 1974) to the article's reprint in *Selected Writings*, Sho'aiyan states that Marx's assertion that the proletarian revolution would take place in advanced capitalist states was true for his time but now the revolutionary epicentre has shifted away from capitalist countries to the periphery. Interestingly, he sardonically remarks, 'although Iran is laden with natural-born (*madarzad*) Marxists, nonetheless no one ever pointed out this error [of Marx]' ('The Life and Burial' in SW 1). This is evidence of how his writings were ignored.

Sho'aiyan criticises 'peaceful coexistence' as a revisionist claim against Marx's concept of the proletarian 'world revolution': it began by Lenin's emphasis that if a country could break away from the capitalist system, then the socialist bastion should preserve itself while remaining in conflict with the capitalist states ('The Life and Burial' in SW 4). For Lenin, however, since the two systems inevitably remain in conflict, such coexistence cannot continue forever. Thus, although Lenin abandoned the idea of 'permanent revolution' (Trotsky), he still approved of revolutions and wars in a 'periodical way' ('The Life and Burial' in SW 5). This idea was then contorted beyond recognition by Khrushchev and was forged into a banal policy ('The Life and Burial' in SW 6). Thus, Sho'aiyan continues, peaceful coexistence has been Leninist right from the start: Khrushchev only removed Lenin's revolutionary rhetoric and exposed its naked essence for what it really was ('The Life and Burial' in SW 10, n. 5). The national liberation movements, however, showed that peaceful transition was impossible. Likewise, the 1968 crisis in Czechoslovakia brought the internal problems of the socialist camp to the forefront ('The Life and Burial' in SW 7–8). That the 'peaceful coexistence' policies of Lenin and the USSR were detrimental to the liberation movements will further take shape in his historical work on the Jangali movement. Later, these positions earn Sho'aiyan Fadaiyan's criticism.

In 'The Words' (1969), Sho'aiyan offers a new approach: he offers an analysis of the shared formation of anti-colonial *discourses* through an analysis of their *rhetoric*. Here he unwittingly sketches an elementary version of what today we call 'critical discourse analysis'—an extension of Gramscian theory.[69] He critically examines the way the term 'development' has been deployed to mean 'backward' (*aqabmandeh*), undeveloped (*tose'eh nayafteh*), developing (*dar hal-e tose'eh*), backwardly held (*aqab negahdashteh shodeh*), or slow-growth (*kamroshd*) in those countries in which capitalism has not grown to the level of advanced nations. In retrospect, this shows that in a way Sho'aiyan, a non-academic, is one of the forgotten and marginal precursors of critical studies of 'development.'[70] The aforementioned terms are loaded with emotional and notional connotations that normatively define these countries in terms of a 'lack'—i.e. what these countries are *not* in contrast to the western, colonial inventors of 'development'. These terms serve to hide the true reason behind these nations' maldevelopment. He identifies how each term captures the flaws and mechanisms behind the imperialist-imposed conditions on Asian and African societies. *Words are not innocent.* 'For the revolutionary nations, words should be alerting, clarify the tasks of their movement, help people to identify their friends and enemies, in short, words should be politically (political in the widest sense)… "guiding" [*rahnama*]' ('The Words' in SW 6). 'Although the economic base has been most fundamental to human efforts throughout history, from the vantage point of [our] struggle… the realization of the [economic] objective depends upon the triumphant outcome of political activities. Consequently, politics always stands prior to economy, although it derives from economy' ('The Words' in SW 6). Instead, he proposes a new term to designate these societies: 'reactionary-colonized' (*erteja'i-este'marzadeh*) ('The Words' in SW 1)—which Momeni later calls un-Marxist. *Sho'aiyan argues that the rhetorical construction of the political discourse takes precedence over the economic reality of a colonised nation, and such constructs are capable of giving direction and momentum to liberation movements. He thus breaks away with the conventional Marxist paradigm that views politics as superstructural* (a position reminiscent of that of Gramsci).

He continues with this line of thinking in 'A Glance at the General Disarmament Conspiracy' (1970), which can be read as a sequel to 'The Words'. In these two articles, Sho'aiyan offers an elementary theory of *discourse: words can capture ideas*, he submits, *that have no external reality and convey them to others as part of reality*. When words are detached from reality, they are deployed at the service of betrayal (*khiyanat*) ('Disarmament Conspiracy' in SW 1–2). A prominent example is 'peace.' Long-lasting peace requires the elimination of all factors that destroy peace. So long as such factors linger on, the 'logical word of history' will not be peace but war, not 'security' but 'revolution' ('Disarmament Conspiracy' in SW 3). Disarmament (mutual or otherwise) does not bring peace: arms are not the cause of war but its product ('Disarmament Conspiracy' in SW 4). There are good and bad wars: the wars in Palestine and Vietnam are 'approvable' ('Disarmament Conspiracy' in SW 7). *Only revolutionary violence can unseat the capitalist state* (see 'Disarmament Conspiracy,' in SW 14, 18). We must demand disarmaments that would not undermine liberation movements ('Disarmament Conspiracy' in SW 12)—that is, we should disarm imperialism ('Disarmament Conspiracy' in SW 20). Consequently, the Soviet disarmament pacts are imperialistic in essence, intended to maintain equilibrium between two forces of strategic power ('Disarmament Conspiracy' in SW 20, 38).

'*Pardehdari*' (exposing or unveiling), dated 1968, and signed by Serteq (his pen-name), and unpublished, offers an analysis of the Shah's White Revolution article on the allocation of factory share profits with the workers.[71] In his February 1973 foreword to the article, Sho'aiyan admits he had originally held a 'dogmatic approach' to the reforms as he 'did not believe they had any anti-feudal (*arbab-ra'iyati*) essence' ('Unveiling' in SW i). Then he wrote the present essay on the factory workers' profit-sharing component of reforms ('Unveiling' in SW i). Although not agreeing with all of his earlier analyses in the article (in SW), he decided to publish it because 'as examples and documents of our query and progress [*puyeh va seyr*] these [works] have their own place' ('Unveiling' in SW ii). The article offers extensive research and presents numerous tables. He was aided in this research by other individuals ('Unveiling' in SW ii), namely Ali Akbar Akbari and Houshang Keshavarz Sadr (from old Jaryan connections).[72]

The fourth article in the White Revolution mandated that factory workers receive dividends based on the company's reported annual profits. The article was intended to legalise labor unions (so-called 'yellow unions') and bring the workers in line with the state's developmental plans, thus nullifying potential workers' grievances. In the absence of 'red unions,' this article was exceptionally important for Sho'aiyan. In the 'Introduction' (dated 1966), he writes that the 'painful history' of the Iranian revolutionary movement has hindered a proper understanding of the revolutionary and the counter-revolutionary forces, which relates to the theoretical weakness of the movement ('Exposing' in SW 1). The concept of 'oriental despotism' (*estebdad-e sharqi*), while not entirely inapplicable, misses the fact that despotism in Iran is class-based ('Exposing' in SW 3). Only the ruling class enjoys political organisation, and the oppressed classes cannot express themselves: 'without the party, the class is an eye without vision' ('Exposing' in SW 4). Regrettably, though, the working class has long suffered from 'soviet-stricken' (*showravizadegi*) disease and Tudehism—i.e. the 'chimera of the worst and most devilish ideological deviationism' and an offspring of Sovietism. Challenging Sovietism is as important as fighting imperialism ('Exposing' in SW 4), and the Chinese alternative belongs to the same genus as Sovietism ('Exposing' in SW 5). Clearly referring to the pro-Soviet Tudeh and pro-China ROTPI, he argues, the problem facing Iranian Marxists is that they fight the counter-revolution (*zedd-e enqelab*) with counter-revolutionary (Soviet or Chinese ideological) weapons. But today's sterility will give birth to tomorrow's revolutionary movement, thanks to the intellectuals. 'In our view, under the present conditions the weight and pressure of struggle is on the shoulders of revolutionary intellectuals of Iran.' In other words, the 'intellectual is the teacher (*amuzgar*) of the class' ('Exposing' in SW 6). This requires the acquisition of knowledge from the anti-colonial movements.

Sho'aiyan points out that the Tudeh Party supported the Shah's profit-sharing reform for the workers—an extension of the fourth article of the White Revolution implemented in 1972—but was critical of its rules and implementation.[73] This means the reform has disarmed the Marxist opposition. But the Shah's reforms should not simply be dismissed as demagogical ('Exposing' in SW 9–10). The roots of the White Revolution should therefore be sought in the three conflicts between (a) dependent capitalism and pre-capitalistic system(s), (b) private and public sectors, and (c) British and American imperialisms ('Exposing' in SW 11). Originally, the reforms had their roots in Iran's authoritarian capitalist modernisation. The Constitutional Movement was initiated by the urban petite bourgeoisie, and, in response, the British installed the Pahlavi dynasty. Reza Shah modernised Iran's infrastructure so as to allow the country to adopt a capitalist economy ('Exposing' in SW 13). The 1953 coup marked the defeat of the nationalist bourgeoisie and the decisive dominance of dependent capitalism. The government emerged as the sole agent of capitalism and thus state capitalism grew. The Iranian state was therefore the political agent which would mobilise the economy as well as politics ('Exposing' in SW 15). But the economy soon ruled and reshaped politics: 'it was now economic considerations that guided politics' ('Exposing' in

SW 16). Sho'aiyan does not adequately explain this process, but state capitalism grew in Iran because of the autocratic shape of the regime that rendered it the sole agent of development. Here Sho'aiyan finally releases himself from the spell of Tavakkoli's thesis of UK–US conflict and professes that the authoritarian capitalist reforms in Iran in fact positioned the United States as the dominant imperialism in Iran ('Exposing' in SW 26).

In a final tally, Sho'aiyan appraises the profit-sharing reform as allowing the state to encroach on the private sector ('Exposing' in SW 43), which he regards as the 'more authentic and progressive' sector of capitalism ('Exposing' in SW 19). More importantly, he finds the policy to be a ploy of the state so that 'the workers imagine the regime (*dastgah*) as their supporter and advocate (*havakhah*),' and since the factory owners will use every possible means not to share profits with workers, 'the workers find their immediate and primary enemy in the face of this or that factory owner and not in the regime' ('Exposing' in SW 43).

This analysis also invites a critique of pseudo-Marxisms that in the 1960s dominated the leftist analyses of the Shah's reforms: namely, Tudeh and ROTPI. In his signature idiosyncratically meticulous way, Sho'aiyan contrasts 'popularisation' (*amiyaneh shodan*) with the 'massification' (*tudeh`i shodan*) of Marxism: the massification of Marxist teachings preserves its principles and applies them creatively, whereas popularised versions of Marxism tend to abandon Marxist principles ('Exposing' in SW 20–21). A legacy of Tudeh, a popularised notion is to pose public (state) ownership of the means of production as a non-capitalist or socialist phenomenon (as in the Soviet Union), and, by that token, evaluating the fourth article of the Shah's reforms as an inherently 'socialist' step ('Exposing' in SW 21).[74] However, Sho'aiyan rightly contends, 'The "socialization" (*sosiyalizeh kardan*) of the means of production or nationalization of resources can mean "socialist" or "nationalist" only when the leading apparatus is truly a social-ist or nationalist one. By itself, "state" ownership of the means of production can neither mean "socialist" nor "nationalist." It can be either or neither' ('Exposing' in SW 21).

Here Sho'aiyan is onto an important theoretical proposition: *he develops a concept of hegemony akin to that of Gramsci before this idea found its way into the Persian language.* Attending to dates is important for our observation. The 'Introduction' to 'Exposing' is dated 1966 (the undated article itself is attributed to 1968), while Gramsci appeared in Iran through a number of translations (from French) by Manouchehr Hezarkhani in *Arash* in February–March 1968.[75] This suggests that Sho'aiyan must have come up with the idea on his own. Co-founder of the Italian Communist Party and Member of Parliament, Antonio Gramsci (1891–1937) proposed the concept of hegemony in his analysis of the rise of fascism in Italy in his prison notebooks. We could see the Shah's reforms as maneuvers for total control by targeted countering of the cleri-cal influence (land reform, women's suffrage), the nationalists (nationalisation of the forests and public resources), and the Left (land distribution, workers' profit-sharing). Gramsci would call the taking over of popular, subaltern demands by the ruling class a 'passive revolution' (or 'revolution/restoration').[76] Indeed, the White Revolution did entail an unmistakable element of passive revolution. The Tudeh Party, following Soviet foreign policy, regarded the reforms as serving Iran's entry into the capitalist periphery but did not reject them. By the mid-1960s, only Jazani and Sho'aiyan offered genuine analyses about the reforms. For Jazani, in a manner reminiscent of the theories of Paul Baran and Andre Gunder Frank,[77] the land reform represents neo-colonial industrialisation as a precondition for Iran's entry into the world capitalist system as a peripheral economy. The democratic social reforms such as women's suffrage, while necessary, did not affect the repressive nature of the state.[78] For us, of course, this latter point unjustifiably glosses over the advocacy of women's rights by the state simultaneously as a necessary step for the incorporation of women by Iran's growing peripheral capitalist economy and the state's passive revolution to bring women, as a formidable social force, into the hegemonic orbit of the state and its democratic-reformist gestures. The reforms resolved the conflicts within the ruling classes by pushing feudalism under the leadership of the comprador bourgeoisie.[79] The reforms also augmented the general welfare of the working classes, especially rural workers, in order to diminish the perceived revolutionary potential of these classes.[80]

Sho'aiyan confirms that the White Revolution represents the state's way of channeling all transactions through its owner-ship of resources ('Exposing' in SW 29). But he understands that against the backdrop of what Gramsci would call 'war of maneuvre' during the oil nationalisation movement and the Shah's crackdown on the anti-colonial movement, as well as the half-baked and ill-fated 'war of position' launched by the Second National Front, the reforms enabled a 'passive revolution' finally to achieve an imperial hegemony in the country. Once I decode these terms, Sho'aiyan's insights will shine forth. For Gramsci, the socialist movement can employ a number of strategies for the victory of the workers'/peasants' alliance led by the Communist Party. Using World War One analogy to bypass prison censor-ship, Gramsci argues, the subaltern classes can confront and possibly overwhelm the ruling class and the state through a 'frontal attack' or 'war of maneuvre.' This was Lenin's strategy for the Russian Social Democratic Workers' Party in the Russian Revolution. This is not precisely what happened during Iran's anti-colonial movement, but Mosaddeq's two key demands—oil nationalisation and the enactment of constitutional restrictions on Shah's power—did indeed produce (counter-hegemonic) 'frontal attacks' against Iran's old oligarchy and its imperialist supporters. On the other hand, Gramsci contends, in western, liberal societies this strategy may not apply as the ruling classes govern not by being dominant (*dominante*) but as leaders (*dirigente*)—a political configuration he called 'hegemony.' Under these conditions, the subaltern classes may have to turn, normally under democratic conditions but also and in particular under repressive conditions (fascism), to a 'war of maneuvre' in which they gradually take over the political 'trenches'—i.e. become dominant in their moral and intellectual leadership of different classes across the social terrain over specific demands—until such time as the subaltern classes become hegemonic, thus imposing a political crisis upon the ruling class that will subvert it.[81] The attempts made by the Second, and especially Third, National Front and the student movement of 1960–3 represent a confused specter of 'war of position': they intended to remain politically active as legal opposition by making specific demands, but as Maleki, Tavakkoli, and Sho'aiyan pointed out, the Second National Front's demands, to put it in Gramscian terms, were not intended to mobilise and thus fill in the 'trenches' and demands of workers, peasants, women, and students. So the Second National Front devolved into haggling with the regime with no cards to play. After 1963, the Shah, who by now had borrowed many key ideas for reforms from the Left or anti-colonial movement (including women's suffrage and land reform),[82] championed the reforms, thus applying a 'passive revolution' or 'revolution/restoration' in which he took the key demands of various opposition forces and implemented them in a partial or diluted fashion, thereby foreclosing 'trench warfare' on all opposition. Through this process, the regime was no longer a purely repressive regime but one that tried to establish its own social bases through (partially) meeting the organic demands of the subaltern.[83] The White Revolution thus restored the Pahlavi's hegemony by taking (structurally) revolutionary reforms, and it worked, more or less, for the next fifteen years. *The Shah's reforms effectively disarmed the opposition.*

A man who admittedly knew no foreign language (OLM 83, n. 13)[84] and thus could not simply have borrowed these ideas unless they had been published in Persian (which is not the case here), Sho'aiyan saw this process through *his own* Gramscian lens. What is important is that the Shah's 'passive revolution' hegemonised the political terrain. *For the new generation of anti-colonial activists, therefore, no option remained other than dehegemonising the regime by pushing it to its historical roots in brutal dictatorship and the regional gendarme of imperialism and thus exposing it for what it really was: armed struggle served precisely that purpose.* This strategy of the young militant leftists in the 1960s succeeded.[85]

THE JANGALI STUDY AND THE RADICALISATION OF HIS THOUGHT

Sho'aiyan's 500-page historical work, *A Review of the Relations Between the Soviet Union and the Revolutionary Movement of Jungle,* certainly stands out as his most extensive, scholarly researched work in the 1960s. The book was written in 1968 and printed in 1970 but it did not receive a publication permit reportedly because 'the views of the writer were false' (OLM 51; see also SURMJ i). The printed copies were seized and destroyed by the authorities before distribution. Clearly, SAVAK had been monitoring Sho'aiyan's activities closely and intended to curb his public output after his *Jahan-e Naw* excursions. A rescued typeset copy eventually found its way to Florence where Mazdak (Chaqueri) published the entire book in 1976. While he was writing this book Jaryan no longer existed (OLM 52), but Sho'aiyan admits that he still held nationalistic sentiments (OLM 66).

It is not possible, nor is it my task here, to review the scholarly contributions of this book. Despite its many factual errors brought about by a lack of proper sources, the book has yet to receive the attention it deserves. As Cosroe Chaqueri, the author of the most extensive scholarly research on the Jangali movement, states, Sho'aiyan offered 'a long, interpretive analysis of the Jangali Movement.'[86] The book, however, paved the way for his opus, *Revolution* (see OLM 51), and, aside from being a worthwhile study, it was a turning point in Sho'aiyan's intellectual development. In his 1973 preface Sho'aiyan reflects, 'The book itself became a kind of life. As the book progressed step-by-step my eyes opened to new landscapes' (SURMJ v–vi). He started the book as a 'believer' in Leninism (i.e. an unexamined adherent to Marxism-Leninism, a legacy of Jaryan) but ended up rejecting Leninism (SURMJ vi). The book documents and analyses, among other things, how the then young Soviet Union and its leaders Vladimir Ilich Lenin and Leon Trotsky betrayed Mirza Kuchek Khan's Jangali movement in the Caspian province of Gilan. But the study guided him further than he had originally imagined it would: a historical study turned up serious theoretical implications. So, before sending the manuscript for printing, Sho'aiyan decided to take out the last chapter titled 'October and Lenin's Ideas on the Revolution' only to continue working on it over the next four years. *Revolution* was thus born (Chapter 6).

To summarise it briefly, the Jangali movement emerged in about 1915 in the aftermath of the failure of the Constitutional Revolution to meet the masses' key demand of land distribution, in reaction to the old land-owning class maintaining control in the post-constitutional period, and against the intrigues of Russian and British imperialisms. The movement was founded by the progressive constitutionalists Mirza Kuchek Khan, Mirza Hassan Kasmai, and Dr Ebrahim Heshmat. In the absence of a strong central government, Cossack troops had occupied Gilan, but they failed to suppress the movement and the Jangali guerrillas gradually took control of most of the region. The 1917 Russian Revolution radicalised the Jangalis, and the Bolsheviks promised to evacuate Russian forces from Gilan, which they postponed for fear of further British encroachment. At this time, Gilan had become a hub for the British-supported White Russian troops. As the movement progressed, its leadership became 'frontal', manned by both revolutionary democrats such as Kuchek Khan and communists related to Edalat (Justice) Party and Iranian Communist Party (ICP) like Heydar Amu Oghli. After the Anglo-Persian Agreement of 1919, British troops occupied Gilan and were supported by land-owners.[87] This caused Gilani peasants to join the Jangalis, and, with the influence of socialist figures from ICP and Bolshevik military support, the Soviet Socialist Republic of Iran was established in June 1920. Kuchek Khan entered Rasht with the support of Edalat Party and the Soviet troops, but soon, because of disagreements with the communists, he left the seat of government in Rasht. After the British-supported coup of 1921 by Reza Khan (later Reza Shah), Iran reached an agreement with the Soviets to withdraw in return for the British ending their support for Russian White Guards in Gilan. After a number of campaigns, Reza Khan's troops entered Gilan, terminating the Republic, and Kuchek Khan froze to death near Khalkhal.

The last component—that revolutionary Russia first supported and then abandoned the Soviet Republic of Iran—stood out for Sho'aiyan as historically and theoretically significant. The Soviets, he showed, sent arms to the revolutionary government but as a gesture of goodwill did not accept payment (SURMJ 181–2). They also brought members of the social-democratic Edalat

Party to Rasht (SURMJ 187–8). The social-democratic figure Ehsanollah Khan joined Kuchek Khan and brought radical ideas (SURMJ 310), a trend continued by the deployment of the revolutionary agitator Heydar Amu Oghli to create a Revolutionary Committee (SURMJ 350). But then the Bolsheviks detrimentally affected the movement: the Jangalis split as the Russian and Iranian socialists tried to control the movement, which led to the resignation of Kuchek Khan from the revolutionary government and his departure from Rasht (SURMJ 239, 243). Although he clearly recognised their betrayal, Kuchek Khan did not criticise the Soviet leaders (SURMJ 502). In any case, the Soviets treasonously switched sides when, on 26 February 1921, the Irano-Soviet Friendship Treaty annulled Tsarist loans and treaties with Iran[88] and effectively ended the Soviet presence in Gilan, leaving the movement at the mercy of British and Iranian troops. To Sho'aiyan, this treaty proves the Soviet and British collaboration against the Jangalis (SURMJ 343–4).

Sho'aiyan did not have access to historical documents in Russian (or other non-Persian sources), so his *only* evidence of what he regards as the Soviets' betrayal remains the undeniable fact that the Soviets withdrew support and left the Jangalis to their own meager devices. In fact, in order to preserve their precarious revolution, leaders of the young Bolshevik state used the Gilan revolution as a bargaining chip in their dealings with the British and Iranian states. Confirming Sho'aiyan's position (at that time he did not have access to the following document), a top-secret telegram from Trotsky to Lenin shows that this move was part of a calculated step by the Soviets to make concessions to the British as they regarded the revolution in the East objectively implausible: Trotsky and Lenin believed that at the time the East—Trotsky specifically names Persia—did not have revolutionary potential. The telegram was sent in June 1920, around the time the Soviet

Socialist Republic of Iran had already been established. This shows that just as the Jangali movement had succeeded, the Soviets were already contemplating abandoning it and using the Jangalis as bargaining chips, theoretically justifying their move by *attributing* to the East a lack of revolutionary potential, despite the fact that a revolution had occurred in Gilan before their very eyes. In Trotsky's own words: 'All the information about the situation in Chiva, Persia, Buchara and Afghanistan testifies to the fact that a Soviet revolution in these countries would at the present moment cause us the greatest possible difficulties.' So the sly theorist behind the 'permanent revolution' recommends: 'It follows from this that a *potential Soviet revolution in the east* is now advantageous for us chiefly as a major item of *diplomatic barter with England*.'[89] This suggests that the Soviets simply sold out the Jangali movement, despite their rhetoric of internationalism. Of course, for the Soviet state representing a vastly feudal society's transition to socialism through a communist putsch, it is a *paradoxical* position to belittle a grassroots revolutionary momentum in Iran enlivened by popular support. For Sho'aiyan, though, the gravity of the revolution had shifted from the West to the East (SURMJ 107). Trotsky's assessment therefore did not apply. In his meticulous and comprehensive study of the Jangali movement, Chaqueri calls the Soviet move a 'game' played masterfully to reinforce the Soviet position in the region.[90] 'Lenin himself was ready to go far in exploiting the inter-imperialist contradictions to salvage his regime from the quandary following "war communism".'[91] Sho'aiyan's hunch about the Soviets proved right, so he boldly declared that Lenin became a counter-revolutionary around 1920 (Rev 260, n. 135). Lenin's betrayal of the Jangali movement provided enough evidence for Sho'aiyan to dismiss altogether the leader of the Russian Revolution as a revolutionary communist. *From this point onwards, 'Leninism' began to signify something entirely different to Sho'aiyan than to his contemporary revolutionaries.* Remember that Sho'aiyan had mentioned that when he wrote the Jangali book he was not entirely free of nationalistic sentiments. We can now observe that his criticism of the Lenin–Trotsky decision to withdraw support from the Jangali movement is certainly informed by his nationalistic view. But we will see this is the moment when the Leninist taboo is scattered in his thinking. Unlike his contemporaries, he no longer views Leninism uncritically, although his approach to Leninism remains at times reductive.

The last chapter of *Jungle*, as mentioned, was removed so that Sho'aiyan could develop this historical observation into theoretical arguments. For him, the common justification that Lenin's decision to desert the Jangalis was down to pragmatic reasons such as protecting the battered Bolshevik country besieged by world imperialisms and caught in a bloody civil war were just that: *justifications* for counter-revolutionary measures perpetrated by the so-called revolutionaries. The Jangali movement was defeated because the Soviet Union played the role of an 'external counter-revolutionary.' Because the revolutionaries regarded the Bolsheviks as friends and allies, declares Sho'aiyan, they never probed it scientifically. To Iranian revolutionaries, the Russian Revolution carried a certain spiritualism (*ma'naviyyat*), and the Soviets' abuse of this 'spirit' created a Trojan Horse (SURMJ 141). Sho'aiyan criticises Kuchek Khan for lacking a 'correct, scientific outlook' (SURMJ 135), but he recognises that while Mirza was defeated, he saved the movement's *ma'naviyyat* by preferring to die instead of submitting either to the Soviets or the regime. 'The Revolution was defeated but it did not degenerate. The leaders did not succumb' (SURMJ 505).

'Among the enemies of Iran,' Sho'aiyan suggests, 'the Soviet Union is the only one that has appeared (or appears) with a friend's face' (SURMJ 15). And yet, Sho'aiyan does not entirely dismiss the USSR as a potential ally of liberation movements. He still believes that, although the USSR is driven primarily by its own interests, the Soviet interests might sometimes overlap those of revolutionary movements. Strangely, this means one should follow the same rule applied to exploiting the imperialist conflicts for the benefit of the movement (SURMJ 526–7). Undoubtedly, this view smacks of Tavakkoli's interpretation of Mosaddeq's policies. Nonetheless, Sho'aiyan's warning remains unequivocal: 'Our intention is that in its progressive relations and struggles the Iranian nation must never rely on the foreign policy of the Soviet Union as an internationalist proletarian politics' (SURMJ 529). 'It is a fatal mistake to descend into the well with the Soviets' rope. A tried and fatal mistake' (SURMJ 529). The subsequent Iranian movements did not learn this lesson from the Gilan experience: both the Autonomous Azerbaijan Government (November 1945–December 1946) and the Mahabad Republic (in Iranian Kurdistan; January–December 1946) were established under Soviet occupation and were lost in the aftermath of the Soviet about-face involving a pact with, and withdrawal from, Iran.

Beneath Sho'aiyan's study of the Jangali movement was indeed his first-hand, lived experience of Tudeh's betrayal of the nationalist movement. The study intended to expose the roots of Tudeh's irrecoverable fiasco: had we properly analysed the Jangali movement, we likely would have understood Tudeh's position in the early 1950s for what it really was. The Tudeh Party was not just dependent upon Stalin's policies; Stalin's and the Cominform's policy had its roots in the 'peaceful coexistence' thesis that originated with Lenin. *A Review* therefore intends to return to an option closed by history—the Jangali movement—and find out about how Leninism—the very quintessence of Iranian socialism and the hitherto unshakable bulwark against various 'deviationist' offensives—was indeed the root cause of problems within the Iranian socialism and liberation movement.

WHAT IS TO BE DONE?

I have previously shown that throughout most of the 1960s Sho'aiyan maintained a double life: while known to the authorities, he maintained a public persona as a (mildly) dissident intellectual and writer and allowed the police to monitor his activities, while he clandestinely organised militant networks and logistical support for future long-term urban guerrilla warfare. Not surprisingly, around the time when he 'published' his first (confiscated) book, *A Review*, he also wrote a secret pamphlet for his first group (with Sadri and Nabavi) and future militant cells on how to *conceive* a 'rebel' (*shureshi*) group. Signed Bumareh (his alias, appropriately meaning a 'mystical bird'), the pamphlet's original, handwritten version is dated 1968, typewritten version 1971, and mimeographed one 1972. This unpublished work shows that he contemplated armed struggle as early as 1968 in terms of his 'rebellious thought.' Two streams of thought—conceptual and practical—run through *What Is To Be Done?* While I leave the first stream—his concept of *shuresh*, or rebellion—for Chapter 6, here I will show how he envisioned an underground militant organisation in his instructional text.

Coming from a decade during which open activists (early 1960s) transformed themselves into underground militants (mid- to late 1960s), Sho'aiyan warns that such acquaintances cannot simply be transformed into clandestine organisational contacts (WBD 19). The same principle applies to the non-militant groups, as the latter will only expose the militants. At this time, he expressly rejects political activism (WBD 20–1): this is why he and Sadri began recruiting from among university freshmen or high-school students, young people with no security record (Chapter 1).

By the vanguard (*pishahang*) organisation he envisions an 'iron organisation' steadfastly recruiting and training only members who reveal a 'rebellious essence' (or 'essence of rebellion': *gohar-e shuresh*) (WBD 2). Sho'aiyan deploys both *organik* (the body and its organs) (WBD 4, 2) and family metaphors to envisage the group, emphasising that the rebel group must only recruit when it can accommodate new members (WBD 2). In recruiting, the group must seek the sparkling diamonds that are hidden in the darkness of the mine of society (WBD 3), and it should admit only individuals not groups (WBD 14) and only 'those in whom life has already cultivated the love for fighting, ability to sacrifice, and courage in their blood and the love for the masses' (WBD 3). Indeed, for this group, dedication (*fadakari*) goes deeper than sacrificing one's life (*janbazi*) (WBD 12). In Sho'aiyan's often cryptic lexicon, here *fadakari* should mean relinquishing the old individual in the interest of becoming a fully dedicated member, a militant-human, one with new qualities required for a new era now in its embryonic form and waiting to be born out of revolutionary action. This is the very struggle that, as Frantz Fanon said with his dying breath, 'endeavor[s] to create a new man.'[92] The organisation Mostafa contemplates is entirely secretive (WBD 3) and reminiscent of the Clandestine Centre (*markaz-e gheibi*) of Iranian Social Democrats that carried out political assassinations through its militant members known as 'Fadai' during the Constitutional Revolution. The group must therefore operate on the principle of 'absolute distrust' (WBD 15). This militant group must stash weapons in order to launch guerrilla warfare for the dual purposes of destroying the military machine of the enemy and constructing the front (WBD 4). This is achieved through preparatory and operational stages (WBD 5). Just as police work is based on scientific principles (WBD 6), so should the group be (WBD 8). His example is the SAVAK-created Tehran Organisation of the Tudeh Party during the 1960s that entrapped many activists and was responsible for the arrest of several members of Jazani's group.[93] This example shows that the police create 'resistance' groups in order to net the activists (WBD 7). But we, the activists, are the ones who actually lead the police to our groups (WBD 7). How? In response, Sho'aiyan points out one of the most illuminating maladies of the intellectual type: self-exhibitionism. Since the intellectuals and university students are the pillars of urban, armed struggle, they are the ones leading the police to the clandestine groups they join. The intellectual loves to engage in public exhibitions of dissent, 'spreading books' (*ketabparakani*) and 'sharing writings' (*neveshtehbazi*) (WBD 14, 16–17). Handing out banned books will only expose the activists (WBD 24), and Sho'aiyan proposes theoretical training based on the books available in the market (WBD 18), a recommendation that reflects his own experience.

In light of Sho'aiyan's uncompromising rejection of Leninism, there may be an objection that Sho'aiyan disregards that within the history of revolutionary communist movement this kind of clandestine organisation is owed to the Bolshevik party. I argue that this criticism is misinformed and mostly inapplicable as it reveals a certain constructed memory of revolutionary Marxism sanctioned by specific readings of revolutionary history. The vanguard party had indeed become the *normative* form of dissident political organisation in the postcolonial era. So one inevitably finds oneself adhering to it without necessarily adhering to Leninism, or even Marxism (e.g. Iranian

Mojahedin-e Khalq, a 'vanguard,' clandestine Muslim organisation). It must be noted that Lenin and his comrades were not the originators of the vanguard party as an 'iron organisation' but are often erroneously credited for it. I should remind the readers that the Bolsheviks had borrowed the idea of a vanguard party from the Narodniks, a populist and militant movement, rooted in middle-class radicalism, in the second half of nineteenth-century Russia that engaged in revolutionary agitation against the Tsar. The Narodniks are the forgotten originators of both secret, vanguard organisation and militant activism in the modern world—both elements present in urban guerrilla warfare globally. The Narodnik assassination attempt on Tsar Alexander II in 1881 led to their demise. This allowed Lenin and the Bolsheviks to take their ideas, rather opportunistically and without giving due credit (since the Narodniks no longer existed) and heretically change Marx's concept of proletarian organisation from a union-based workers' communist party into a vanguard party manned primarily by intellectuals and professional revolutionaries. All clandestine vanguard groups inevitably belong to that tradition but not necessarily to the ideological allegiances compacted in that history. One cannot expect any revolutionary to reinvent the wheel; the point, however, is that in vernacular engagements with an already existing tradition, the new is born. The three major socialist revolutions of the twentieth century—Russian, Chinese, and Cuban—emerged while rethinking and applying the tradition according to the requisites of their own specific conditions. Sho'aiyan's contribution, marginal as it really is, is epistemologically no exception.

What Is To Be Done? is more than just an instructional pamphlet. It captures some of the fundamental views that Sho'aiyan would develop in later works and in relation to future turns of events. However desirable, the seamless organisation he envisions *does not seem realistic*; it is almost a mystical entity. Sho'aiyan's idea reflects his judiciously but exceedingly cautious approach to clandestine organising for which he was later blamed (Chapter 3). Anyhow, as it turned out it was the lack of such principles that led to his two groups being raided. Furthermore, certain naive determinism—reminiscent of Ahmadzadeh's views and typical of the activists of the late 1960s generation—galvanises his hope that armed struggle will quickly lead to popular uprising (WBD 7). Most interestingly, though, is that a wanted revolutionary who wrote, published, and distributed more than 2,300 pages under a police state— a good proportion of which documented the state of affairs of underground activities—finds the intellectual culture of recording activity details against the pillars of a 'rebel' group and insists on reducing the 'paper-load' of the revolution (WBD 17). History is indeed full of ironies.

CONCLUSION: THE FLUX OF TIME

Resurfacing in open activities after a decade of disappointment between the 1953 coup and the 1963 crackdown, the intellectuals of the 1960s brought the cosmopolitan (*jahanshahri*)[94] character of Iranian culture to the fore through publications. In our context, publications such as *Jahan-e Naw, Arash, Ketab-e Hafteh,* to name but a few, show how Iran stands at the crossroads of its own intellectual ways of grappling with its particular conditions and the contributions of European, African, and Latin American revolutionaries, philosophers, poets, novelists, and commentators. Translations of revolutionary literature and other works immensely influenced the way Iranian intellectuals approached their conditions. For the leftist activists of these unkind times, there emerged an opportunity to reflect on their experience and find a way out of the political impasse by obtaining, to varying degrees, a new language—heterogeneous and internationalist by character and from sources other than those sanctioned by Soviet or Chinese Marxisms—that released them from the legacy of the Tudeh Party and its splinters. Jazani, Zia Zarifi, and their group, Sho'aiyan and his comrades, and later Ahmadzadeh, Puyan and their circle each found in the internationalist discourses theoretical and practical ways to challenge the regime. The whiplash of the June 1963 crackdown inadvertently but logically convinced these activists to abandon legalist-constitutionalist means as well as Tudeh, ROTPI, Jaryan, and the Socialist League's methods. The discursive breakthroughs of Iranian intellectuals—accessed through published and underground materials—allowed this generation to emerge with a new torch. *The master code of the era had changed. New modalities of activism had become possible.*

The Shah's autocratic rule, partially rendered hegemonic through the reforms, was to be challenged through armed struggle—an innovation of Jazani and Sho'aiyan with the influence of Algeria, Vietnam, and Peru (and generally Latin America). In retrospect, we observe the rift between two generations of self-declared Marxists. If Iran's Social Democrats (*Ferqeh-ye Ejtam'iyun Ammiyun*) and later the ICP were part of the national self-assertion movement crystallised by the Constitutional Revolution and its aftermath (the Soviet Socialist Republic of Iran), the Tudeh Party had abandoned the national liberation question in light of its adherence to the policies of Stalin and Cominform, despite the Party's undeniable and lasting contributions to organising labor, creating the leftist public discourse, and bringing awareness of women's status and minority rights. The militant generation galvanised into armed struggle in the 1960s needed to reconnect communism to national liberation: this is evident most vividly through the discourses of Sho'aiyan and the PFG. Sho'aiyan's assertion that Tudeh had never been a communist party reveals the expectation that *communism in Iran primarily received its identity from its radical (Marxist) role in the liberation movement* (rather than allegiance to the socialist homeland). We can observe *the history of the Iranian Left as partaking in (roughly) two periods of national liberation movements*: the Social Democrats, ICP, the Gilan Republic (1905–20s) and the 'guerrilla period' (1970s). Viewed as such, the once largest socialist party in the Middle East (the Tudeh Party) was indeed an anomaly within the Iranian Left. For Sho'aiyan and Jazani, their significant differences aside, the Tudeh Party's legacy had to be bypassed in order for the Iranian Left to return to its foundational mandates, as perceived by the Marxist founders of the guerrilla movement: the liberation of the Iranian people from neo-colonialism.

The *intertextual* and *cosmopolitan* character of Sho'aiyan's writings in this decade illustrate that his frontal politics was conceptually internationalist. In order to be situated at this particular nexus, Sho'aiyan needed to critically engage with Leninism despite the limited literature available to him. To compensate, he relied on his experience, resentment against the Tudeh, and his Jangali studies. This renders his view of Leninism rather reductive, but posing this critique, while valid, reveals the pedantic gesture of armchair academics, not the necessities of a militant practitioner. Whatever his shortcomings, his critical stance against Leninism forced him to stand outside the shared language and discourse of the Iranian Left, including the 1970s militant Left with which he unwaveringly identified. Sho'aiyan challenged the *common idiom* of the Left of his time. The rejection of Tudeh legacy constituted only one element to convince him that a fresh departure for the Left was needed: the other two elements were the failure of the Second National Front to mobilise the people and the reluctance of Shi'i clerics to partake in a nationwide economic mobilisation effort. However, like Jazani, Zia Zarifi, and their comrades, who also came from Mostafa's generation, *Sho'aiyan needed to have experimented and appraised the potential of existing leftist, nationalist, and (in Mostafa's case) Islamist forces for mobilising the masses* before arriving at the conclusion that legalist opposition had been completely exhausted. Moreover, his works in the 1960s still show his inclination toward frontal politics: indeed, had his experiments been successful, he would have been able to forge frontal *relations of equivalence* between heterogeneous social forces of the leftist, nationalist, and Shi'i activists and overcome their *relations of difference*, a requirement for frontal politics, to counteract the Shah's 'passive revolution.' Being ahead of his time, Sho'aiyan perceived his role as the constructor, through *articulatory practices*, of a frontal nodal point that would allow the articulation of demands of heterogeneous social groups (see Chapter 5).[95] This, in addition to the fact that Iran had never been colonised by foreign powers, meant for Sho'aiyan that in Iran identifying the people's enemy was difficult. Here he points out the problem, one that I call *public epistemology*: that popular and common notions of colonisation do not fit the Iranian reality, and, in the context of the Shah's calculated moves to grow culturally and socially hegemonic, the decolonisation of Iran required a surgical incision. Since the social and political signs available to the public had no meaning in and by themselves, and their referents could switch from progressive discourses to repressive ones (e.g. the land reform, as a sign, first emerged in the socialist discourse and only then became the hallmark of the White Revolution), the new generation's politics require the *key public signs* to be strictly fixed across divided political discourses.[96] Sho'aiyan's frontal politics and his advocacy of armed struggle (the latter also pioneered by Jazani) must be viewed as an effort to produce clusters of signs of resistance without allowing these signs to transmute across the discursive boundaries that set the dissidents apart from their common enemy. Armed struggle divides the public discourse across politically articulated antagonistic relations. His meticulous attention to 'the words' is indicative of this sensibility: it was a rudimentary theory of political discourse.

No wonder the decade of steel and blood was still to come.

3

FACING THE FADAIYAN

As long as you have not lived something, you have no right to write [about it].
Sho'aiyan, SOLI 135

To accept or reject something, I do not need verses [ayeh]. Anyone who states something that articulates the inner relations of reality and sheds light on the objective realties—that is acceptable to me, even when [such articulations] clearly negate the verses of anyone, including Marx.
Sho'aiyan, SOLI 52

After the People's Democratic Front was raided by SAVAK, in June 1973 Sho'aiyan and the surviving members of the PDF joined the People's Fadai Guerrilla—a group he admired for having initiated armed struggle in Iran after the many false starts in the 1960s by groups that did not understand *armed struggle as a movement*. The PFG founders did, and so did Sho'aiyan. However, to paraphrase the poetry of Hafez, in the goblet (of wine) Sho'aiyan had seen the lineaments of the profile of the beloved. He had perceived the Fadai Guerrillas as a 'frontal' group for militant Marxists, a de facto embodiment of his perceived 'frontal rebellious' group, and certainly not as an ideological organisation. His apprehending the true essence of Fadaiyan through personal experience proved tremendously painful for him. In any case, the in-group perspective of Fadaiyan granted to him by the unfortunate turn of events summoned ghosts from the past he thought he had exorcised for good.

Sho'aiyan consequently found himself in three different engagements with the Fadai Guerrillas: over his status within the group, in a debate about the intellectuals (Chapter 4), and over his theory of *shuresh* (Chapter 6) (in addition to a minor exchange on the 'front'). As such, for better or worse, *Fadaiyan had a more profound dialectical influence upon his thought than he had ever imagined.* As expected, though, Sho'aiyan's engagements with Fadaiyan precede the PDF formation. As he was acquainted with Puyan, co-founder of Group Two and PFG, he observed, from afar, the formation of the PFG through the original underground literature of Group Two.

A DIALOGICAL ENGAGEMENT

Signed by Bumareh and dated May 1971, 'Some Pure Criticisms' contains a critique of *Armed Struggle: Both Strategy and Tactic* (summer 1970), written by Massoud Ahmadzadeh, co-founder of Group Two and the PFG, and the latter's original theorist during its first phase. When the PFG was co-founded by Group Two (Ahmadzadeh, Puyan, Meftahi) and Group One's survivors (in particular, Ashraf), Fadaiyan adopted Ahmadzadeh and Puyan's theories, not Jazani's. In its first three years, the PFG operations bore the signature of Ahmadzadeh's thought.

It was Ahmadzadeh who had organised the largest clandestine network of militants in the 1960s–1970s with fifty individuals, recruited in 1969–70, who made up the absolute majority of PFG members in 1971.[1] In *Armed Struggle*, Ahmadzadeh heralded the advent of Iran's New Communist Movement and rejected that establishing a working-class party was a prerequisite for taking action against the Shah's dictatorship. We should note that, according to Ahmadzadeh, the Tudeh Party 'was only a carica-ture of a Marxist-Leninist party.'[2] He was influenced by the Latin American guerrillas and in particular Régis Debray's *Revolution in the Revolution?* (1967). Having fought alongside Che Guevara in Bolivia and later been arrested, the French philosopher argued that the Cuban Revolution and Che's theory of *foco*—which Ahmadzadeh translated as *kanun-e shureshi* (the rebel base)—opened up genuine possibilities to revolutionaries.[3] In a nutshell, in his very influential book Debray argues that the victory of the Cuban Revolution proves that the Leninist requirement for the party as the vanguard of the working class and the masses—a pillar of the international communist movement up to and including the Chinese Revolution—is no longer necessary, given the reality of Latin America. Instead, a band of armed, dedicated intellectuals can be a substitute for the Leninist vanguard party, and instead of the party, these committed intellectuals can set up a revolutionary *foco*, a guerrilla base in the mountains, and pro-ceed to liberate areas and mobilise the peasantry in the liberated zones. Debray questions the orthodoxy that the proletariat can only be represented through the party.[4] Thus, *foco* is a vanguard substitute for the communist party. Readers should be reminded that, although Cuban revolutionaries clearly called themselves communists, it was not until 1961, two years after the victory of the Revolution, that Fidel Castro declared Marxism-Leninism the official ideology of the Cuban state. Thus, Debray shows,

Cuba introduced a model of vanguardism without the party in the formal sense. Interestingly, like most post-Cuban Revolution revolutionaries in Latin America, Ahmadzadeh declared a *nominal* adherence to Marxism-Leninism while in fact aiming to implement an urban model of *foco* in Iran. In his book, Ahmadzadeh deploys Debray's theory to argue that Iranian intellectuals can create *foco* and launch armed struggle. As armed struggle expands, it achieves two objectives: first, it creates the 'objective conditions of the revolution,' and, second, it leads to a popular uprising, or to use his terminology, the small motor ignites the large motor.[5] Already alarmed by manifestations of Leninism after his Jangali study, Sho'aiyan endorses this view (Rev 94). This idea clearly goes against the Leninist model of the vanguard party, in which the party expands its constituency through (Leninist) propaganda and agitation. Nowhere in his writings does Lenin endorse the likes of the Cuban-style action.[6] Lenin would have appraised as 'petty-bourgeois intelligentsia'[7] Debray and the Latin American revolutionaries who followed the *foco* model, and Iranians like Ahmadzadeh and Jazani, who made attempts to instigate a revolutionary movement without the organised presence of the proletariat—through the Communist Party. A simple reading of Lenin's criticisms of the Russian Socialist-Revolutionaries (who to some extent can cautiously be said to prefigure the 1960s guerrilla movements) would reveal that Lenin would not have approved of the bypassing of the party by the guerrilla insurgents. The careful reader can appreciate the chasm, in the 1960s, between the *revolutionary practice* of a generation that goes against the grain of an ideologically sanctioned *revolutionary theory*. Ahmadzadeh and Sho'aiyan both belong in this rift: the former bypassed it through a *nominal* theoretical adherence to Marxism-Leninism while in practice committing to the Latin American revolutionary path; the latter upheld the

Latin American path as practice and disavowed Leninism, thus opening himself to a lot of criticism.

Chronologically, Ahmadzadeh's work was not the first revolutionary treatise of the rising militant generation of post-1963 era. The *Thesis of Jazani's Group* dates back to 1967. *What a Revolutionary Must Know*, dated 1969, was written by Jazani and smuggled out of Qom prison by his wife Mihan in 1970. The former was not published until years later while the latter was distributed in small numbers.[8] Even within the group, Puyan's pamphlet *The Necessity of Armed Struggle and the Refutation of the Theory of Survival* was published in the spring of 1970 and had effectively convinced the new generation of activists that the older ways—political activism—were not viable in Iran's police state.[9] Sho'aiyan also wrote a defense of Puyan's work alongside his work on Ahmadzadeh ('What Is Not To Be Done?' in SW).[10] Undoubtedly, though, it was Ahmadzadeh's treatise that was widely distributed. It achieved what other works had not: *Ahmadzadeh articulated the concept of armed struggle for an entirely new generation of activists waiting to partake in the struggle for Iran's liberation. He rendered armed struggle intelligible, indeed desirable.*

According to Sho'aiyan, he was not aware of the author's identity when he read Ahmadzadeh's book. What is unique about Sho'aiyan's essay is its platonic, dialogical narrative: an imaginary debate, at times polemical, between the two, with Ahmadzadeh's positions represented by excerpts from his book. The essay was reportedly sent to Ahmadzadeh who might have seen it, but his arrest on 27 July 1971[11] would obviously not permit a rejoinder ('Some Pure Criticisms' in SW 1). He was executed in March 1972.

The 'Preface' captures the essence of Sho'aiyan's approach: he writes his essay in the aftermath of the momentous Siahkal. 'Once upon a time there was a long period in which the revolution, and grabbing weapons for the revolution, would be postponed to a future that never arrived' ('Some Pure Criticisms' in SW 2). But the courageous uprising of 'Siahkal-Tehran' was a turning point that put armed uprising on the activists' agenda. By this he is referring to the attack on a gendarmerie post in the village of Siahkal in Gilan Province by the survivors of the Jazani–Zarifi group in February 1971, an operation that launched the guerrillas onto the Iranian political scene. The fact that in this essay (May 1971), as well as in 'What Is Not To Be Done?' (July 1971), Sho'aiyan refers to the militants as the 'Siahkal-Tehran' group shows he was not aware of the PFG formation (April 1971), although by this time the PFG had issued several communiqués beginning with its inaugural operation, the assassination of Lieutenant General Zia Farsiu (7 April 1971) in retaliation for his handing down the death sentences to the Siahkal militants. In any case, Sho'aiyan argues that soon afterwards 'communiqués, books, and articles' on armed struggle were hastily put together. But the Iranian 'enlighteners' (*rowshangaran*) had not yet offered a refined and cohesive theory. 'A vivid example of such haste combined with confusion can be found plentifully in a book entitled *Armed Struggle: Both Strategy and Tactic...*' ('Some Pure Criticisms' in SW 2). While praising the author's efforts, Sho'aiyan expresses his disappointment: 'how can a person or a group that is unable to wrap up a fifty-page book with sophistication (*darchidehgi*)... lead a popular revolution with all its twists, unpredictable problems, and *terra incognita* to its conclusion?' ('Some Pure Criticisms' in SW 3)

The imaginary dialogue begins in the middle of the night when the narrator wakes the author of *Armed Struggle* with a sense of urgency, asking him to present his theory. At the heart of Sho'aiyan's critique is Ahmadzadeh's adoption of Debray's theory. He had already written a critique of the Persian translation of

Debray's book ('Party and Partisan,' September 1969, signed by Ensan, Persian for 'human'), in which Sho'aiyan rejects Debray's reliance on the *foco* theory as a springboard for the revolutionary party, as explained above. But more importantly, he problematises revolutionary models and argues that a theory about the Cuban Revolution cannot be applied to Iranian conditions ('Party and Partisan' in SW 55). In short, revolutions are particularities defying universalisation (Chapter 6). He agrees with Debray and Ahmadzadeh that at the heart of oppression is the military might which must be confronted by the people's army. He also sees why Ahmadzadeh calls armed struggle both tactical and strategic: the militants' armed engagements today will grow into armed popular uprising tomorrow. But he objects that *armed struggle cannot be a tactic* since it is geared toward a popular revolt ('Some Pure Criticisms' in SW 7–9). Then he diverts the critique to Debray's *foco* theory—which is at the heart of Ahmadzadeh's small and large motor metaphors[12]—a view Sho'aiyan endorses in his work (Rev 94, 167), while dedicating an extensive critical note to Ahmadzadeh's theory (Rev 251–7, n. 110). The issue is that neither Debray nor Ahmadzadeh deny the importance of the party but they view it in terms of the guerrilla *foco* ('Some Pure Criticisms' in SW 31). This means that, although Ahmadzadeh adopts a rearranged model following the Cuban experience, he still thinks in Leninist terms whereby the presence of the party is the prerequisite for revolutionary action. The party, however, has no organic place in this theory because, according to Sho'aiyan, if the proletariat could be organised by the vanguard there would not have been a need for the armed action of the intellectuals. This is the rift between theory and practice that I flagged earlier.

Sho'aiyan observes a conceptual gap here: the claim that *foco* will lead to the people's army remains untheorised. It is, rather, an *assumption* against the facts: 'apparently "armed struggle" automatically "guarantees"... the presence (*hasti*) of [the guer-rillas]... against any harm (*gazandi*) in their confrontation' ('Some Pure Criticisms' in SW 11). The Cubans did not theorise their struggle before actually engaging in it. If Ahmadzadeh's assumption is correct, then why the need for all the hair-splitting? (Sho'aiyan, 'Some Pure Criticisms,' p. 11) If action guarantees the outcome, then the revolutionary theoretician will be redundant, which means Ahmadzadeh's work is inherently contradictory ('Some Pure Criticisms' in SW 13). In contrast, Sho'aiyan insists that we need theory. 'Revolutionary theory is ground-breaking and the guide for [our] deed, not a formula for inactivity (*bikari*) or idleness, nor a rhetorical tool' ('Some Pure Criticisms' in SW 20). The problem with Iranian society rests with the weakness of revolutionary theory. Had Iranians had the slightest idea about how to proceed at the opportune historical moment, the outcome of the nation's struggles between 1941 and 1953 would have been very different. 'To say the least, we would not have been a colony' ('Some Pure Criticisms' in SW 23). Sho'aiyan's point regarding the need for revolutionary theory is well taken: he is alarmed by Ahmadzadeh's disregard for a roadmap, a sensibil-ity reflecting Ahmadzadeh's shared horizon with the 'practice-leaning generation' (*nasl-e amalgara*) to which he belonged (Rev 288–90, n. 247, 167). He attributes such disregard for theory to Latin American revolutionaries (Rev 168). But Sho'aiyan, too, developed his theory in *Shuresh* only after he had already engaged in underground activism. To summarise, Sho'aiyan misses the point that a certain degree of live engagement is required for revolutionary *practice* before revolutionary *theory* is conceived.

Moreover, we are facing two movements: one against capital-ism (championed by the proletariat), another against imperial-ism that involves the convergence of various classes. *As such, liberation movement and defeating imperialism is not the same as defeating capitalism.* The victory of the working class and the defeat of capitalism are never conclusive, and capitalism can always return, as it did in the Soviet Union ('Some Pure Criticisms' in SW 17–18). Here is where Sho'aiyan offers hints of his theory of *shuresh* that he was developing at this time. Being a revolutionary—that is, *acting in fidelity to the essence of revolution* (Chapter 6)—does not require being a communist or a worker ('Some Pure Criticisms' in SW 27). Ideology does not bestow revolutionary action: Marxist-Leninists are not necessarily revolutionaries, the Tudeh Party being a prime example. By the same token, a non-communist is not automatically a counter-revolutionary ('Some Pure Criticisms' in SW 28–9, 32).

Sho'aiyan's critique of Ahmadzadeh trails his earlier critique of Debray. The engagement anticipates his theory of 'front' and 'revolution' as he makes a distinction between liberation movement and workers' revolution for the purposes of unifying them through rebellious action. Sho'aiyan's emphasis on the necessity of systematic theorisation is irrefutable. However, coming from an older generation, he misses the point that Ahmadzadeh's declaration 'that more than anything we need practitioners rather than theoreticians'[13] is in fact *not* refusing to theorise, but articulating the experiences of a rebellious generation that came of age after 1963. Ahmadzadeh conclusively challenged the requirement, epitomised by Lenin, that 'without revolutionary theory there can be no revolutionary movement,'[14] through a clever *inversion*: *without the revolutionary movement there can be no revolutionary theory. Ahmadzadeh's theory is essentially a negation of the Leninist 'uprising' model* (Chapter 6) despite Ahmadzadeh's crediting Leninism (Rev 254, n. 110). Fadaiyan avoided this contradiction for three years until they adopted Jazani's theory circa 1974. Jazani had used armed struggle as tactical and as a preparatory action for constituting a 'political wing' of the movement as the nucleus of a liberation front. As mentioned, it was Ahmadzadeh alone who unified the concept of armed struggle for his defiant generation. The fact that Sho'aiyan wrote his response in a dialogical fashion, however, shows that he deeply related to this generation, regarding the original Fadaiyan as younger comrades-in-arms.

THE INSIDER'S VIEW: LIVING WITH FADAIYAN

Sho'aiyan unreservedly praised the Fadai Guerrillas as audacious pathfinders and the founders of the armed struggle proper in Iran—those who *in practice redefined the Iranian political life* ('Let Us Not Kill Marxist Criticism' in TCE 1) through careful strategy and tactics. 'There were other groups and organizations, of course, that generally believed in armed confrontation, but their programs and tactics for action practically held them back from military confrontation with the counter-revolution [the Iranian state]. Among them, *this author and [his] group are no exception*' (Rev 209, n. 3; emphasis added). Although he had reservations about the PFG's discursive references to Marxism-Leninism, he regarded the PFG as an umbrella group—a 'front' of sorts for militant Marxists—and the potential core of a national front of militant challengers of the Shah's regime (SOLF 37, n. 1). This presupposition thus encouraged him to join Fadaiyan in June 1973 alongside the surviving PDF members, following SAVAK raids on the group that left Nader Shayegan and some key members dead, many arrested, and several without support and safe houses. Mostafa hoped to convince PFG leaders—in particular, Hamid Ashraf but also the theoretician Hamid Momeni—to adopt his *Shuresh* as the guiding theory of Fadaiyan.

Obviously, his joining the PFG did not occur under ideal circumstances or on equal terms, and despite Sho'aiyan's *assumption*, clearly it was not unification. Fadaiyan sheltered fugitive PDF members within their hermetically sealed network. In return, they gained zealous and experienced militants. Joining the PFG were two surviving PDF teams: one from Tehran, which included Marzieh Ahmadi Oskui and Saba Bizhanzadeh, and another from Tabriz, led by Oskui, which included Ahsan Nahid, Houshang Isabegloo, Yusef Keshizadeh, Dr Mahbubi and his sister (name unknown) (SOLF 43–4, n. 17).[15] SAVAK did not trace the Tabriz cell until several months later, which led to Oskui's death in April 1974.[16] Also joining the PFG were Shayegan's mother, Fatemeh Sa'idi (aka Comrade Mother), and her three young sons, Abolhassan (aka Shokufeh/blossom), Arzhang (aka Daneh/seed), and Nasser (aka Javaneh/sprout). The mother and the children supplied Fadaiyan with fantastic organisational cover: the boys in particular would deflect suspicion from the Fadai safe houses by presenting themselves as the children of the young 'couple' (members of the Fadai Guerrillas) in their rented accommodation.

The tumultuous joining of Sho'aiyan to PFG also exposed the inner conflicts within the PDF. A reasonably detailed review of the dynamics involved will show why this turn of events was important for Sho'aiyan. Following his bitter departure in response to his discriminatory treatment by Fadaiyan, Sho'aiyan wrote six open letters reflecting on his experience within the PFG, letters that provide a unique window into his insider's view. Ashraf refused to respond in writing (SOLF 4). It is *ironic* for a man who had insisted, circa 1968, that revolutionary intellectuals must cultivate an oral culture to avoid security risks (WBD 14, 16–17) to state in 1974 that: 'I don't agree with oral games [*shafahi-bazi*]; all must be in writing' (SOLF 4; see also SURMJ iv). Naturally, his letters would not compromise anyone's safety. By now, he truly had learned how words befriend the forsaken. Experience is an astute teacher.

Sho'aiyan had begun recruiting for the future PDF long before its formation and while he was still collaborating with Sadri and Nabavi. He notes his interest in the oil-rich province of Khuzestan and wanted to recruit cadres from the Literary Corps and deploy them to Khuzestan for future operations. What exactly he had in mind with this interest in the 'oil wells' remains unclear, but given the failed Isfahan steel plant sabotage (which exposed his first group)—a plan he later scorned as a 'quasi-coup d'état' (Rev 209, n. 3)—and his debate with Momeni,[17] we can surmise that he primarily (though not exclusively) understood militant action as spectacular sabotage operations. To recruit new members, he published in the magazine *Jahan-e Naw*, which led him to a certain public talk: when writer and translator Baqer Parham was invited for a public lecture by students at the Literary Corps Institute at Mamazan, Sho'aiyan accompanied him. This was when he became acquainted with Marzieh Ahmadi Oskui, who later recruited Sediqeh Serafat for the PDF. Oskui was expected to volunteer for Khuzestan after receiving her certificate, but instead she chose her home province of Azerbaijan (SOLF 44, n. 18).[18]

The PDF was dissolved upon joining the PFG. In retrospect, its joining exposed the already tumultuous relationships within the PDF. According to Sho'aiyan, Oskui was critical of PDF inaction and wanted to part ways with them and join Fadaiyan (SOLI 40), possibly even before the PDF's formation. While Shayegan was still alive, joining Fadaiyan was on the PDF's agenda (SOLF 24). Sho'aiyan claims that he was the one to propose unification with Fadaiyan and had designated Oskui as the contact person, but, before the group approved this, Shayegan was killed (SOLF 23, 41). Reportedly, the rendezvous failed but, after joining, it turned out that Fadaiyan already knew Oskui (SOLF 24). This is Mostafa's version. Ashraf's own version contradicts it: he reports that Oskui had told Ashraf that before Shayegan's death she and

Shayegan had decided to expel Mostafa from the PDF (SOLF 34) and Shayegan regarded Oskui as the PDF's second-in-command (SOLI 63). These accounts may be exaggerated, but Sho'aiyan does acknowledge that, even before joining Fadaiyan, he and Oskui were supposed to part ways (SOLI 64). Paradoxically, joining the PFG put an end to their bitter relationship.

Sho'aiyan joined the PFG with one condition: that his work, *Revolution*, would be debated among Fadai cadres. Given an opportunity to recruit some competent militants, as the PFG had done many times in the past, the PFG leadership must have accepted Sho'aiyan's condition (SOLI 113, n. 5), or else, *logically*, Sho'aiyan would not have joined. This point is important. The PDF members were placed in various Fadai teams. Oskui and Bizhanzadeh rose to prominence within the PFG ranks. Bizhanzadeh became the only female member in Fadaiyan's CC after the loss of leadership in June 1976 until her death in February 1977.

Sho'aiyan, Sa'idi, Arzhang, and Nasser were deployed to Mashhad as a team and under the surveillance of Ashraf's lieutenant, Ali Akbar Ja'fari (SOLI 43–4). Thirteen-year-old Abolhassan Shayegan was assigned to Tehran teams instead of being housed with his family. In Tehran and Mashhad he was deployed as cover and sentinel, accompanied in Mashhad by Oskui and Momeni on two different occasions. Abolhassan was arrested in 1976 at the age of fifteen. Records of his interrogations do exist,[19] but some time after his arrest he vanished entirely. Alas, the sad fate of the Shayegan youngsters would not end there.

The recruitment of Sho'aiyan did not escape the concerned gaze of Jazani, who had now established regular contact with Ashraf from prison. He approached the PDF prisoners Abdollah Anduri and Bizhan Farhang Azad in order to probe the PDF's ideological stance and Sho'aiyan's *Shuresh*, but the two refused to reveal information.[20] Then the recently arrested Mehdi Fatapour met Jazani in prison in 1973 and confirmed that the PDF had joined the PFG. Jazani warned him about this, calling Sho'aiyan's presence 'dangerous' because his 'radical and Trotskyist ideas' could dominate Ashraf and others, which would result in Sho'aiyan taking over the PFG. After his release, Fatapour was informed by Anushirvan Lotfi and Ashraf that, because the relationship between the two parties was unsavory, Sho'aiyan had been expelled from the group. It is still unknown if it was Jazani's warning that had persuaded Ashraf to oust Sho'aiyan.[21]

Reportedly, Sho'aiyan's tasks within the PFG were: 'Going to Mashhad. Engaging in theoretical works. Collaborating on creating a publication (*nashriyyeh*). Collaborating to make some weapons (*jangafazarha*)' (SOLI 43). The suggested 'weapons' duty must have pertained to Sho'aiyan's experience with Sadri in making the grenade shells. Purportedly, though, he did not do anything significant in Mashhad. He worked on *Shuresh* and engaged in face-to-face and then written debates with Momeni, PFG's mid-career theoretician, on the issue of intellectuals (Chapter 4). It was during Mostafa's last months in Mashhad that the PFG published the first issue (February 1974) of its publication *Nabard-e Khalq* (The People's Combat); while he was aware of its publication and proposed a special issue dedicated to documenting the comrades' experiences with opportunism (SOLI 28), he never mentions if he had helped with its publication. *Nabard-e Khalq* was published shortly before his dismissal from the PFG. Indeed, although the PFG may have thought Sho'aiyan would be useful in the group's efforts to publish, the diverging tendencies between Momeni and Sho'aiyan would not have allowed for the latter's contributing to the publication that later turned out as *Nabard-e Khalq*.

When a copy of *Nabard-e Khalq* went missing, Ja'fari issued a security alert, which inadvertently led to the arrest of two members. Then, strangely, and contrary to the basic security rules of underground activism, Ja'fari ordered Sa'idi to return to a dubious, vacated safe house to collect the 'organisational property,' while he and a comrade kept lookout. With the house occupied by SAVAK agents, Sa'idi was arrested after a short chase while Ja'fari and his comrade remained passive bystanders instead of trying to rescue her (SOLF 16–18, 27). Comrade Mother's arrest took place on 14 February 1974.[22] Mostafa was infuriated by the incident: he interpreted it as evidence of Fadaiyan's discriminatory treatment of him and those associated with him. He shrewdly understood that the reason for his placement in Mashhad was Fadaiyan's suspicion toward him: 'I realised that comrades believed that I have been engaged in a brand-new organising in Tehran' (SOLI 56; see also 59). To ensure that he did not secretly return to Tehran, Sho'aiyan was given a specific assignment: to stay by the telephone at their safe house, receive coded messages from Ashraf, and convey them to Ja'fari. This happened only once (SOLI 57–8). In Sho'aiyan's colorful language: 'since the comrades believed I was about to engage secretly in the fabled organising in Tehran, they decided to ground me by fastening my tether to the barn-spike of the telephone' (SOLI 58). Sa'idi's arrest ended Sho'aiyan's association with the PFG: he was ordered to hand over Arzhang and Nasser to Ashraf in Tehran, which he did on 28 February 1974 (SOLI 119, n. 14). And then Sho'aiyan, one of Iran's most wanted dissidents, was abandoned with no proper support. He survived this turn of events by being sheltered by his few dedicated comrades.

Sa'idi was destined to experience the saddest fate. She was severely tortured.[23] She also met her arrested son Abolhassan while they were both in prison and received the news of the tragic death of her two young sons.[24] The two youngsters—Nasser was eleven, Arzhang thirteen at the time of their death—were killed in a Fadai base on 15 May 1976 in Tehran-Naw District. Of the guerrillas, two men and two women were also killed. A security report mentions simply that six individuals were killed; although it names the Shayegan brothers among the casualties, it does not give their ages. This is one of the saddest chapters in the history of the militant movement in Iran. The children were clearly in no position to engage in a gun battle. In retrospect, it is clear that Ashraf, Sa'idi, and Shayegan were ultimately responsible for the fate of the children. What exactly happened to them on that calamitous day remains unclear, but we owe it to them to examine the details of that day and and to discover why the lives of these three youngsters, who did not choose to be in eye of the storm, were taken in this direction and who was responsible for it.[25]

This is how Sho'aiyan became the lonely guerrilla (*cherik-e tanha*). He was too much of a maverick for any dissident group to recruit him, too exhausted to organise yet another cell on his own. We shall soon see why. His reflections on this experience, and his exchanges with Ashraf in 1974 left very little breathing space for him. 'I truly tremble,' he wrote, 'for I indeed feel myself to be gradually worn out and immobilised, fatigued and dead' (SOLI 102). As if speaking of this experience, he wrote in a 1974 poem:

My other refuge is death.
And isn't death the purest bosom for the homeless?
(PFB 10)

SPECTERS OF STALINISM AND SECTARIANISM

His eight-month residence (June 1973–February 1974) with Fadaiyan turned out to be an eye-opener for Sho'aiyan, and his documentation of his lived experience remains a unique feat within the Iranian Left. He noticed that while being kept from any meaningful duty in Mashhad his comrades were asked by Ashraf to write about his character and actions. In these 'memoirs' Sho'aiyan detected traces of the Stalinist purges. From a Foucaultian analytical perspective, we can see the rationalistic similarities between the organisationally required reports on the self (and self-criticism) and the written interrogation records (*taknevisi*) extracted by SAVAK, which I have discussed in a previous work.[26] His first-hand observations about the way he was marginalised and then abandoned was, interestingly, more than a personal issue. He turned his experience into a theoretical and historical pathology of sectarianism and Stalinism within the Iranian Left, a tendency that still persisted despite the generational forging of the 'New Communist Movement,' which by definition must have entailed the rejection *in toto* of Soviet-style organisational policies. With this experience, all the pieces fell into place: his earlier critique of the Tudeh Party (along with Jaryan) and his critique of Lenin's betrayal of the Jangali movement was now connected with his treatise, *Revolution*, enabling him to offer his pathology. He had lived long enough alongside the leftists to know that the only way to challenge what he regarded as Stalinist methods—which for him were epitomised by the organisation's orders that a member write statements about her other comrades (a common practice among all militants)—was to take his accusers to the court of public opinion, although in his case 'public' only meant the mere possibility that his writings would reach Chaqueri (Mazdak) in Europe. Secrecy has always been repression's best ally.

So he began: he wrote a total of six open letters to Fadaiyan, documenting in minute detail his observations and analyses.[27] A wanted man and without support, he wrote his open letters in the corners of city parks and buried them in remote locations on the outskirts of Tehran for safekeeping (SOLI 99). Sho'aiyan had realised that Oskui, Bizhanzadeh, and the two boys had been asked to write about him. In Sho'aiyan's unforgiving opinion, they were pressured into *taknevisi*. We have seen already that Oskui had told Ashraf she and Shayegan would have expelled Sho'aiyan but police raids had caused the plan to be postponed (SOLF 20, 23). Sho'aiyan believed that Oskui's celebrated posthumous book, *Memoirs of a Comrade* (1974), was originally written on Ashraf's orders and contained her (unpublished) account of her time within the PDF, and, despite Ashraf's promise to provide him with a copy of the full version, Sho'aiyan never received one (SOLF 42). Sho'aiyan accused Oskui of having destroyed his relations with Fadaiyan (SOLI 133).[28] He also believed that Arzhang and Nasser Shayegan had been asked to write about him (SOLI 133). A veteran of the Iranian underground Left, he could see clearly that these 'memoirs were nothing but an intra-organ-isational tribunal' (SOLF 42–3, n. 14), indeed a Stalinist-style tribunal backed by *parvandehsazi*—literally 'dossier-making'—against him. He had to challenge these charges out in the open.

Since he was simply 'cut off' without proper notice after hand-ing over the young Shayegan brothers to Ashraf (SOLI 96), he gave the PFG an ultimatum: to offer an explanation by 22 July 1974 (SOLI 106). His last meeting with Ashraf, arranged by Mojahedin (SOLI 96–7), took place on 8 September 1974 at 2 p.m. (SOLF 3). Ashraf refused to meet his deadline, so Sho'aiyan in turn refused to meet him during the summer, but he was even-tually lured into this last meeting when Ashraf messaged him that he would return to him writings of his that the PFG had in their possession. This, of course, never happened (SOLF 3; 38, n. 2). The reason Ashraf insisted on this (last) meeting was to respond to his first, extensive open letter. We may surmise that Ashraf also wished these letters to stop and sought a compromise (see SOLI 50). Evidently, Ashraf became both pragmatic and flexible about finding a solution. We would have benefited from any PFG source concerning Sho'aiyan's allegations, but, alas, no such sources exist. Thus, we are left with Sho'aiyan's account, according to which Ashraf confirms the details of Sho'aiyan's observations but rejects the suggestion that these actions were intended to put him on trial *in absentia*.

This minutely documented conversation begins with Ashraf's threat: 'Your [first] letter was read by those comrades who needed to read it. Our comrades believe that we cannot be in the same organisation. In addition, we are not each other's immediate enemy. Of course, if it comes... to a clash—whose day will inevitably come—then we will confront each other' (SOLF 5). To this, Sho'aiyan's rebuttal is exacting: 'Whatever your decision, it is impossible that I live together with you in a party-like organisation... As regards friendship and enmity, I think just like you do. Our immediate enemy is reaction-colonialism (*erteja'-este'mar*) [the Shah's regime]. I have always believed in frontal struggles... I view you not as comrades but as friends. On the possible clash... well I have no illusions about it and no fears either' (SOLF 5). The torrent of written accusations by Sho'aiyan's former comrades—which we cannot inspect since Fadaiyan destroyed them all—boils down to Ashraf citing three character flaws responsible for Sho'aiyan's expulsion: being opportunistic, being irresponsible, and being cowardly and idle (SOLF 5). Among militant activists in the 1970s there was a typology that separated members into *tip-e amali* (the practitioner type, like Ashraf) and *tip-e nazari* (the theoretical type, like Momeni). Sho'aiyan's record of actual engagement in armed action was certainly a fiasco (to be precise, it was nonexistent),[29] despite his brilliant escape plan for Reza'i: this is because, employing this typology, he belonged to the 'theoretical type,' as did his interlocutor, Momeni. Ashraf had recognised this. But this was not the issue here. Sho'aiyan argues that if these character flaws were right, why would Fadaiyan have recruited him in the first place (SOLF 10, 8). The truth is, he contends, they recruited him so that they would recruit others and then abandon him (SOLF 10).

But then the discussion turns up interesting points about the future of the movement. Here we reach the *implicit* theoretical bedrock of the whole affair, and see why Sho'aiyan's singularity clashes with the normative epistemology of running a revolutionary movement—a legacy of the Left in Iran and elsewhere. At its core, Sho'aiyan's notion was a game changer, which other Iranian (or non-Iranian) revolutionaries did not understand, let alone prepare for. What Sho'aiyan had in mind was to unfold decades later in a land far, far away (see Conclusion). The confrontation, therefore, is encapsulated in one key epistemological antagonism within the militant Marxists: Leninism and *Revolution* (SOLI 40). The question was whether the New Communist Movement, spearheaded by the PFG, encompassed pluralism, organisationally and ideologically. As expected, the answer was no.

It is important for us to recognise that *Sho'aiyan (mis)understood the PFG because he regarded Fadaiyan in light of his own theory of the revolutionary front.* 'The designation "People's Fadai Guerrillas" was chosen so anyone who was prepared to partake in guerrilla operations like a people's fadai [self-sacrificing militant] would find oneself, as a people's fadai guerrilla, a part of (*hambasteh*) the People's Fadai Guerrillas,' he proclaims. 'On this basis, as a humble man, I criticised Fadaiyan's treatment of myself in regard to the printing and distributing of *Shuresh*' (SOLF 37, n. 1). Was Sho'aiyan right? Perhaps not in his implied sense that *anyone* acting in the manner of the PFG would be considered 'a part of' (*hambasteh*) the Fadai Guerrillas. And yet, there is a reason for his claim.

Fadaiyan exerted a magnetic, moral power over the secular militants. Many groups joined the PFG, and absorbing militant Marxists was a PFG objective: 'With regard to all revolutionary combatants (*razmandegan*) and particularly the Marxist-Leninist ones, our organisation has two main duties: first, to absorb (*jazb*) these groups insofar as our power and resources allow and train them directly, and second, to supply all revolutionary groups with our experiences through pamphlets, publications, communiqués, and the radio [program].'[30] Historically, Arman-e Khalq (The People's Ideal) was the first group to plan to join the PFG in 1971 but SAVAK raids aborted the unification. The PFG also housed and integrated the militants from Dr Houshang Azami's group in Lurestan Province in the early 1970s, allowing him and some members to return to Lurestan (where Azami was killed in 1974) and integrating the surviving members. The PFG also integrated some members of the Azerbaijan-based group colloquially known as *Goruh-e Mohandesan* (the Engineers' Group) upon their release from prison. Behruz Armaghani stood out among these recruits as he brought Jazani's ideas to PFG, and, joining the PFG CC, he took Fadaiyan into new directions with Ashraf's support. Momeni was also a member of a group associated with a small circle that joined the PFG (see Chapter 4). Lastly, the PFG integrated, in 1973, a small group outside Iran known as Setareh (Star; later, Group for Communist Unity) that contributed enormously to mobilising financial and logistical support for the PFG through the revolutionary movements or states in the Middle East. Interestingly, though, this group also broke ranks with Fadaiyan in 1976, accusing PFG leadership of Stalinism.[31] Sho'aiyan's confrontation and exchanges with the PFG took place in 1974. Incidentally, around this time there was an internal discussion within the PFG about the very point Sho'aiyan raises. Later in 1975, in an issue of *Nashriyeh-ye Dakheli* (*The Internal*

Bulletin; strictly for PFG members) a member advocated a position similar to Sho'aiyan's: 'The Marxist-Leninist groups that could not contact the People's Fadai Guerrillas should operate under the designation "People's Fadai Guerrillas" (with a suitable addition)'. The leadership expressly rejected this proposal.[32]

Sho'aiyan's proposal was based on the expectation of pluralism and theoretical diversity (SOLI 41). He *misunderstood* Fadaiyan, it is clear, as an umbrella group (a frontal organisation) in which the plurality of ideas would be debated (SOLF 37, n. 1). For Sho'aiyan, 'Ideological [*marami*] questions and conflicting opinions within the people's ranks can only be resolved through democratic means, that is, through discussion, criticism, convincing, and educating, not through enforcement and pressure' (SOLI 104). Thus, he proposed: 'organisational unity along with freedom of thought and creating an environment for debating ideas' (SOLI 42). For Ashraf, that was not the case. The PFG had accepted having *Revolution* debated but *accepting Sho'aiyan's work was not a condition for unification*, as is implicit in Sho'aiyan's own reflections (see SOLI 42). The fact of the matter is that Sho'aiyan was in no position to impose a condition for his joining, but he was under the impression that one had been imposed anyway, and Fadaiyan opportunistically took in the PDF militants only to marginalise him and then cut him off altogether. In all fairness, though, the Fadaiyan did engage with Sho'aiyan: Ashraf designated Momeni to debate him. Fortunately, these debates are documented and have survived. But it would be naive to think that, given their ideological inclinations, Fadaiyan would accept Sho'aiyan's theory just to keep him in their ranks or allow his theory to become the guiding one of the PFG. However original his thought, *Sho'aiyan overestimated his own theoretical weight* vis-à-vis Iran's most popular underground group. Yes, he had a condition for joining the Fadaiyan, but did it ever occur to him that Ashraf and Momeni were unquestionably already cautious about him by virtue of Jazani's earlier views of Jaryan (i.e. the American Marxists), if not, possibly, Jazani's intervention from prison?

So it is no surprise that in response to Sho'aiyan's advocacy of internal pluralism, Ashraf had purportedly said, 'there cannot be several theories (*nazar*) within an organisation' (SOLI 48, 55). Sho'aiyan reports that in a previous conversation with Ja'fari in Mashhad over the PFG's refusal to publish his works, Ja'fari had said: 'Look, comrade, the movement is still weak. Let us grow and gain strength. Then, well, anyone will be free to express his/her opinions.' Sho'aiyan replied with the immortal words: 'Comrade, the organisation that bans the distribution of ideas it does not approve at the time of weakness, when strong, will smash the brain that wishes to the think ideas other than those dictated by the organisation' (SOLI 49). Sho'aiyan's point is admirable and well taken, but it requires open conditions to have a group that can freely discuss ideas. The instrumental rationality of secretive organisations is not set up to provide democratic venues for debate. This is a structural issue that has very little to do with the individual's will. To be fair, it must be asked, was is really practical to have a theoretically divided PFG under Iran's police state? The answer is clear, but the trajectory of this question leads us to cheap pragmatism unworthy of a revolutionary movement that intends to create a new world, despite the reality of the situation. This is why, I argue, we must unwaveringly respect Sho'aiyan's recognition of internal democracy, practical or not, at the height of the dictatorship. This is what makes Sho'aiyan a singular thinker, indeed our contemporary: he rejected the forces of reality in favor of a higher value.

Where Sho'aiyan sees a contradiction, the Fadai leaders see consistency: the PFG designates a venue for any leftist dissident to join, a 'front' of sorts (SOLI 55). For Ashraf, anyone is welcome to join the guerrillas, but this does not mean the group is a 'front' (SOLI 56). Ashraf's point is *logical*, although ideologically driven. As late as 1974, when he completed the third version of *Revolution*, Sho'aiyan still considered himself a Fadai Guerrilla (Rev 173) in the particular sense by which he understood the term. At this time, Fadaiyan changed their designation from the People's Fadai Guerrillas (PFG) to the Organisation of People's Fadai Guerrillas (OFPG). Adding the word 'organisation' meant that Fadaiyan had decided to identify themselves as a political party, Sho'aiyan claims, in response to his perceptions and objections (SOLF 4).[33] But this claim seems overly exaggerated. We should remember that both Jazani and Ahmadzadeh regarded the PFG as an organisation. This is particularly explicit in Jazani's writings. What is more, until February 1974 Fadaiyan signed their communiqués as the PFG. Beginning in April 1974 the communiqués bore both PFG and OFPG signatures and this continued for about two years. So Sho'aiyan's claim that Fadaiyan's changing the group's designation was in response to his critique is not accurate. We must recall also that, as of 1973, the PFG had been working with Setareh, and it needed to officiate its outward appearance for its contacts with the Middle Eastern revolutionary movements.[34] Perhaps Sho'aiyan's observation helped the PFG to improve on its official appearance, but nothing more.

Now the whole affair assumed a greater clarity for Sho'aiyan: his being isolated in Mashhad, his comrades being asked to write confession-like 'memoirs' about him, and his being suddenly expelled and left to the mercy of circumstance which could have spelled this wanted man's demise—these all pointed to one thing alone: Stalinist methods. The PFG had not planned to purge Sho'aiyan, but leaving him exposed amounted to endangering his life.[35] 'The dossier the People's Fadaiyan were making for me, they never revealed to me even a fraction of it, until they had already issued their guilty verdict... only verbally and only after the letters were distributed by this humble man' (SOLF 7). The character flaws attributed to him were mere excuses, he avers. 'Fadaiyan who, on the one hand, had desperately hung on to their Leninism—which has nothing to do with Leninism—and, on the other hand, clearly saw their ideological bankruptcy contra *Revolution*, had no other option but to turn their ideological confrontation into dossier-making against my person (*parvandeh-saziha-ye shakhsi*)... And this, in the history of the Left, is the common Soviet method, and in particular Beria-Stalinist method' (SOLF 8). Sho'aiyan also regards Fadaiyan's response to *Revolution*, in Momeni's *Not Rebellion, Judicious Steps Toward the Revolution*, as a dossier-making rejoinder (SOLF 8). The fact that the roots of his expulsion were ideological, he concludes, renders the PFG approach Stalinist. It represents an ideological purging. Of course, the reader is aware that here 'Stalinism' has come to signify the ideologically sanctioned repression of diversity through secretive and conspiratorial methods, not the phenomenon that defined the Soviet Union for about three decades. Sho'aiyan was around long enough to recall the stories of Tavakkoli and Maleki about the way they had been treated by the Tudeh Party. These stories and his own experience seemed parallel. Furthermore, perceiving the PFG as a strictly ideological party, Fadaiyan revealed their sectarianism, which annulled the possibility of a liberation front and hence the suppression of diverse ideas. In this bitter but eye-opening affair, Sho'aiyan sensed that the (Stalinist) 'tradition of killing thinking' (Rev 19) had crept up on the PFG that he cherished so unwaveringly. This experience enabled Sho'aiyan to theorise his observation and offer a diagnosis: 'the long spectrum of colourful Soviet partisans (*showravist-ha*)' reached 'from the

North to pure Stalinists, from the East to the new Maoists, from the West to the ancient Tudehists, from the South to the judicious Fadaiyan' (SOLF 6–7). The common denominator was the Soviet-like (*showravisti*) opportunism that revealed itself in the form of sectarianism and ideological purges. For Sho'aiyan, the PFG's use of methods the Tudeh Party had employed in its heyday two decades earlier to silence or purge its critics was not just an error of judgment. It amounted to the contraction of a *disease*. Hence his pathology. 'It is here,' he avers in his criticism of the PFG's version of Tudeh history, 'that once again one can understand how Tudehism, in spite of the organisational decline of the Tudeh Party, has dominated the minds and judgments and engagements (*barkhord*) of many individuals or organisations, including the Organisation of People's Fadai Guerrillas' ('Let Us Not Kill Marxist Criticism' in TCE 19). The generation that came into being out of severing ties with the Tudeh Party and aimed at a genuine communist *refoundation*, Sho'aiyan observed, seemed to be pulled back into the whirlpool of sectarianism and Stalinist methods of its disavowed predecessor.

CONCLUSION: OF RADICAL CRITIQUE AND ITS ISSUES

Strangely, in the Iranian context Leninism, regardless of its historical origins, significance, and nuances, represented, as an unquestionable *master signifier*, the normative theoretical signpost for an entire rebellious generation's rather *rhetorical* identification with the Russian communist tradition, while in fact armed struggle had nothing to do with Leninism or the Bolshevik (or Chinese) Revolution (see Chapter 6). Sho'aiyan's attacks on Leninism rendered it, possibly for the first time, a *floating signifier* within the Iranian revolutionary-communist discourse.

Armed struggle became *intelligible and actable* in the revolutionary ambiance of the 1960s with two world-historical resistances—those of the Viet Cong and the Palestinians—emerging as *decisive* signposts for revolutionary action. In spirit and approach, the Iranian armed struggle in particular was indebted to the Algerian war of liberation and the Latin American urban guerrilla movement that inadvertently received a conceptual boost after Che's death in Bolivia in 1967.

Movements emerge out of tacit and collective knowledge that gives the actors and activists a worldview (*Weltanschauung*) that, as Karl Mannheim has shown us, constitutes a reality for those divided by class struggles. Mannheim's concept of 'utopia' designates 'that certain oppressed groups are intellectually so strongly interested in the destruction and transformation of a given condition of society that they unwittingly see only those elements in the situation which tend to negate it.'[36] An objectivist point of view cannot account for the Fadaiyan's constructed worldview that enabled them to perceive themselves as the vanguard of societal change in Iran; sociology of knowledge, à la Mannheim, can. Ahmadzadeh rendered armed struggle intelligible for his generation in the manner not achieved by pre-Fadaiyan militants. Such intelligibility sets apart Fadaiyan from preceding militants and is conceptualised by Jazani's brilliant distinction between 'violent action' (*amal-e qahramiz*) and 'armed struggle' (*mobarezeh-ye mosallahaneh*): armed struggle involves violent operations but armed struggle is not reducible to violent action: 'Armed struggle is the pivotal strategy of the liberation movement. As such, armed struggle basically relies on violent operations and this is why it is called "armed struggle" although in this form of struggle peaceful methods [*ashkal-e mosalematamiz*] are also utilized.'[37] For Jazani, the pre-Fadai groups' 'violent methods' involved little or no conceptualisation of the movement that the militants needed to *create*. I can refer the reader to the Maoists (ROTPI in particular) who relied on general discontent among the people (in Kurdistan or among the Qashqai tribesmen) to launch an armed uprising in the vague hope that their challenge to the state would grow. These groups did not create a movement after their own image. Fadaiyan, on the contrary, shaped the student movement in their own image (since they came from the university students), and had planned, following Jazani's theory, to create networks of workers and other social groups. For Jazani armed struggle did not signify a putsch, but the nucleus of a popular movement. For this generation, identification with Marxism-Leninism had very little theoretical basis, and it revealed the Tudeh's legacy at the time when the Party was practically dead within the political scene while still exerting a ghostly but measurable influence over the generation that had abandoned Tudeh but was nonetheless tied to it through leftist lexicon and literature. To this tradition, Sho'aiyan was an *anomaly*. And the nail that sticks out gets hammered down.

According to Sho'aiyan, as mentioned, the Iranian revolutionary movement had two options: Leninism and *Revolution* (SOLI 40). Based on his experience, observations, and studies, he strongly believed that Leninism (even claims to it), as he understood the word, would only bring the struggle to a theoretical impasse. He feared the New Communist Movement might succumb to the toothless Tudeh-style politics of defeatism and compromise (being dependent on the USSR's foreign policy) with the regime. In fact, this did happen: a group known as the *Monsha'ebin* (splitters) broke ranks with the OIPFG in 1977 and later joined the Tudeh Party.[38] The other option was to uphold a *nominal* adherence to Leninism and carry out urban guerrilla warfare, à la Latin America militants, *in practice*, regardless of the theoretical contradictions of this course of action. As we saw, Lenin would reject armed struggle of the 'petty-bourgeois intelligentsia.' For PFG theorists, Leninism enabled vanguardism, regardless of the method they used, and, although contradictory, they were correct. Coming from a generation of 'practitioners,' Fadaiyan chose the latter. Inevitably. Sho'aiyan's penetrating gaze picked out the contradiction in the PFG position, and he argued in favor of the theoretical consistency for the movement about which he cared. But the PFG leadership, especially with the growing influence of Jazani over Fadaiyan under Ashraf, was reluctant even to identify the problem, let alone resolve it. This reluctance is epitomised by Sho'aiyan's dismissal—a man who was as critical toward Fadaiyan as he unwaveringly praised them as the Promethean instigators of a heroic era for the liberation of Iran.

By the time Fadaiyan emerged onto the political scene, there remained only memories of the Iranian Communist Party (ICP). With the ICP leaders killed in the Stalinist purges in the 1930s, the tradition founded by ICP was eradicated. When the Tudeh Party was founded upon the direct involvement of the Soviet Union,[39] it was intended, as confirmed by the Tudeh leaders,[40] to function as a pro-Soviet, anti-fascist united front, following the Comintern-Dimitrov doctrine guided by Stalin.[41] Here is where we understand the curse of foundations: with the original founding moment of Iranian communism by the ICP totally eradicated, the tradition of the Tudeh Party—its literature, language, sectarianism, mannerisms, and policies—overshadowed the next generation, since the Tudeh had given the Left its *discourse*—one that had sedimented into the particular *accent* of Marxism that Fadaiyan's generation had internalised. Sho'aiyan represented a *genuine departure* from this tradition.

So the 'choice' between Leninism or *Revolution* was really whether we wanted to stay within the already established discourse of the Left, a legacy of Tudeh, that had given the New

Communist Movement its discourse (but *not* its content), or make a radical departure from it. The latter would have constituted the challenging issue of communist-liberatory *refoundation*. It would require not only abandoning the Tudeh, Leninism, *Showravism*, and opportunism, but also exiting the already established and prevalent theoretical discourses that fixed phenomena to the discursively generated algorithms of Truth and Action. This seemed to be too bold a move for the Fadai leaders to make. But, more importantly, with the PFG's armed struggle aiming to inspire a popular uprising against the Shah, I ask, *would adopting Sho'aiyan's theory measurably lead the PFG closer to victory? Sho'aiyan's theory provided no actual or practical contribution to the movement that had already established itself in Iran.* But this observation, while true, is still contaminated with pragmatism, and not concerned with the principled argument that a movement so radical as Fadaiyan's is expected to be equally radical in its theory. On the other hand, it was clear the PFG would not accept Sho'aiyan's anti-Leninist theory. At the personal level, the fact that they recruited Sho'aiyan only to isolate and abandon him without support suggests a lack of respect for his life. The PFG could have taken in other PDF members and let go of Sho'aiyan from the outset. Ashraf's decision, therefore, remains morally questionable.

With the gift of hindsight, though, we can observe the 'magic of dialectic' (Sho'aiyan) in the whole affair: the personal and organisational conflicts narrated in this chapter gave birth to two interesting written debates: one on the intellectuals (Chapter 4), the other on his *Shuresh* (Chapter 6). In a way, Fadaiyan delivered what they had promised—they allowed these debates to take place. But for the PFG leadership, Ashraf in particular, the group was too precious to be endangered and potentially paralysed through ideological debates.

When Sho'aiyan charges Fadaiyan, quite justifiably, with sectarianism and actions that remind him (and us) of Stalinist methods (specifically, secretly profiling Sho'aiyan for the purpose of his later dismissal), he does not mean to single them out as 'evil' guerrillas—the position taken by right-wing yellow journalism in Iran nowadays, although the Fadai leaders were utterly responsible for their poor treatment of Sho'aiyan and endangering his life. Sho'aiyan regarded Fadaiyan's sectarianism and Stalinism as *symptomatic of the ideological positions* they had uncritically adopted. What Fadaiyan did *not* learn from Sho'aiyan, they learned bitterly from the tumultuous post-revolutionary circumstances when OIPFG underwent endless splits that were exacerbated by Stalinist (especially 'dossier-making') methods,[42] megalomaniac leaders, and the state's brutal repression. This diagnosis further reinforces Sho'aiyan's argument in favor of the *liberation front*, and it anticipates both the overly ideological and sectarian public re-emergence of the leftist groups after 1979 and the need for pluralism, democracy, and dialogue that became key to the Left's rebuilding after the repression of the 1980s. Therefore, far from being purely ideological, Sho'aiyan's critique of Fadaiyan was *principled*. He must be credited as being a *singular* leftist revolutionary who advocated pluralism and democracy in the unkindests of times. In this regard, he was at least two decades ahead of his generation. In spirit, he belonged to a future chapter of the Iranian Left.

4

ON INTELLECTUALS

*These [leftist] activists circulate outlawed books
ineptly and without taking intellectual lessons
from them. At most, they feel content reading and
finishing them... They read these books only to
memorise some passages word for word... Faced
with the actual events, they only seek out models
rather than exercising their brains... That is why
the tendency* (jenah) *that calls itself 'the Left' so
far has been the most uncreative tendency.*

Sho'aiyan, WBD 17

The exchange between Sho'aiyan and Momeni on the
ontological position of the revolutionary intellectuals
remains an important but overlooked debate within
twentieth-century Iranian intellectual history. The central concern of this debate is the *agency of Iranian intellectuals fighting
for national liberation and democracy (and socialism) while no
popular movement exists for them to represent.* For Sho'aiyan, in
particular, the *intellectuals' agency and subjectivity* constitutes one

pillar of his *tripartite theory of rebellion* or revolution (Chapter 6), which also includes *the front* (Chapter 5). This debate is largely forgotten due to its neglect by scholars and activists alike, as the emerging discourses of secularism and democracy—in the aftermath of repressive and turbulent post-revolutionary times—have dominated Iranian intellectual imagination. Thus, key issues within this debate that pertain to the intellectuals' social and political position under the Shah's repressive development have been relegated to oblivion. This is how discursive shifts take place.

The exchange represents a conceptual disagreement in situating the leftist intellectuals within the liberation movement. Its importance rests with the fact that the *absolute majority* of militant activists in the 1970s were university students and educated professionals from the middle or lower classes. A pivotal guiding idiom of the New Communist Movement was 'liberation' as championed (however conceptually) by the (self-declared) militant vanguards of the 'working class'—another key idiom. Given the Left's (often only nominal) allegiance to Marxism-Leninism, the class analysis of the intellectuals was deemed a priority, for the guerrillas who mostly came from non-working-class backgrounds needed to probe their very own *raison d'être* within the envisaged liberation movement of Iran. Beneath the hard and uninviting shell of algorithmic Marxist prose used by Fadaiyan and other leftists, as well as Sho'aiyan's idiosyncratic (and often polemical) prose, there did indeed simmer *the quest of Iranian revolutionary intellectuals for self-understanding* within the country's rapid, repressive development, forced by the state, in which the social relations were shifting due to social mobility between classes and displacement of population from country to town.

FROM TEHRAN TO MASHHAD

To understand the trajectory of Sho'aiyan's maverick approach to the revolutionary intellectuals, we need to trace his thoughts back to the mid-1960s. Sho'aiyan's specific understanding of the intellectuals' role within the liberation movement is partly due to his professed lack of knowledge about Marxist class analysis (RRC 32). As is well known, Marxism holds that educated individuals and the intelligentsia serve as the professionals who run the bureaucratic, managerial, and technical machinery of capitalist production and state. They do not directly participate in the relations of production between the bourgeoisie and the proletariat (and the petite bourgeoisie, for that matter) but they feed off the productive, proletarian class, while serving, for the most part, as cultural and intellectual representatives of the capitalist ruling class. Such class analysis is not present in Sho'aiyan's theory, and Momeni's criticism sharply flags this absence.

Already in his 1968 article '*Pardehdari*' Sho'aiyan announces, '*Rowshanfekr amuzgar-e tabaqeh ast*': 'the intellectual is the teacher of the class' ('Exposing' in SW 6; IRJS 26). We need to pay careful attention to Sho'aiyan's unique lexicon and semantics here. In this article, he still uses the common Persian word for 'intellectual'—'*rowshanfekr*.' The French word *intellectuel* entered Iranian modernist intellectual circles during the late Qajar Dynasty (1785–1925) and especially after the humiliating defeats of the Qajars in the Russo-Persian Wars (ending in 1828) when these educated Iranians pondered the root causes of their homeland's seemingly irremediable backwardness. An Arabic import borrowed from the Ottoman cultural milieu where this term was used by Turkish modernist intellectuals, Iranian intellectuals first used '*monawarolfekr*'—literally, 'enlightened-minded'—to translate *intellectuel*. During the state-sponsored Persian revivalism under Reza Shah Pahlavi and later, the term was gradually transformed into *rowshanfekr*, also meaning 'enlightened-minded.' It is a catch-all term to refer to a vast array of individuals engaged in mental work—from the intelligentsia to philosophers and social scientists, university students, lay intellectuals, poets, writers, professors, and social commentators. One component, though not an exclusive one, is the *implied* critical stance of *rowshanfekr*.

Although published in 1968, Sho'aiyan dates the article 1966. Incidentally, the Persian translation (from French) of Antonio Gramsci's famous essay 'On Intellectuals' was published in *Arash* (February–March 1968) through the translation of Manouchehr Hezarkhani (b. 1934)—a pro-Maleki activist and member of the Iranian Socialist League in Europe. The translation was published with the intervention of Jalal Al Ahmad who had been interested in the subject since his 1964 book on intellectuals (published in 1978), in which he included a chapter on Gramsci's 'The Formation of Intellectuals.'[1] The essay was followed by a few more of Gramsci's translated articles.[2] Sho'aiyan's association with the intellectual magazines and, cautiously, with Maleki's circle render it likely that, as an autodidact, he relied on sources like *Arash* and *Jahan-e Naw* to study the latest developments in the world's intellectual trends. We must also mention *Andisheh va Honar* (*Thought and Art*), edited by pro-Maleki Nasser Vosuqi, that published the works of critics of the Soviet Union including Isaac Deutscher. Anyway, *surprisingly* Sho'aiyan does not acknowledge Gramsci in his writings, except twice and in passing (IRJS 22, 348, n. 4). So I offer a lexical-conceptual analysis to probe the possible connection. Rather than being a direct influence, I argue, this is a process of contemplation.

Sho'aiyan's *conceptual* encounter with the *problématique* of the 'revolutionary intellectual' goes back to his watershed pamphlet

What Is To Be Done? This is where the two key concepts of *shuresh* and front emerge alongside his idea of the intellectuals (Chapter 2).

In 1972 he still uses the term 'rowshanfekr' (WBD 9) although conceptually the term captures the ideas he soon developed through his debate with Momeni. Here he submits that the agency of armed struggle rests with the intellectuals.

> The weight of struggles against the regime (*dastgah*) is still upon the shoulders of the educated and intellectuals (*rowshanfekran*) in Iran. Our anti-reaction, anti-coloni-alism struggle has not yet expanded beyond the domain of the intellectuals and has not reached the masses. In its most expansive moments, [the struggle] has paid a visit to a handful of craftsmen and workers and has withdrawn faster than we had imagined. [This is true] to the extent that the share of other forces, layers, and classes in this effort is so little that one could simply ignore it. (WBD 9)

In short, the intellectuals lead the revolutionary movement, since the share of non-intellectuals—in particular, the working class—is simply negligible. To a probing gaze, though, this obser-vation problematises the issue of *representation*: the intellectuals largely man the liberation movement but *on behalf of* the working and exploited classes. Obviously, this position is sanctioned by the Marxist proclivity of Iranian dissidents. 'That the educated (*darskhandegan*) are representatives and intellectuals of which classes and layers is another question' (WBD 9). Sho'aiyan does not provide an answer yet, but he knows that the intellectuals are expected to convey 'the struggle to the masses' (WBD 9). These lines emphasise the concept of intellectuals as *representatives* of classes—in this case the colonised masses with revolutionary potential. Gramsci speaks of intellectuals not as independent social groups but as 'strata' attached to the classes. Hezarkhani translates the word 'strata' into '*layehha*' (layers), the very word Sho'aiyan later deploys in his debate with Momeni.[3] At this time, though, Sho'aiyan does not go any further with his concept of intellectuals. Instead, he takes a detour to launch the pathology of 'intellectualism' manifested through self-aggrandising and ostentatious self-exhibitionism endemic to Iranian intellectuals. Revolutionary intellectuals have no control over their linguistic and non-linguistic gestures, and this is how they endanger the movement (WBD 9–12).

These symptoms reveal a *bimari* (disease, illness) (WBD 12). Sho'aiyan argues that the Iranian revolutionary intellectuals' love of books is superficial: they remain heedless of the lessons to be learned and are certainly without creative application of what they learn. The leftists only memorise books. 'Just like the [Shi'i] clerics (*mollayan*) that treat the Koran in the same miserable way, they [activists] do not reflect on them [the books they read]…, only memorising them.' This is a symptom of 'intellectualism' with serious consequences. When confronted with concrete cases, as the epigraph to this chapter confirms, 'they only seek templates (*olgu*) and do not exercise their brains' (WBD 17). This is why the Left has produced, by and large, theoretically uncreative (*bihonar*; literally, 'artless') responses to the conditions that have hurt the movement. We are, then, dealing with a polar opposite: read-a-lot and think-little as opposed to read-and-think-a-lot (WBD 17).

By April 1973, in response to Fadaiyan on the issue of the revolutionary front (Chapter 5), the term *rowshangar* makes its debut in Sho'aiyan's writings ('Inquiry about a Critique' in HSW 7). In June 1973, targeting the lack of theoretical training among the militants, Sho'aiyan writes his dialogical 'An Outline on How to Study' and submits it to Fadaiyan. This imaginary conversation between Nader Shayegan and Hassan Rumina is where his term 'rowshangar'—literally, 'enlightener'—replaces the common term 'rowshanfekr', or 'intellectual.' This neologism allows Sho'aiyan to semantically mark off his concept of the revolutionary vanguard from the commonplace notion shared by a vast array of political groups, past and present. Arguing that studying should be concomitant with fighting ('An Outline' in SW 9), he proposes a practical way for incorporating systematic study into the minutely scheduled daily life of the underground militants. He appraises the underground lifespan of a militant to be three to five years, which is actually too generous an estimation compared to Fadaiyans' realistic projection: six months. Given that, contends Sho'aiyan, a militant can read only about ten to fifteen books in his or her entire underground life ('An Outline' in SW 12, 15). Sho'aiyan's view of training the militants was quite mechanistic. He wished to forge cadres in the shortest possible time and deploy them to operations. In effect, the way he conceives of the theoretical training of the militant stands out as a rite of passage of sorts without any practical use for the theory learned. Beyond his intentions perhaps, what he suggests resembles the ideological training of party cadres reminiscent of such programs under communist parties in socialist countries. In terms of the mechanics of the cadres' function and from a Foucaultian viewpoint, the militant is not much different from the docile subject of authoritarian state machinery and its security agents. In other words, *the 'matrix of subjection' of the state and the 'matrix of liberation' of the guerrilla both function based on the instrumental deployment of the purposive subjectivity of the individual.*[4] I have discussed this issue to some extent elsewhere[5]; what *radically* separates the two matrices is the social imaginary that propels the militant, and thereby (potentially) the masses, toward a future society in which there won't be any need for the militant. The militants are not only self-sacrificing (*fadai*) but *self-dissolving*. The liberated world has no need for the vanguard. The militant vanguard's *raison d'être* is linked to the process of liberation. Thus, in the post-revolutionary era, the militant will be transformed into military personnel to fend off counter-revolution. There is no continuity between the two modes of existence.[6] But Sho'aiyan had not yet come to this conclusion.

Not surprisingly, for Sho'aiyan the issue of (lack of) educating the militants goes deeper than just offering training schedules. He views the ultimate militant in his own image. 'In my view, soldier and philosopher, warrior and enlightener of the working class should not be on separate wings. As long as the enlightener and the soldier of the working class are in two separate divisions of the workers' army, the hope of salvation (*rastgari*) of the working class and reaching communism, however pleasant, remains only imaginary (*pendarin*)' ('An Outline' in SW 11). This statement reflects Mostafa's own lived experience as a revolutionary intellectual.

THE PERPLEXING EXISTENCE OF REVOLUTIONARY INTELLECTUALS

I have mentioned that Ashraf did indeed fulfil his promise to Sho'aiyan: however limited in its reach, this provided him with an unprecedented opportunity to debate his ideas. The PFG mid-career theoretician Momeni was assigned to this debate. Hamid Momeni was born in 1942 in the Kurdish province of Kermanshah. He graduated from the University of Tehran with an honours degree in economics and was employed by the Centre for the Intellectual Cultivation of Children and Youth (*Kanun-e*

Parvarsh-e Fekri-ye Kudakan va Nojavanan), founded in 1965 by Empress Farah Pahlavi. Momeni knew Russian and was the author of books on human evolution and the translator of a treatise on Nader Shah Afshar (1688–1747). He joined the PFG in late 1972 and soon grew into the PFG's mid-career theoretician and a key figure in the publication of *Nabard-e Khalq*, for which he anonymously wrote editorials. Momeni adhered to the Soviet version of Marxism-Leninism, rejected the de-Stalinisation process that had begun under Nikita Khrushchev, and advocated the critique of Soviet revisionism launched by Mao Zedong. These ideas appeared in the pages of *Nabard-e Khalq*. While in the PFG ranks, Momeni wrote a treatise defending Ahmadzadeh's theory but Ashraf refused to publish it under the PFG banner. From prison, Jazani reacted to the Maoist tendencies in Momeni's writings. Momeni was assigned to debate both Setareh and Sho'aiyan. In response to Setareh he wrote four controversial essays on China and Stalinism.[7] Aside from his exchange with Sho'aiyan on the intellectuals, Momeni is also the author of a critical book on Sho'aiyan's *Shuresh*.[8]

The documented exchanges between Momeni and Sho'aiyan follow their face-to-face debates in Tehran.[9] Their meetings did not go well as the two did not have the patience for each other's mannerisms and ideas and thus agreed on written exchanges instead. For Sho'aiyan, Momeni exemplified a classic case of pedantic intellectualism,[10] while Momeni, confessing that his ire at *Revolution* had caused him to lose patience,[11] accused Sho'aiyan of exhibitionism: 'Our comrade [Sho'aiyan] supposes if he curses Lenin he becomes a Lenin.'[12] The debate published in *An Inquiry into the Intellectual or Enlightener of the Working Class* includes two texts by Momeni and three by Sho'aiyan (dated between 5 and 19 August 1973). It was instigated by Momeni's ruthless criticism of *Shuresh* (*Revolution*) in which the concept of 'rowshangar' or 'enlightener' plays a key role.[13] A copy of *Revolution* (second edition) had been given to the PFG by March/ April 1973, before the PDF had 'joined' the PFG.[14] Momeni was assigned to Mashhad shortly after Sho'aiyan had settled there, and although the two apparently did not meet in Mashhad, Momeni spent his time writing his rejoinder to Sho'aiyan's *Shuresh*.[15] (The debate continued in two additional volumes about *Revolution*.[16]) Two issues dominate this debate: the *first issue* is Sho'aiyan's *neologisms and puritan Persian*—a legacy of Iranian historian and reformer Ahmad Kasravi (1890–1946) who had promoted and used a prose purified of avoidable Arabic imports. Sho'aiyan had chosen (possibly around 1968) the Kasravite prose, he claims, exclusively for the underground literature he authored so he would avoid being identified by SAVAK through his prose, as his writings had already appeared in cultural magazines by this time (Rev 11). The proof is his *A Review of the Relations Between the Soviet Union and the Revolutionary Movement of Jungle* (written 1968, printed 1970), written using common jargon, compared to his underground manual, *What Is To Be Done?* (written 1968, distributed 1972), which uses his distinct Kasravite prose. The dates indicate that in 1968 the two styles of prose began to emerge in his writing. Whatever his motivation, I argue, *Kasravite prose enabled him to articulate a revolutionary theory that radically departed from the common lexis of Iranian Marxism, originated with, and popularised by, the Tudeh Party*. Momeni in particular objects to Sho'aiyan's Kasravite neologisms and argues that Sho'aiyan's 'arbitrary' (*mandaravardi*) terminology carries 'no historical and cultural' significance, thus causing him to confuse the meanings of key, common concepts of Marxism and revolutionary literature.[17] The *second issue is Sho'aiyan's lack of Marxist knowledge about the formation of intellectuals*. The lack of sufficient knowledge of Marx and relying only on translations available to him (Rev 103) forces

Sho'aiyan to reflect on his own experience and the knowledge he had gathered from hybrid and diverse sources and expressed through his eccentric prose. Momeni argued that Sho'aiyan could have used the Marxist analysis critically and advanced his position. Sho'aiyan did the opposite. And this irritated Momeni.

I have said that Sho'aiyan's concept of *rowshangar* is owed to Gramsci. This observation results from my close, intertextual reading, and thus it is more than just conjecture. Let me offer some clue as to why this should be: in the debate Sho'aiyan asks, 'Does each class have its own particular enlightener (*rowshangar*), or else, do the enlighteners constitute a specific class, and not all classes have their own particular enlighteners?'[18] Momeni confirms that the debate was launched by this question, which he regards as a sign of Sho'aiyan's deep misunderstanding.[19] Now compare Sho'aiyan's question to the opening line of Gramsci's 'On Intellectuals': 'Are intellectuals an autonomous and independent social group, or does every social group have its own particular specialised category of intellectuals?'[20] The questions are *identical*. In conjunction with the word '*layehha*' (the Persian rendition of 'strata'), this causes Sho'aiyan to 'deviate' from the Soviet-Marxist understanding of the intellectuals, which Momeni intercepts.

Gramsci argues that intellectuals are *not* a distinct social category and do *not* stand free from class relations. In fact, all classes have their own *strata* of intellectuals. Categorically, intellectuals comprise 'organic' and 'traditional' intellectuals (as well as 'conjectural' ones). 'Every social group, coming into existence on the original terrain of an essential function in the world of economic production, creates together with itself, organically, one or more strata.'[21] Note that 'strata' is *plural*: there is always more than one group of 'intellectuals' attached to any particular class. For instance, the entrepreneurial class finds itself attached to accountants and managers who are organic to its function. Every class also finds itself historically and culturally attached to strata of intellectuals that Gramsci calls *traditional*. The peasants, for instance, have been attached to the church. But this categorisation begs the question, what constitutes the intellectuals? Gramsci's conception goes against the Marxist canon: 'The most widespread error of method seems to me that of having looked for this criterion of distinction in the intrinsic nature of intellectual activities, rather than in the ensemble of the system of relations in which these activities (and therefore the intellectual groups who personify them) have their place within the general complex of social relations.'[22] The distinct nature of intellectual, cerebral activity can only be analysed in relation to the social relations in which the intellectual is inserted. This collapses the Marxist distinction between manual and mental labor: 'Indeed the worker or proletarian... is not specifically characterised by his manual or instrumental work, but by performing this work in specific conditions and in specific social relations.'[23] Then comes the true Gramscian moment: 'All men are intellectuals, one could therefore say: but not all men have in society the function of intellectuals,' Gramsci submits. 'When one distinguishes between intellectuals and nonintellectuals, one is referring in reality only to the immediate social function of the professional category of the intellectuals...'[24] In other words, since all humans hold worldviews and conceptions of the world, they are inevitably 'intellectuals.' As such, '*Homo faber* cannot be separated from *homo sapiens*,'[25] and thus the relationship between the intellectuals and production is a mediated one.[26] The political party is nothing but the organisation of the organic intellectuals of the working class.[27] Sho'aiyan's position, *with caution*, is similar to Gramsci's. In fact, Sho'aiyan credits Gramsci only once in this context, when he refers to Gramsci's statement that manual labor involves more

150

muscular than cerebral activity (IRJS 22), suggesting that the two are not mutually exclusive.[28]

Momeni's position comes from Marx's distinction between manual and mental labor, in particular the way this distinction is read through Lenin and the Soviet academy of Marxism-Leninism. Since under capitalism mental labor feeds off the manual labor of the proletariat, the intelligentsia structurally belongs to the exploiting, bourgeois class. The proletarian revolution will gradually render the expert class redundant as 'society regulates the general production,' causing the division between mental and manual labor to wither away.[29] Clearly, the materialist concept of history cannot understand the intelligentsia outside of the material relations of production, i.e. class relations, since the intellectuals can only exist within the social institutions of capitalist economy.[30] But then there is the problem of the 'revolutionary intellectuals' through whose articulation the unity of theory and practice is achieved. Regarding the revolutionary intellectuals, however, Marx's position was ambivalent.

> On the one hand, Marx's general perspective was that the working class itself, as the social agency of historical change, would organically generate through long years of struggle the necessary cultural and political conditions for socialism... On the other hand, ... there are repeated references to the need for leading or vanguard forces and to the idea that, through their own self-activity, workers could never escape their social immediacy enough to arrive at a total picture of capitalist society.[31]

The debate between Sho'aiyan and Momeni does not represent the Gramscian versus the Leninist view, since these two positions are not entirely mutually exclusive. Gramsci's position is quite 'materialist' but he brilliantly resolves the Marxist dilemma by refusing to separate mental activity from material life and by proposing that all humans are intellectual regardless of their function. Here we are dealing with a certain intellectual geneal-ogy: Marx himself did not promote a rigid division of mental and manual labor, but the complex processes that unfolded through the Bolshevik Revolution, in particular Stalin's purges in which he accused (fellow Marxist) intellectuals of betraying the Soviet Union, led to a certain concept that found its way into Iran through the Tudeh Party and in particular through the experience of the split led by Maleki. In this view, the intel-lectual uncommitted to the Soviet Union becomes ancillary to imperialism and the bourgeoisie. In our case, both interlocutors cut through the Marxist-Gramscian positions: Momeni due to his rigid understanding of Marxism, and Sho'aiyan due to his lack of proper knowledge of Marxism. But they converge on the theoretical arena that reveals 'the Marxist tradition struggled with the contradiction between a theoretical identity rooted in the vision of proletarian self-emancipation and the political reality of a movement dominated by intellectuals.'[32] Put another way, the two encounter one another over a predicament of Marxism that is larger than their context and more complex than they could address. The responses of each, of course, have theoretical and practical ramifications.

The exchange begins with Momeni, following the approach he calls Marxist, defining the intellectuals (*rowshanfekran*): they carry out mental work in all divisions of labor within history. Under capitalism, they ultimately belong to the bourgeois class, but some intellectuals come into conflict with capitalism both economically and culturally, as they are 'influenced by the great reality of their time, the working class' and transform into revo-lutionary or proletarian intellectuals. Thus, the task of 'resolving the technical leadership of the proletarian revolution' falls upon the intellectuals. They are the last remnant of the bourgeoisie to be eliminated under socialism as communist society emerges.[33] 'Any danger threatening socialist society comes from intellectuals who are the only residue of the bourgeoisie in the socialist society.'[34] For Momeni, I note, while the 'revolutionary intellectual' is inevitable, it must be transcended.

In contrast, Sho'aiyan coins the term 'enlighteners' (*rowshangaran*) to refer to the strata or layers (*layehha*) *attached* to each class and yet *distinct* from them. Since 'every manifestation reveals a being,'[35] the enlightener is different from the class economically by not 'directly participating in the process of production' and politically by being the 'mentor [or teacher; *amuzgar*] of the class' toward the revolution. The enlighteners arise from the class as it is constituted by the material foundations of history. They 'are the products of the class and class conflict.' Every class has its own internal plurality and characteristics ('Inquiry about a Critique' in HSW 7) and thus multiple layers of enlighteners. Social mobility indicates that 'class essence' [*seresht-e tabaqati*], which determines class existence [*zendegi-ye tabaqati*], is not determined simply by being born into a class. Rather, 'living the life of a class determines one's class essence.' Moreover, "The key (*asl*) is not that who is born into which class, but that in which class one lives and for which class one fights' (SURMJ 59–60). The intellectuals who are not workers '*ideologically* belong to the working *class*, [they are] the ideological elements and enlighteners of the proletariat' (IRJS 86; emphasis in the original). Sho'aiyan charges Momeni with reducing the 'worker' to a vocational concept, devoid of meaningful, actable content (IRJS 87). I put Sho'aiyan's statement in contemporary terms: *class position determines class belonging, not vice versa*. And yet, following Marxist principles, he submits that the proletarian *essence* is distinct from other classes. This means that class positions, in regard to production but in the Iranian context also colonialism, pre-exist the revolutionary agent, and any activist taking this position will be joining class warfare and in Iran, in particular, the anti-imperialist war of liberation. Of course, the position remains paradoxical for someone who wishes to do away with rigid class analysis based on class belonging. It does away, however, with the 'demographic' and 'employment' conceptions of class, insinuated by Momeni. And, of course, this is a convenient stance for Sho'aiyan to take: *rowshangaran* absorb the characteristics of the class they represent without losing their own distinctive characteristics.[36] For Sho'aiyan, the enlightener is the necessary catalyst for transforming the working class from a 'class in itself' into a 'class for itself.' When the latter appears, we surmise, the distinction between the enlighteners and the class they represent will wither away.

In response to Momeni's position—that the intellectuals belong to the dominant classes—Sho'aiyan asks: if engaging in mental activity causes the intellectuals to belong to the exploiting classes, how can we speak of revolutionary or proletarian classes? How, in other words, can the inherently bourgeois intellectuals become proletarian intellectuals? Was Che Guevara a 'bourgeois intellectual'? If Momeni is right, whence arise the intellectuals of the oppressed classes? Is there not a contradiction in Momeni's concept? Momeni's schoolish understanding shows the 'ugliest form of university-stricken (*daneshgahzadegi*) conduct.' [37] Moreover, he argues, Momeni's equation of 'revolutionary intellectuals' with 'proletarian intellectuals' is problematic. Were revolutionary intellectuals such as Yasser Arafat or Mirza Kuchek Khan also proletarian intellectuals?[38] These errors, Sho'aiyan polemicises, indicate Momeni's uncritical adherence to Leninism and Chinese communism.[39] For us, the last identification is interesting: too general to stick but evident from Momeni's future editorials in *Nabard-e Khalq*. In any case, this is where the concept of *enlightener* shows its merits: the European philosophical connotations of *les intellectuels* are lost in the Persian *rowshanfekr*, which has acquired a *political connotation* in Persian. *Rowshangar*, proposes Sho'aiyan, strictly signifies the political intellectual and thereby preserves the vast, neutral implications of *rowshanfekr*, which Sho'aiyan intends to de-politicise.[40]

The debate becomes more intense when in his reply Momeni accuses Sho'aiyan of confusing three Marxist concepts in his neologised term: 'conscious layer (*qeshr-e agah*) of the [working] class,' 'revolutionary vanguard,' and 'professional revolutionary.' The problem, Momeni argues, is that proletarian intellectuals learn from the masses, analyse and summarise that knowledge, and then return their findings, through teaching and guiding, to the masses. Sho'aiyan's 'enlightener' only refers to the teaching component of the intellectuals' function.[41] Following Marxist analysis of the petite bourgeoisie, Momeni refers to the intellectuals' 'dual character' (*kheslat-e doganeh*): a small number of intellectuals become the 'greatest advocates of the masses' while the majority of them constitute 'a major obstacle for the revolution and socialist society.' Both the working class and liberation vanguards consist of revolutionary intellectuals and conscious layers of workers. This is because historical materialism has enabled the proletarian agency under capitalism (unlike slaves and peasants).[42] To maintain his distinction, Momeni avers, the 'proletarian intellectual' is the one who is linked to the 'political life and struggles of the proletariat': a revolutionary intellectual who actually labours as a worker is in fact a 'revolutionary worker.'[43] 'The proletarian intellectuals make up only a small layer of the large layer of intellectuals. The vast majority of intellectuals simply submit to the socialist revolution without believing it in their hearts.'[44] If the small layer of intellectuals loses contact with the masses and stops learning from them, they lose their 'organic' connection and thus degenerate back to their own class origins. Examples of such degeneration within the socialist movement include Trotsky, Soviet leaders from Khrushchev onwards, Tito, Dubček, etc.[45] What does Momeni mean by learning from the masses? It is true, he argues, that all intellectuals feed off the 'surplus value' produced by workers, but then there is an internal diversity within this group: 'Some of them have risen from the masses and are in continued contact with the masses in their private lives. Such and such Harvard professor and Samad Behrangi are both intellectuals. Can one use the stereotypical statement that "the intellectuals do not understand the masses" to refer to both of them?'[46] Yet, because of his rigid class analysis, Momeni inevitably *mystifies* the so-called organic connection and the 'learning from the masses'; he offers no concrete example of how intellectuals can 'learn' from the working class. Anything other than this class analysis, he maintains, constitutes petite bourgeois deviationism, and to prevent it, there is only one solution:

Lenin says that the only way to overcome bureaucracy is to hold bureaucracy answerable directly to people. This means people have the right to go straight to [the office] without filing a complaint or writing letters to his superiors and yank mister intellectual from behind his desk and take him to the street where they argue and quarrel with him and even beat him up (*kotakkari konand*). On the other hand, [our] intellectuals, deviated intellectuals in particular, should go and labour through physical work. A sentimental intellectual, for example, who says, 'Machinism is evil, it enslaves humans, etc.,' must go and furrow land using an ox or dig a well using shovel and pick to understand his mistake. Moreover, the masses' surveillance over intellectuals and specially the masses' cultural revolution can prevent bourgeois tendency in science, arts, and politics.[47]

The passage vividly conjures up the images of the Chinese Cultural Revolution in its first part. And while the second part depicts Momeni's fascination with the gulag-style 'rehabilitation' of intellectuals, it also reveals an intertextual (sardonic) intimation to Jalal Al Ahmad's *Gharbzadegi* (*Westoxication*; 1962) in which Al Ahmad launched a critique of rapid (and shallow) modernisation without society's cultural preparedness for it, a process through which Iranian masses, dazed by the glamor of mushrooming cities and imported western objects and culture, wandering helplessly to make sense of a world alien to them, have lost their connection to traditional (religious) identity. The result is the scaphised Self that is neither modern nor traditional. Momeni attacks Mostafa Rahimi and Al Ahmad 'who have written books on intellectuals in a cheeky way (*ba kamal-e porrui*) without knowing anything.'[48] This is meant to attack Sho'aiyan's association with the (allegedly, 'liberal') cultural circles of the 1960s. Yet Momeni's position is actually useful: it 'resolves' the theoretical impasse of his class analysis, as it represents his Stalinist thinking. Undoubtedly, the remark is aimed at Sho'aiyan. Sadly, though, Sho'aiyan registers no scruples about Momeni's Stalinism. In fact, he implicitly endorses it by responding that when the people beat up the intellectual, that will be the moment of *shuresh*.[49]

Sho'aiyan's extensive 'open letter' to Momeni concludes this round of debates. In his 'open letter,' Sho'aiyan clarifies that he coined the term 'enlightener' to exclusively signify the 'political intellectual,' thus leaving the signifier 'intellectual' to encompass the vast array of signifieds from educated professionals to philosophers. Thus, he submits, the 'class enlightener is the guide of the working class in its class struggle, in its political battle, in philosophical knowledge, in its revolutionary (*shureshi*) war, as well as in its assuming power.' 'The class enlightener is the mentor of the class. The party is the guiding organization of the [working] class in class war. Thus the party is the field of organic solidarity of [working] class enlighteners with one another.'[50] Just because the term 'intellectual' is now a part of the political lexicon (Momeni's point) does not mean it is used correctly.[51] Moreover, the claim that revolutionary intellectuals belong to the exploiting classes is absurd. Are the Fadai leaders and martyrs bourgeois intellectuals?[52] If the socialist states are led by intellectuals who, according to Momeni, belong to the bourgeoisie, then these states are not 'dictatorships of the proletariat' but 'capitalist dictatorships.'[53] Momeni has created a class 'multiplication table,' Sho'aiyan charges, a proof of his rigid understanding of Marxism.[54] This is an appalling reminder of the Tudeh Party that, admittedly, evokes only 'a deep hatred' in Mostafa.[55] Remember that Sho'aiyan's criticism of Tudeh's 'political algorithms,' expressed during the 1960s (as I mentioned earlier), was over a decade old:

Basically, the Tudeh Party had created new tables and values and for every notion (*mafhum*)... it had constructed a conceptual frame and when it was confronted by the realities of the outside world, it would place those realities within its frame and if the reality exceeded the limits of the [conceptual] frame, [Tudeh] would cut out the excess, and if it [reality] was smaller than the frame, it would add a few things to its sides. As a result, by distorting reality it [Tudeh] would create major confusions in the country's situation. (YGNF 32–3)

Interestingly, the algorithmic thinking that Sho'aiyan criticises is represented in Momeni's statement about *Revolution*. Momeni reportedly stated, 'I thought that instead of responding myself, I put together a number of statements by Mao and Lenin and others in a column and against them [in the opposite column] write the statements from [Sho'aiyan's] *Revolution* that contradict them. So I can show that these [statements] are not Marxist in any case' (SOLI 46). It is no wonder that in Momeni's canonical and doctrinal thinking Sho'aiyan traces Tudeh's disastrous legacy. Sho'aiyan observes Momeni's approach with a sense of disappointment. It was as if he reflected on this debate when some years earlier he had stated: 'It has not been long since leftist youth have embarked upon new, important paths and have preferred thinking, trying, and experimenting over templates (*olgubardari*). Nonetheless, they have not yet been free from Tudeh-style deductions' (WBD 17).

Rejecting algorithms, Sho'aiyan relies on his own experience, and, as if *suggesting*, asks, 'Is there a deeper measure of knowledge than life itself?'[56] He is a revolutionary intellectual who tries to bring knowledge to the working class as the privileged agent of history by virtue of Marxist theory; in no way can he belong to the bourgeois class. He is, it seems, aided by Gramsci's insights, once again, when Gramsci states:

> The relationship between the intellectuals and the world of production is not as direct as it is with the fundamental social groups but is, in varying degrees, 'mediated' by the whole fabric of society and by the complex of superstructures, of which the intellectuals are, precisely, the 'functionaries.' It should be possible both to measure the 'organic quality' [*organicità*] of the various intellectual strata and their degree of connection with a fundamental

social group, and to establish a gradation of their functions and of the superstructures from the bottom to the top (from the structural base upwards).[57]

In other words, the 'organic connection' between intellectuals and 'fundamental social groups' (bourgeoisie and proletariat) is a 'mediated,' matter-of-degree connection, measured against the (abstract) 'ideal type' (borrowing from Max Weber) organicity. Sho'aiyan's formulation, in its particular expression, points out a very interesting concept of 'subject position,' an important concept popularised by poststructuralist feminism, post-Marxism (Ernesto Laclau and Chantal Mouffe), and postcolonial theory (Gayatri Spivak) in the 1980s, before it gave birth to the now popular concept of 'intersectionality' in the early 2000s. The concept of 'subject position' in fact originated with Gramsci,[58] of which Sho'aiyan could not have had any knowledge since this part of Gramsci was not translated into Persian during his time. So he offers a *similar* concept before poststructuralism's popularity, but *writing from a marginal position in a marginal (non-European) language*, Sho'aiyan's discovery and contribution was not made known until now, here in these lines, over forty years later! And, of course, he had *not* abandoned class essentialism, despite his interesting theoretical errands. About what we call 'subject positions,' he writes: 'It is known that when it is said that generally humans have multiple roles (*chand naqshi*), this does not mean that people have *all* their social and class roles at one and the same time. It merely means that anyone in a class *has some* of his class roles and *does not have some* others' (IRJS 102; emphasis in the original). The conceptualisation resonates with poststructuralism, but, of course, Sho'aiyan was no poststructuralist, and he was still caught in class analysis and did not cut through gender, ethnicity, or sexuality, the loci where the roles are multiplied. His notion of *subject positions* allows Sho'aiyan to locate the *being* of the enlightener with remarkable conceptual accuracy. Because, 'overall humans have multiple roles,' as mentioned, 'the typical working-class enlightener is like this. He does not directly participate in production but *socially belongs* to the working *class*' (IRJS 102; emphasis in the original). Therefore, *class position determines class belonging*, not some rigid 'class multiplication table.' 'It is not the family or class to which an enlightener, indeed anyone, is born that shows her class essence. How an enlightener, or anyone, lives, and thus how she thinks, and therefore, on which side of the battlefield of class struggle she takes position will reveal her essence' ('What Is Not To Be Done?' in SW 17). As mentioned, these positions are treated as a given in his thinking. For him, the struggle against colonialism designates these class positions. The enlightener is the phenomenon of the early stages of struggle: the working class cannot create its world unless it is coherent, united, and self-conscious. It must become its own enlightener by surpassing its vanguard enlighteners ('An Outline' in SW 10). Sho'aiyan's concept reveals that the level of organicity of the class the enlightener represents is determined by the degree to which she takes revolutionary, class action. Put a different way, militant action, as the preparatory stage in the war of liberation, determines political position, and with the growing popularity of the struggle, new enlighteners will grow out of the class as the articulators of its worldview.

Momeni leaves this debate only to return with his harshest critique of *rowshangar* in his rejoinder to *Revolution* (*Shuresh*). Recall Jazani's derogatory labeling of Jaryan as 'American Marxists' to discredit Sho'aiyan. Jazani intentionally conflated Jaryan with a fictitious group in order to pose Jaryan as a SAVAK-made 'underground' group created to entrap activists.[59] Momeni goes even further, speculating that Tavakkoli was connected with the CIA in order to discredit Sho'aiyan's past through guilt by association (SOLI 137).[60] Momeni attributes Sho'aiyan's thinking to the Third Force ideas appearing in *Andisheh va Honar* (*Thought and Art*),[61] and Tavakkoli,[62] thus denying his originality: 'the author [Sho'aiyan] has not even mentioned the origins of his opinions so that the reader would encounter his statements with greater awareness.'[63] Momeni does not shy away from ad hominem attacks, calling Sho'aiyan an 'idealist' and a liar and his thinking 'metaphysical.'[64]

In *Not Rebellion*, Momeni offers a more structured discussion and argues that *rowshangar* 'is a word that the author has selected based on his prejudice in favor of his own language and he conceals roughly seven different economic, political, and organizational concepts under this word.'[65] These include: (a) intellectual, (b) revolutionary intellectual, (c) the conscious members of the class, (d) full-time revolutionary, (e) revolutionary vanguard, (f) revolutionary vanguard organization, and (g) members of the party.[66] Momeni then proceeds to offer Marxist definitions for each term. To show why the intellectuals belong to the bourgeois class, Momeni points out the upward mobility of educated members of the lower classes that enables individuals from the working class and peasantry to become a 'layer' of the bourgeoisie. This process is brought about through education (Gramsci's point, actually). Socialism inherits these intellectuals who pose a danger to communism. 'The dictatorship of proletariat... cannot eliminate intellectuals. The elimination of intellectuals will depend on the full automation of production and the vast and complete reduction of physical labour and this can only be achieved in a communist society.'[67]

Exposed to the realities of the working-class life, lower-class intellectuals (e.g. teachers) experience an 'intellectual and spiritual (*ma'navi*) conflict with the dominant system,' and 'because of their congruity with the masses and reading revolutionary literature…, even under acute repressive conditions, [they] may incline toward the masses and specially the working class and its progressive ideology.'[68] Here we can see that for Momeni the 'intellectual' is an economic category, but the 'revolutionary intellectual' is a political one. Contrary to Sho'aiyan's position, Momeni asserts, these two phenomena cannot be captured through a single concept.[69] In the conditions of 'backward countries,' by learning from the experiences of the revolutionary intellectuals of the 'more advanced countries,' revolutionary movements such as the PFG will be able 'to establish organic relations with the masses.'[70] How this process takes place *concretely* remains obscure to us.

This analysis, Momeni submits, shows why Sho'aiyan's 'sophistry' in fact conceals the bourgeois character of his seemingly revolutionary rhetoric. No class connotations stem from 'rowshan-fekr,' but Sho'aiyan translates this term, following Kasravi, as 'educated' (*darskhandeh*). Sho'aiyan's linguistic formalism allows him to maintain the hegemony of bourgeois intellectuals over the party and revolution.[71] Momeni's verdict could not be clearer: linguistic similarity produces intellectual similarity.[72] Idealism and metaphysical thinking dominate Sho'aiyan's thinking. The revolutionary intellectual who is not guided by Marxism-Leninism will inevitably arrive at anarchism.[73] Red herrings and a slippery slope in Momeni's argument allow him to charge Sho'aiyan with the unthinkable: this underground, revolutionary intellectual and a most wanted man is in fact counter-revolutionary! Once again, the verdict is clear: because of his philosophical 'idealism,' which connects him to bourgeois ideology, Sho'aiyan 'precisely wants to maintain the hegemony of bourgeois intellectuals over the party and the revolution.'[74] If we ignore Momeni's accusations, what he does here is what I am trying to show, too: Sho'aiyan was intertextually indebted to a certain historical-intellectual stream from Kasravi to *Jahan-e Naw*, but for Momeni, intertextual connections outside of his prescribed, canonical Marxist discourse are prohibited.

Sho'aiyan committed suicide upon his arrest on 5 February 1976. Momeni was shot and killed by SAVAK six days later, on 11 February. The two irreconcilable interlocutors were united by their abrupt deaths, less than a week apart. Guerrilla existence is indeed most precarious. What remains is what we carve out for ourselves in history—through action, through thought.

CONCLUSIONS: REVOLUTIONARY INTELLECTUALS IN THE MIRROR

This debate, long ignored by activists and scholars alike, has not been afforded any analytical attention, even in the extensive afterword to its recent reprint.[75] For the activists, this debate seemed to offer no fecundity and was implicitly deemed 'expired' for the post-revolutionary conditions—yet another testimony to the Iranian Left's theoretical dearth of ideas. For the handful of scholars who attended, in passing, to the intellectual history of the Left, the debate apparently seemed too trivial. They often missed the point that the guerrilla warfare inadvertently launched the question of the *agency of intellectuals who fought against the monarchical dictatorship for national liberation and democracy when there was no popular movement for them to represent.*

One study of modern Iranian intellectual history launches the essence of European modernity as the intellectual (and legal) movement toward 'universalisable subjectivity,' emanating only from the individual, and then offers painstaking readings of a vast number of key figures within Iranian modernity whose contributions are measured against the aforesaid *a priori* yard-stick.[76] Reducing a complex phenomenon like modernity to one concept, which remains questionable in itself, the study avoids an effective critique of the dark side of European Enlightenment: colonialism, marginalisation, and oppression—that is, the negation of 'universalisable subjectivity' of the Other so that the European Self could supposedly achieve its own. Offering a reductive summary of the contributions of Bizhan Jazani and Massoud Ahmadzadeh, Farzin Vahdat criticises their turn toward 'the masses' and 'denying the principle of subjectivity' in their critique of 'individual subjectivity.'[77] His verdict? Iran's guerrilla movement deviated from the purported pillar of modern subjectivity due to its adherence to Marxism-Leninism—a judgment achieved by ignoring the fact that Iran's modernity bore a cross-bred freak of autocratic monarchy, repressive development, and the peripheral participation in neo-colonial capitalism. Instead of seeing these conditions as impediments to the emergence of subjectivity, Vahdat blames the intellectuals for not advocating his Eurocentric *a priori* which he upholds as the standard-bearer of modernity.

The point of departure of another study of Iranian intellectuals' encounters with modernity, on the contrary, is the dilemma of Eurocentric concept of modernity's foreclosure on '"local" experiences and their contribution in the realization of modernity.'[78] Problematising the essentialisation of the Third World,[79] Ali Mirsepassi recognises the Iranian Left's social basis,[80] but he blames the Left's 'failure' (whatever this means) on its theoreticians' superstructural understanding of Islam and the clerics as well as its partial understanding of modernity (like Marx).[81] Mirsepassi recognises that the Left's turn toward armed struggle to mobilise the masses reflects the country's repressive political conditions that had prevented the

Left from organising the people through party politics.[82] Still, the contributions of the leftist intellectuals remain nebulous in this study.

As argued in a previous work, the *raison d'être* of armed struggle in Iran must be sought in the neo-colonial conditions in which economic development and modernisation were detached from political development and participatory democracy. I have called this phenomenon 'repressive development.'[83] This maldevelopment had caused the steady growth of working and middle classes while the state, as the privileged and exclusive agent of modernisation, did not allow for their democratic participation as rights-bearing citizens. In this context, educated young people, coming from both modern and urban as well as traditional and rural backgrounds, were propelled into political action while the social classes were still in the process of developing and had not yet found their political weight. University students and the educated, however, had borne the brunt of repression first-hand: they were the trained minds expected to contribute to the modernisation of the country but barred from having an input in its future direction. Where the regime saw glory and opportunity, they largely saw indignation and inequality. The intelligentsia was expected to be ancillary to the regime's authoritarian modernisation, and a segment of it rebelled against it in no uncertain terms. Catapulted into resisting the authoritarian system that had begotten them due to their moral protest against repression, inequality, and injustice, *they had to take action before the developing classes were ready for political participation.* Since party politics and open propagation of ideas were banned, the process of socio-political development of the 'masses' could not be completed. Therefore, *the liberatory action of militant intellectuals, it was hoped, would compensate for the socio-political underdevelopment of the classes.*

166

The Fadai theorists—Ahmadzadeh and Jazani—rightly called this *peratik* (from the French *pratique*) to evoke the Marxian concept of *praxis*. They both stressed the role of revolutionary practitioners (albeit differently) in the New Communist Movement. It was revolutionary *praxis* that would induce the birth of a popular movement, which in turn, upon envisioned victory, would allow for the *socialised* development of classes in Iran. The revolutionary intellectuals regarded themselves as the midwives of this movement. Under these conditions, however, *praxis* also captures the *distance* between the revolutionary intellectuals and the classes they intended to represent.

Praxis is important here: following Che Guevara's theory, it compensates for the lack of objective conditions of the revolution—central to both Ahmadzadeh's and Jazani's theories and a lively debate among the Fadai Guerrillas.[84] Believing that guerrilla warfare would soon lead to popular armed revolt, Che averred, 'one need not always wait for all conditions favorable to the revolution to be present: the insurrection itself can create them.'[85] This situation was not exclusive to Iran: we also witness that Latin American revolutionaries conceived that in its earliest stage (1959–61), 'the guerrilla movements were led principally by students, who believed that victory was the matter of months.'[86] Che's point constitutes the division between traditional communist parties and guerrilla movements. The significance of the *peratik* of Iranian activists now comes to light: it represents a reworking of Che's theory of *foco* that would fit the specific conditions of Marxist urban guerrillas of Iran, following Ahmadzadeh but inspired by the Uruguayan *Tupamaros* that, in 1969, had reworked Che's mountain guerrilla theory into an urban guerrilla movement. Motifs similar to those observed in Latin America and Iran—anti-imperialism, the Vietnam War, Palestinian liberation, and fighting capitalist dictatorship—can be observed in the formation of the Red Army Faction in West Germany and the Weather Underground in the United States, the former radicalised by the protests of Iranian student movement abroad—CISNU affiliates—against the Shah's state visit to Germany, and the latter being, just like Iranian militants, the radical faction of the student movement known as the Students for Democratic Society.[87] Of course, we should note the major differences, in terms of their objectives, between the guerrilla movements in the capitalist core and the movements in the periphery that still struggled for modernisation.

The Momeni–Sho'aiyan debate, contextualised within Iran's 'guerrilla period,' is arguably the *only* internal debate about the *raison d'être* of revolutionary intellectuals in Iran. Other militant theoreticians only assumed the presence of the militant intellectual. The debate represents a rare moment of reflection and self-consciousness, as the two theoreticians pause within the daily life-and-death struggle of the urban guerrillas to articulate who they are, where they come from, and on whose behalf they act. This chapter captures the diverging ontological probings of these revolutionary intellectuals. Two fundamentally different approaches to the revolutionary intellectuals are offered, revealing different epistemological backgrounds. Relying on an orthodox reading of Marxism, Momeni understands the revolutionary intellectual in canonical terms. Sho'aiyan's heterodoxy compensates for his lack of Marxist knowledge by relying on his own experience as a veteran activist through some appropriation of Persianised Gramsci. Here we see the clash of two rival discourses, each one a terrain constituting all the elements and conceptual relations within it. Fastening polysemic words to fixed meanings within a discursive terrain whence all agreed-upon meaning, objectivity, and political analyses arise results in the production of truisms. Inevitably Momeni's having recourse to the dominant Marxist-Leninist canonical phraseology and conceptual algorithms, established within the discourse of the Iranian Left that reduce the complexities of concrete life to *a priori* formulaic solutions, pushes him to dwell in the arcane language of the Left, the legacy of the Tudeh Party, despite the fact that the generation to which he belonged arose out of a radical disowning of the Tudeh legacy—or, to be precise, a certain concept of this legacy. This paradox indicates that the post-Tudeh leftists were not able to release themselves entirely from the discursive heritage of Tudeh and its truisms. It also reveals that language is not simply a medium of communication: *language constitutes the world*. Sho'aiyan had already recognised this in his earlier article 'The Words' (Chapter 2). At the time when discourse analysis was in its nascent stages, he had observed that language could either conceal the world or reveal it. Self-exiled from the discursive legacy of Tudeh that revealed itself through *Showravism* (Sovietism) as an alias for doctrinal, opportunistic adherence to Marxist ideology, Sho'aiyan intuitively understands *the need for the discursive renewal of the Left*: only a new discourse of the Left, uncontaminated by the discursive intimations of the past, would allow the revolutionary intellectual to radically rethink the national liberation project. As such, Sho'aiyan's *rowshangar* is coined as a *linguistic sign*, one whose signifier-signified connection has not acquired the intended social function. In a way, Momeni's criticism is correct when he argues that *rowshangar* is a forged word to capture many concepts with already established (Marxist) meanings attached to it. Momeni is also right that *rowshangar* is reflective of Sho'aiyan's idiosyncrasy and thus extraneous to Marxist lexicon and theoretical culture. On closer inspection, though, Momeni's criticism in fact produces the conditions of its own demise, inadvertently showing that in its origination, Marxism, too, was nothing but a renegade discursive formation, intended to capture the original experience of industrial capitalism in the nineteenth century. Marxist discourse and its various offshoots have gained currency and fixity only through the repeated articulation of Marxists ever since. This last observation is a gift of close and inferential reading of the Momeni–Sho'aiyan debate in the context of Marxist phraseology.

That said, both Momeni and Sho'aiyan remained trapped within the Marxist assumption that the revolutionary intellectual must somehow represent the working class as 'the ontologically privileged position of a "universal class".'[88] In the absence of the workers' movements in Iran, they could not see the problem of representation. For Momeni, in a Leninist vein, the revolutionary intellectual belongs to the exploiting class but emerges out of moral protest against capitalist injustice and inequalities. For Sho'aiyan, in a somewhat Gramscian vein (but without Gramscian analysis), class belonging is determined by class position: those who fight for a cause organically belong to those they advocate. But then the 'problem' of language surfaces: Momeni's reaction against the lexical elitism of Sho'aiyan (and his *Shuresh*) reveals his anxieties about the problem of intellectuals in the workers' movement. Sho'aiyan's *rowshangar*, Momeni believes, is the epitome of the intellectuals muted by a false language that blocks communication with the masses the intellectuals intend to represent. The revolutionary *rowshanfekr* can still use the common lexis of the traditional Left for mobilising the masses, Momeni submits, since there is a history attached to it.

For Sho'aiyan, the New Communist Movement needed a new discourse to match its new, radical, militant departure. To effect a new discourse for the Left is the most daring attempt of

Sho'aiyan, an unthinkable sin that justified his marginalisation by his comrades-in-arms, by a Left accustomed to its old discourse. He would remain unforgiven for this, pushing himself into exile from his co-combatants. The linguistic sign system remains relevant as long as a historical community adheres to it, or so advocated Ferdinand de Saussure. Sho'aiyan's language remains his own. He was a maverick theoretician, a singular figure among only a handful of leftist intellectuals like him in the history of the Iranian Left. We shall see in the next two chapters how his discourse bore two key elements in his later thinking: the rebellious front and rebellious thought and action.

5

FRONTAL POLITICS, FRONTAL THINKING

The 'front' becomes that eternal alembic that, on the one hand, rearranges within itself the anti-reaction-colonialist classes such that they would rise to combat their common enemy shoulder to shoulder, and on the other hand, [it] combines the scattered forces of a class... Thus within a rebellious front (jebheh-ye shureshi) the re-creation of the class begins. All its various centres (kanun) are negated and from their negation there emerges a single... fire-temple.

Sho'aiyan, 'Half-a-Step on the Way', HSW 9

What particularly renders Sho'aiyan our contemporary is not just his critique of the doctrinal, ideological Left, which strikes a chord with our sensibilities in the postcommunist era, but, more importantly, his 'frontal thinking.' His work's relevance today is accentuated when we observe the many social justice-oriented 'frontal movements' since the 1990s.

We have seen how Sho'aiyan's formative experience with the original National Front convinced him that only a vast political alliance could be capable of challenging the Shah's autocracy. For most activists, the National Front's loose alliance of small parties was not a model to emulate, and the Second National Front proved the weakness of frontal politics. For Sho'aiyan, quite to the contrary, the front was a 'way of political life' that he tried to conceptualise. But prior to theorising the front, he quickly transformed his dismay at the Second National Front into a serious attempt in the early 1960s at forging a frontal politics involving the boycott of the regime's financial institutions and state-run companies (Chapter 2). Although crude in vision and lacking in execution (the plan hinged on the leading Shi'i clerics' approval), the influence of Mosaddeq's National Front and Gandhian 'passive resistance' is evident in his 'A Thesis for Mobilisation'. Looking back at the economic boycott from his early-1970s stance, when Sho'aiyan contemplated grand-scale operations like the Isfahan steel plant or the Khuzestan oil sabotage, we can cautiously see that even a decade earlier he would envision resistance in terms of spectacular operations— an eccentric trace of his thinking. His peculiar notion of armed operations (basically large-scale sabotage) was contrary to the PFG's philosophy of armed struggle based on small, manageable operations with a clear message to specific social groups, follow-ing Jazani's brilliant theory of 'armed propaganda.'[1] Fadaiyan were certainly astute tacticians; Sho'aiyan clearly was not. Mind you, Sho'aiyan rejected the assassination of key figures of the regime—signature Fadai operations—regarding them as inef-fective means for mass mobilisation.[2] Sho'aiyan's advocacy of *the front as the highest form of politics* was pragmatically conceived before it was reasonably conceptualised. The economic boycott registers a rudimentary enactment of the idea, but his underground group consisting of Marxists and Muslims was certainly envisioned as a 'front' in the years of the embryonic formation of armed struggle. However, by the late 1960s, on two different occasions he began to theorise the front.

THEORISING THE FRONT

His first attempt at showing the historical precedence of frontal politics in Iran appears in his book on the Jangali movement, in which he claims, rather unwarrantedly, that Mirza Kuchek Khan indeed understood his movement as a 'frontal' struggle (SURMJ 172–3, 176–7). The reference is to the short-lived alliance between the then nascent Communist Party of Iran and Kuchek Khan. Naturally, this observation is colored by Sho'aiyan's interpretive, and partially biased, understanding of the Jangali movement. Notwithstanding, here is where he offers one of his first glances at the concept of 'front.'

> If under non-frontal conditions of the struggle, extensive and comprehensive ideological propaganda constitutes one of the most immediate duties of every party or organisation in order to recruit people in their ranks, in a frontal struggle, through the slogans [pertaining to issues] of the day (*sho'arha-ye ruz*), fitting decisive revolutionary [actions], showing the right ways out of this or that deadlock (*bonbast*), and finally through practical and tactical guidance of the revolution and the front, one can direct the masses (*khalq*) toward the [revolutionary] party, and thus toward the philosophy and ideologies of the party,

and gradually lead the party to become the vanguard (*pishqaravoli*) of the revolution, the front, and the masses. (SURMJ 179)

This dense excerpt needs unpacking. *The front designates two things: a condition and a mode of action. First, I infer, there are ('non-frontal') conditions in which one party is favorably situated to lead the revolutionary struggle*, in which case its duties are clear: it should mobilise the masses by deploying its theoretical or ideological roadmap that articulates the people's demands and gathers the smaller parties under its frontal umbrella as the leading party's struggle expands. *Second*, when the *conditions* deny one party de facto leadership, a 'frontal struggle' becomes necessary. Now *the front represents an actable response to certain conditions in which the plurality of revolutionary forces, which aim for similar, shared, or overlapping objectives, denies any force hegemony over others*. Here, the struggle changes: the party deploys a number of slogans and actions that respond to the practical and immediate demands of diverse groups such that the masses are attracted to the front and to the party that addresses their demands. For shorthand, I call this form of action, following Ernesto Laclau, *articulation*—a *discursive position* that brings into *alignment* the revolutionary party's policy with the *diverse and concrete demands* of the people that the party intends to represent and lead. This clarifies the way I have been using the term 'discourse,' which allows me a conceptual connection between Sho'aiyan's work and some key concepts in today's theories of the Left. Following Michel Foucault and Laclau, a discourse does not merely designate speech.[3] On the contrary, 'a discursive structure is not a merely "cognitive" or "contemplative" entity; *it is an articulatory practice which constitutes and organizes social relations*.'[4] The concept of discourse shows us that in addressing the people's demands through a party program, the party in question engages in discourse building and articulatory practices. These components are *implicit* in Shoʻaiyanʻs thought as he did not have the knowledge to theorise his observations in this way. Articulating the popular demands through party action and declarations thus constitutes concrete, lived relations between the party and the masses. Shoʻaiyan clearly was not equipped with the poststructuralist terminology I utilise here, but, viewed through a poststructuralist lens, one observes how contemporary indeed his ideas are fifty years later. As mentioned previously, he was still caught in some serious essentialisms that did not allow him to go beyond his own perceived truisms.

Two more observations: *first*, the name for the *articulations* of one revolutionary party that leads to the *mobilisation* of the masses is ʻ*hegemony*.ʻ But in order for this to happen, the presence of a common enemy is pivotal. It is in fact the common enemy that unites the popular forces (SURMJ 280). In Shoʻaiyanʻs words, ʻconvergence and unity (*hambastegi va yeganegi*) "between" different organisations, on this or that specific task, is building a *specific united front (jebheh-ye vahed va yeganeh) against an enemy*ʻ (ʻWhat Is Not To Be Done?ʻ in SW 9; emphasis added). Therefore, *a ʻfrontal struggleʻ is essentially a hegemonic struggle*: it pushes a certain revolutionary organisation to the status of ʻmoral and intellectual leadershipʻ[5] of diverse groups among the peoplesʻ forces against, in the Iranian context, the Shahʻs neo-colonial dictatorship. Stated plainly, the masses *identify* with those revolutionaries that ʻspeakʻ their demands in political terms. Note that Shoʻaiyan states ʻa specific united front,ʻ proposing that the *front is always particular in its content, and thus by deduction, there cannot be a generic front*. This is due to the specificity of the frontal demands and articulations. *Second*, the *articulator* of the peopleʻs demands is the *enlightener (rowshangar) of the class*, its ʻorganic intellectual.ʻ Now it all comes together: the front is a response to a condition in which, when fighting a common enemy, no single agent within diverse people's forces is sufficiently popular for assuming leadership, even when one agent is situated to lead the front. As such, the party equipped with 'frontal thinking' will gain popularity and thus leadership through the articulation of the people's concrete demands. This is achieved through the enlightener's reflecting the people's demands through party action and slogan. As the 'educator of the class' (Sho'aiyan), the enlightener's 'organic' relation to, and representation of, a class (or one of its layers) and its demands arises from the 'articulatory practices' (Laclau) of the enlightener and not through a shared economic reality (Momeni rejected this last point). Of course, the connection between the enlightener and the hegemonic articulatory practices in Sho'aiyan's theory is rather *assumed*. The theoretical connection, in terms of the actual political steps to be taken, between the two is missing. However, Sho'aiyan elaborates on a previous proposition:

> Under the conditions of struggle when a class, or a party, has actually attained the leadership (*parchamdari*) of a frontal struggle, other parties and classes that tend to elevate themselves to the highest positions of the revolution, must skillfully, accurately, prudently (*hesab shodeh*), and tirelessly show in practice the merit, soundness (*salamat*), and accuracy of their proposals and tactics, and as such advance step by step to increasingly capture (*tasahob*) the leadership. This is the positive and correct path to gain the leadership (*parchamdari*) of the revolution. (SURMJ 179)

The passage is brilliant: now, *two possibilities* may arise within a frontal struggle: *first*, a party is already leading the front, the circumstances leading to which are not discussed (they should have been). That the leading party still stays within the front (and leads it) suggests that the *plurality and diversity* of the social forces represented by the organisations within the front denies each and every one of them sufficient grounds or social support to lead the struggle alone. In short, the political field will always remain *heterogeneous*. Hence, it is only through the frontal convergence of the people's forces that they can pose a formidable resistance against the common enemy. Elsewhere, Sho'aiyan takes the Viet Cong (National Liberation Front) as an example (SURMJ 209). This possibility is only *implicit* in the above excerpt; it is a *suggestion*, but without it we would not be able to appreciate the *second, explicit* possibility. What if the party in question is not strong enough to achieve leadership of the front? Sho'aiyan's recommendations are clear: by launching carefully devised tactics, the smaller party can gradually rise to prominence within the front and attain its leadership. It is true that the unity of the people's forces depends on their revolution-ary potential for the overall strategic goal of the front (SURMJ 319), but, to this end, tactical positions are more important than ideological positions. In fact, frontal tactics supersede a party's ideologically sanctioned tactics. The right tactics and programs allow the smaller movement to gradually gain frontal leadership. 'Above all else, the party brings the nation along through current slogans, current tactics, and current programs. And often, [the aforesaid]... cannot embody the ultimate ideals and thoughts of the party' (SURMJ 275). Through these slogans and tactics, the party cultivates an organic relationship with the masses. The front must therefore avoid strictly ideological propaganda (SURMJ 177). In retrospect, the fact that he affords this outcome (formerly small parties leading the front) an explicit discussion *suggests* that this is where he envisaged his future presence within the armed movement against the Shah, although the passage is actually about the Jangali movement.

The first possibility necessitates the front as the reflection of the internal diversity of the people's forces, while the second shows that the front is the ground from which any party can rise to leadership should the said party *articulate* the diverse demands of the masses and *mobilise* them under the party's flag. In this case, the necessity of the front is tied to the *distance* between the party and the people. Devising the appropriate tactics should therefore come with the *critique* of the other forces within the ground.

> And since under any condition one cannot and should not ban the proper expression of internal criticisms, the parties and classes that increasingly and rightfully (*beh dorosti*) intend to capture (*tasahob*) leadership (*rahbari*) can point out the incorrect ideas and moves of other parties and elements, their shortcomings and incompetence, and their deficiency or lack of revolutionary knowledge for the revolution and the masses. Consequently, once again [the parties aiming at leadership] prove their being the most capable and appropriate flag-bearer (*parchamdar*) of the struggle and revolution. And this is the correct and negative [i.e. critical] way of attaining the leadership (*parchamdari*) of the revolution. (SURMJ 179)

The internal diversity of the front inevitably activates internal criticism within the front. This means that the forum for dialogue and mutual criticism must remain open. Eerily, this passage anticipates Sho'aiyan's future critical debates with Fadaiyan, debates he would not have been remotely aware of at this time.

All in all, we have a theory of a revolutionary, hegemonic front. It is uncanny to observe the methodological resemblance of Sho'aiyan's conceptual extractions for a theory of front through his study of the historical case of the Jangali movement and Gramsci's conceptual extractions for a theory of hegemony in his 'Notes on Italian History'. We must note that from Lenin to Mao to the Viet Cong and all national liberation movements, the question of hegemony was indeed a part of their overall strategy, and Sho'aiyan is no exception here. But to appreciate Sho'aiyan's originality, let us compare his propositions (excerpted above) with Gramsci's theory of an anti-fascist hegemonic front.

> The methodological criterion on which our own study must be based is the following: that the supremacy of a social group manifests itself in two ways, as 'domination' and as 'intellectual and moral leadership'. A *social group dominates antagonistic groups*, which it tends to 'liquidate,' or to subjugate perhaps even by *armed force*; it *leads kindred and allied groups*. A social group can, and indeed must, already exercise 'leadership' before winning governmental power (this indeed is one of the principal conditions for the winning of such power); it subsequently becomes dominant when it exercises power, but even if it holds it firmly in its grasp, it must continue to 'lead' as well.[6]

I rest my case. Had Sho'aiyan been born to any of the imperial-scientific languages of Europe, his name would probably have been universally recognisable within political theory. 'That you're born in Asia is called geographic determinism,' sings maverick Iranian musician Mohsen Namjoo in a famous song, 'Geographic Determinism'. Writing in a language that falls outside the orbit of scientific imperialism inevitably begets intellectual margin-alisation.[7] This is how Sho'aiyan has remained the forgotten revolutionary intellectual of Iran.

THE FAILED FRONT

Following Siahkal, Sho'aiyan tried his frontal politics, yet again, but this time in an entirely new form and with the newly emerged militant actors: Fadaiyan and Mojahedin. He was guided by the experience of his underground 'frontal' group (with Nabavi and Sadri).

From early on, Sho'aiyan's efforts to create the militant front had not escaped Iranian security. A SAVAK security bulletin (no. 311/955, dated 22 June 1972) states: 'Acquired intelligence has confirmed for some time that in the leadership ranks of two active subversive and terrorist (*kharabkar*) organisations, that is, Organisation of the "People's Mojahedin"... (religious extremists) and the "People's Fadai Guerrillas" (a communist group...), the preparatory steps have been taken for a coalition for joint activities...'[8] The bulletin continues that the coalition had been traced to 'an individual named Mostafa Sho'aiyan.' Reportedly, a SAVAK informant has been instrumental in acquiring this information: 'In the continued contacts of the source with Mostafa Sho'aiyan he has made statements confirming a series of intensive, secret activities by him and most probably he is instrumental in connecting the leadership elements of the two aforesaid organisations for the coalition.'[9] Note that such an informant must have been very close to, and trusted by, Sho'aiyan to have reportedly heard such a statement from a secretive man such as Mostafa.

The idea of creating a *new militant front* must have dawned on Sho'aiyan around 1972. In 'A New Threshold' (January 1973; in SW)—a short essay filled with tropes pertaining to birthing, rearing, and caring—he commemorates the second anniversary of the Siahkal operation, proposing that *unified action* (armed struggle) provides a common ground for unification. 'Guerrilla warfare has brought together the guerrilla *focos*' ('The New

Threshold' in SW 2). Now that armed struggle has been established, he argues, armed movement must temporarily retreat in order to prepare for a new start ('The New Threshold' in SW 3). 'Based on such appraisals the movement reduced its military operations—the continuation of which in the same manner would have been suicide—in order to increase the volume of its analytical, organizational, educational, and propaganda activities' ('The New Threshold' in SW 4). No concrete proposal follows.

Then, in March 1973, he registers his hopes for the formation of a new militant front in 'Half-a-Step on the Way: The People's Liberation Front' (in HSW).[10] 'A New Threshold,' 'Half-a-Step on the Way,' and 'Some Hasty Glances' all belong to the PDF's short-lived heyday, suggesting that Sho'aiyan regarded the PDF as a 'balancing force' that would bring Fadaiyan and Mojahedin together within his envisioned front. This is also the time when the concept of 'enlightener' is born and gains significance in his thinking. 'Half-a-Step on the Way' was written and submitted to the PFG in anticipation of a shared platform for the two groups' *perceived* (by Sho'aiyan, *not* Fadaiyan) merger before the PDF's demise, when the latter could regard itself as an independent underground cell ready to grow and partake in militant action. This article brought Sho'aiyan to his first exchange with Fadaiyan.

Heavily Kasravite and at times poetic in its prose, 'Half-a-Step on the Way' (dated 24 February 1973) begins by celebrating Iran's joining the world revolutionary movement through the 'rebellion (*shuresh*) of "The Revolution"' (referring to his book *Shuresh/ Rebellion*, renamed *Enqelab/Revolution*). The 'vanguard's armed movement' indicates the 'embryonic stage of rebellion,' taking place in Iran's 'reactionary-colonised' society ('Half-a-Step' in HSW 1). This strange designation of Iran's revolutionary stage— definitely *not Marxist*—is meant to indicate that 'the system of production and class domination is not only in the hands of the reactionary and retrograde (*erteja'i va vapasgara*) classes but [also that] this system and domination can only sustain itself by connecting to external colonialism' ('Half-a-Step' in HSW 1–2). Sho'aiyan's invented term 'reactionary-colonised' merely reflects the reality of Iran's dependent capitalism, but it hardly provides any structural analysis for determining the correct revolutionary stage—that is, democratic or socialist stage, using the model proposed by Lenin in 1905.[11] The term reflects Sho'aiyan's lack of knowledge of Marxist political theory. In any case, the armed movement must target 'reaction-colonialism' ('Half-a-Step' in HSW 2), but what this means remains unclear because it suggests diverging modes of action.[12] This common enemy—following his previous, thoughtful conceptualisation—provides the common ground for the frontal convergence of militant groups. Thus, at this time *the front is a response to a condition* (in the first sense of front mentioned above). This is why the 'rebellious vanguard' (*pishtaz-e shureshi*)—*implicitly the PDF*—must unify all anti-reaction-colonial forces 'regardless of their ideological (*armani*) and class origins' ('Half-a-Step' in HSW 2, see also 4). Because 'the rebellious vanguard in this society does not have a single-organisational profile (*chehreh-ye tak sazmani*)' ('Half-a-Step' in HSW 6), he envisions a supra-organisational mission for the PDF and thus himself as the originator of the theory of the rebellious front. Organisational diversity does not cancel out the possibility of the front due to the fact that a single class can have multiple vanguard organisations ('Half-a-Step' in HSW 7). Rebellious action, nonetheless, minimises the organisational singularities of the frontal groups ('Half-a-Step' in HSW 9). 'The organisational contexture (*baft*) of a popular liberatory rebellion... is a "frontal" structure' ('Half-a-Step' in HSW 3). This is achieved through the front's program and slogans that function as the thread that strings diverse forces together ('Half-a-Step' in HSW 4).

The centrality of *revolutionary praxis* (*peratik*) requires the frontal organisations to be vanguards in action (SURMJ 178). So Sho'aiyan regards armed struggle as the unifying *principle* of the front. *Note that this unifying principle is not theoretical: it is practical.* The rebellious essence leads the militants toward their frontal unity ('Half-a-Step' in HSW 8). 'Rebellious spawning' (*tokhmrizi-ye shureshi*; a polysemic word, *tokhomrizi*, could also mean 'seeding' or 'sowing') stems from the contradictions within society and is constitutive of the intellectuals' armed struggle. It is unclear what 'spawning' means: one can *infer* it refers to the objective conditions of armed struggle that beget the subjective conditions ('Half-a-Step' in HSW 8). But in a country where the two leading militant groups were Marxist and Muslim (proletarian and petite bourgeoisie, respectively, to use Marxist jargon), as a self-declared Marxist, Sho'aiyan must make the distinction between revolutionary forces and the proletarian forces. How can proletarian groups ensure their hegemony over non-proletarian revolutionary groups? Frontal participation of the communist militants will hinge, we shall see, on answering the question properly. Sho'aiyan falls short in providing a thoughtful answer. Yes, *the front unifies both the people's forces and the working-class forces* ('Half-a-Step' in HSW 10). Yet he simply reassures the reader that the communists will lead national liberation from the few to the many ('Half-a-Step' in HSW 9, 10). He does not explain how.

In the end, Sho'aiyan proposes a joint periodical as the first step toward the frontal alliance of Fadaiyan and Mojahedin (he assumes he would be the editor). 'This publication must not allow the roaming of diverging aspects of the vanguard forces and rebellious guerrillas. On the contrary, it must showcase the affinities and unity of the armed movement' ('Half-a-Step' in HSW 14). The joint publication—for which he proposes the title *Cherik* (*The Guerrilla*)—must cover topics relating to rural-dwellers, workers, soldiers, history, global analysis, economic, culture, arts, poetry, and fiction ('Half-a-Step' in HSW 25–6). Clearly, these topics are intended to address issues that can potentially mobilise wide-ranging social groups and create *relations of equivalence* among them. However, anticipating that Mojahedin's religious beliefs might cause objections among the Marxists, Sho'aiyan goes to unnecessary lengths to prove that metaphysical questions are irrelevant to communism and signs of scholastic-stricken sickness (*bimari-ye daneshgahzadegi*) ('Half-a-Step' in HSW 17, 14–15). He minimises the extent of Mojahedin's religious beliefs by highlighting their quasi-Marxist doctrines ('Half-a-Step' in HSW 21).

The PFG's critique (undated) of Sho'aiyan's proposal is sharp and observant. Their rejoinder (probably written by Momeni) points out that 'reactionary-colonised' does not provide a Marxist analysis of Iranian reality, best characterised as bourgeois-comprador. The term 'reactionary' does not capture relations of production. 'So when a Marxist wishes to explain the most vivid profile of a society he must use terms that designate the relations of production in that society and the class that rules it' ('The PFG Critique' in HSW 1). Fadaiyan's stance reflects Jazani's extensive analytical works on Iranian society. Suffice it to say that Jazani brings together Marxist analysis with elements of dependency theory and world-system theory.[13] According to his Fadai critic, Sho'aiyan misunderstands the front: *his notion* of front actually signifies the communist party, because *Sho'aiyan assumes the communists will lead the front*. 'That in a united front consisting of different classes from the opposition [to the Shah] the proletarian organisation must maintain its hegemony, does this mean that the front is the same as the communist party?' ('The PFG Critique' in HSW 3). The PFG is right: Sho'aiyan is silent about how to achieve communist hegemony over the front. His zeal does not justify this short-coming. Indeed, his Fadai interlocutor asks, why would any noncommunist join the front at all? 'The fact of the matter is that non-proletarian organisations join the front only and only because they perceive that by joining the front they might regain their lost or imperiled [class] interests (*manafe'*)' ('The PFG Critique' in HSW 3). So, contrary to Sho'aiyan's discussion, the ideological difference between Fadaiyan and Mojahedin does not stem from the question of God; the two groups represent two different classes. Will Mojahedin abolish private property? ('The PFG Critique' in HSW 5, 7). Let us recall that Fadaiyan unswervingly regarded Mojahedin as petite bourgeois. This opinion never changed, not even after the bloody coup within the OIPM in 1975 through which secret Marxist cadres within the group took over the organisation by murdering, exposing to security forces, or otherwise marginalising their Muslim comrades.[14] Mojahedin are revolutionaries but they are not communists. However, this does not mean that the OIPM and the PFG cannot cooperate ('The PFG Critique' in HSW 8). If, as Sho'aiyan claims, Mojahedin have affinity with Marxist ideas they must join a communist party (i.e. Fadaiyan) not the front ('The PFG Critique' in HSW 10). In the end, the PFG does not reject the idea of a joint bulletin but emphasises that this publication can only discuss concrete not theoretical issues ('The PFG Critique' in HSW 12–13).

Sho'aiyan was clearly unsettled and offended by the PFG's criticisms, but his rejoinder (dated 17 May 1973) is mostly formalistic and irrelevant. He retreats from many positions and admits that his 'reactionary-colonised' is a generic designation also applicable to African and Latin American countries ('Inquiry' in HSW 3), unwarrantedly blaming his choice of concept on lack of sufficient resources. He justifies that because the alternative term, 'comprador bourgeoisie,' also has its problems (he does not mention what they are), he invented a new term ('Inquiry' in HSW 4–5). Sho'aiyan forgets to point out that the term, however problematic from the Marxist-Leninist stance, has affinities with Tricontinental approach that has been informing Mostafa's melange of liberationist and Marxist approaches. In any case, reasserting the internal characteristics (*khodvizhegi-ha*) of every class ('Inquiry' in HSW 7), he unduly repeats that the 'two political organisations' of the working class (as if anticipating the Marxist coup within the OIPM) may converge in the front through united action—armed struggle ('Inquiry' in HSW 9). He unduly insists that *shuresh* may be led by a single class or multiple classes because the 'rebellious spawning' (*tokhmrizi-ye shureshi*) is also plural ('Inquiry' in HSW 16). His sophistry sours when he makes the outlandish claim that because rebellion (*shuresh*) is the essence of working-class politics, then every armed movement is a working-class movement ('Inquiry' in HSW 12–13). He pointedly reveals that he has not given serious thought to the leadership issue.

But then he admits he has no concrete or theoretical reason for supporting the OIPM ('Inquiry' in HSW 17) and withdraws his previous advocacy of Mojahedin ('Inquiry' in HSW 28). Since the petite bourgeoisie will retreat before the advancing proletarian culture, he implies surprisingly, in the process of frontal action the petite bourgeoisie (read the OIPM) will acquire a working-class character ('Inquiry' in HSW 24–5). Did he know about the secretive ideological shift within Mojahedin when writing these lines? In any case, he declares, 'Now we are fighting specifically against "reaction-colonialism." So, despite ideological differences (*jodai-ha-ye armani*) we can selflessly create a united front with all anti-reaction-colonialism' ('Inquiry' in HSW 27).

Despite his previous theorisation, in the early 1970s Sho'aiyan's attitude toward the front is at times naive. Consider this:

Although 'People's Fadai Guerrillas' have chosen their designation such that all revolutionary and anti-colonial-reaction forces and elements can be a part of it [PFG] should they pick up arms, they nonetheless in practice only shake hands with the elements that they consider Marxist. The fact, however, is that the present anti-colonial-[anti-] reaction struggle needs such an organization and process that enables it to embrace and draw to the battle all revolutionary and anti-colonial forces regardless of their ideal and objectives (*maram*): a frontal organisation! ('Some Hasty Glances' in SW 52)

He makes a case for the front, although the first argument apropos the PFG is simply an assumption. Yes, the PFG opened a new path for revolutionary action but this does not necessarily mean it is a 'frontal organisation.' Sho'aiyan then proceeds with an astonishing oversimplification: 'Anyone living like us is one of us! Anyone fighting like us is one of us! Anyone dying like us is one of us! He is our battlefield comrade! That one throws his grenade while crying out "Ali" [the first Shi'i Imam] or "Marx" is not important; what is important is to throw the grenade' ('Some Hasty Glances' in SW 52). Really? The entire complex question of ideologically informed strategy and tactic of the movement is reduced, however metaphorically, to throwing the grenade? Does this attitude work for the frontal unification of a movement that is engaged in a life and death struggle on the daily basis? How can we account for such practical and political naivety in the case of a man who, in his Jangali book, offered the contours of a formidable theory of the front? Sho'aiyan writes the above lines in 1972, and his attitude reflects the zeitgeist of a generation; he shows the unfounded but (to some extent) shared belief (popular especially among militant prisoners) that *peratik* unifies us. This attitude is memorably announced in the heroic defense statements of the Marxist poet Khosrow Golesorkhi (January 1974) in the only televised military court proceedings in the 1970s Iran. Golesorkhi averred, 'As a Marxist-Leninist, I first found social justice in the school of Islam and then I arrived at socialism.' He then continued, 'The life of Imam Hossein [third Shi'i Imam, killed in the Battle of Karbala in CE 680] embodies the current life of us who... are being tried in this court for defending our people... Therefore, in a Marxist society, true Islam is regarded as a superstructure, and we endorse this Islam, the Islam of Ali and Hossein.'[15] Will this comradely attitude, however, compensate for the theoretical shortcomings of a theory of the front with all its complexities?

The exchange belonged to the time when the Sho'aiyan–Shayegan PDF seemed to be emerging as a new player in the armed movement—a perceived potential 'balancing force.' I believe this is why Fadaiyan appeared interested in the idea of the front, although their understanding was different. Sho'aiyan praises the short-lived group Arman-e Khalq (The People's Ideal) for opening a new front, a necessary step the OIPM did not take. In contrast to Fadaiyan, Mojahedin mostly regarded armed struggle as assassination and sabotage, and, in addition to their problematic aspects ('Some Hasty Glances' in SW 54), they did not have a 'militant character' (*kheslat-e nezami*) (SOLF

40, n. 10). The danger is that without proper theory, armed movement can degenerate into terrorism, and to point that out he makes a distinction between assassination (in Persian: *teror*) and terrorism (Rev 216–17, n. 25). Looking back in 1974, Sho'aiyan attributes the failure of the joint periodical to Mojahedin's refusal, stating that 'Mojahedin's retraction had no basic and progressive principle and was instead full of craftiness (*hesabgari*)' ('Two Responses to Two Nonsenses' in SW 1). In the end, despite his earlier, brilliant formulation of the front, in practice Sho'aiyan leaves the question of the frontal leadership, arguably the most important aspect of any frontal coalition, to a leap of faith. A muddy meadow lies between theory and practice indeed.

THE FRONT REVISITED

The PFG was certainly right: Sho'aiyan had not worked out the conceptual distinction between the party and the front, despite his theory in 1970. In fact, when it comes to actual politics, Sho'aiyan shows a tendency to collapse the party into frontal structure, as evidenced by his two (unsuccessful) groups. Perhaps there is a specific reason for it in this particular context. Recall (Chapter 3) Sho'aiyan's tumultuous presence within the PFG ranks (June 1973–February 1974) and his idea that the PFG designates a 'front' and not a political party. *Allegedly* in reaction to this claim, the PFG added 'organisation' to their designation (OPFG) by April 1974. Sho'aiyan's idea is based on a clever observation: the two founding groups of the PFG were heterogeneous, coming from two different generations and two different formative experiences (Chapter 1). Their nominal adherence to Marxism-Leninism allowed them to converge but what in reality unified them was their *peratik-e enqelabi* (revolutionary *praxis*).[16] So, in a specific sense, Sho'aiyan's claim is correct that the PFG originally emerged as what we might call a 'frontal group' (an antinomy). The exigencies of founding guerrilla warfare in Iran, we may observe in retrospect, pushed for the organisational (not frontal) unification of the two formative groups. This means that when Sho'aiyan wrote about the practical steps toward the 'rebellious front,' he still regarded Fadaiyan as the umbrella group for all militant Marxists and now wished to extend that umbrella to non-Marxist militants. Nonetheless, Sho'aiyan's *interpretive* view of PFG foundation, however clever, must not overshadow the fact of the matter: the founders and cadres of Fadaiyan never regarded the PFG as anything but a militant, party-like organisation.

The Fadaiyan's prominence was due to their unique, almost unattainable stance in the armed movement as the praiseworthy inaugurators of a new era—indeed, audacious path-openers. Also aware of the PFG's unique position, Ashraf reportedly and expectedly refuted the organisational unification of different ideological groups (SOLI 54)—a position that reflects Jazani's theory.[17] Jazani dwells in the *primacy of praxis* in determining the essence of frontal unification, thus holding the PFG as the standard-bearer of a potential front, and he echoes Sho'aiyan's point regarding the plurality of actors: 'Although these [militant] groups have differences in their understanding of Marxism-Leninism and their policies (*mashy*), together they take on the role of the working-class "Vanguard" [he uses the English word].'[18] The argument continues: '*For Communists, unity is never achieved in closed rooms or by signing unity charters. Communists achieve unity through revolutionary practice* [amal-e enqelabi] *in the streets and* [under the] *arcades along with the masses and force the right-wing leaders in the movement to accept it.*'[19] Once again, here we have a certain articulation of the hegemonic front. To register how this approach is a hallmark of the international guerrilla movement, let me quote a passage from a founding figure of *El Ejército de Liberación Nacional* (ELN) of Peru and an original theorist of urban guerrilla warfare, Héctor Béjar, in 1965: 'The immediate objective of our policy of unity is to form a broad front that will bring the entire people together. The front will not be the result of bureaucratic negotiations behind the backs of the masses. It will be the culmination of a stage of armed struggle on the part of the people in which action will bring all the popular forces together in deeds.' Béjar continues, 'No one can claim the leadership of the revolution for himself if he does not demonstrate in practice that he is at the forefront of the masses and that he is capable of leading them to victory.'[20] I rest my case. The propositions of ELN, Jazani, and Sho'aiyan, their differences aside, belong to the *same genus of revolutionary ideas.* This is *the code of the epoch, the common idiom of revolutionary horizon.* What in our case separates Fadaiyan from Sho'aiyan is the particular junction of the front in their theories.

Now compare this more or less shared position on the front with that of the Tudeh Party: in June 1976 (incidentally, in that same month the PFG leadership was eradicated), the Tudeh CC called upon *all* Iranian opposition to 'overthrow the autocracy of Mohammad Reza Shah' through an 'anti-dictatorship front.' The Party declared: 'In our opinion the only and only necessary and sufficient condition for joining this front is being ready to actively fight for overthrowing the autocratic regime.'[21] The Tudeh Party holds that the common struggle against dictatorship and for social justice provides the grounds for the alliance of Marxists and 'religious activists' (*mobarezan-e mazhabi*).[22] If you think this is vague and unprincipled, read this: 'In its analysis of the anti-dictatorship front, the Tudeh Party of

Iran has declared that in addition to workers, peasants, petite bourgeoisie, and nationalist bourgeoisie, all other elements and layers and even groups within the ruling class (*hey'at-e hake-meh*) that oppose the Shah's autocratic regime can participate in the front.'[23] Quite rightly, the Tudeh's call for the front was never taken seriously. But it shows why we should appreciate the due care afforded to probing and theorising the front by the militant opposition.

Back to Sho'aiyan, we are now able to see his reasoning: his 'front' would have the PFG at its core, but due to Fadaiyan's de facto leadership over armed movement, the front could include Mojahedin. This last point becomes the source of disagreement. In *What Is To Be Done?* he points out, 'we had declared the organisational structure compatible with present condition of revolution in this land to be a frontal structure and... we believed in the unification of the [militant] groups after their operation [*amal*]' (SOLF 39, n. 10). This *suggests* that as the founder of the *praxis* of armed struggle, the PFG leadership would not be contested in the future front. This *assumption*, though, disallows Sho'aiyan from exploring the question of leadership in this particular case. Of the two senses of the front discussed earlier—as a condition and as a mode of action—Sho'aiyan appears to suggest that in the 1970s the front is a *condition* already in favor of the militant communists' leadership due to their well-established armed *praxis*. Since the *frontal core* (Fadaiyan) is already in place, he does not theorise it, and that causes him, inadvertently, to collapse the distinction between the Party and the front (the PFG criticism).

The distinction between the Party and the front brings us to the classical question of 'particular unity' (of proletarian forces; *vahdat-e khas*) and 'general unity' (of the frontal forces; *vahdat-e* 'amm). Sho'aiyan knows the significance of this distinction: 'the unified and "frontal" struggle against this regime, on the one hand, and the unified organisation of the proletarian forces for leading (*parchamdari*) this "front," on the other, caused me to be fascinated by the unification of proletarian forces while being interested in the frontal struggles of all revolutionary forces' (SOLI 39). For Jazani, too, the 'particular unity' of militant Marxists, due to the primacy of *praxis*, will form the hegemonic core that would lead all liberation forces.[24] Only the unified vanguard can unify the people's forces.[25] In short, the hegemonic core must already be in place before other groups can be called into alliance (unlike Tudeh's idea). Note that, as quoted earlier, Sho'aiyan refers to 'building a *specific united front against an enemy*,' thus proposing that the *front is always particular in its content*, thus *by deduction*, there cannot be a generic front.

Let us measure these theoretical postulations against a concrete, historical case of frontal politics: the Confederation of Iranian Students-National Union (abroad), CISNU, was founded in 1962 through the unification of Marxist, Muslim, and nationalist student opposition to the Shah. CISNU was an exemplary embodiment of democratic pluralism. Then it gradually began to shed its many colors as the Marxists and Maoists contentiously monopolised its leadership and the nationalists and Muslims left CISNU. It was eventually dissolved in 1975 due to sectarian politics and in particular Fadaiyan's push to transform CISNU into their exclusive support network abroad, thus in effect ending it as a democratic student union.[26] The lesson is clear: the front needs farsighted leadership since *any front is by constitution precarious and prone to the whims and interests of its constituents*. It is not known whether Sho'aiyan followed the CISNU affairs, but one can regard his theory of the front as an attempt to supersede the front's precarious nature. He wished the front to be a way of life, a political embodiment of Iran's irreducible plurality.

CONCLUSION: THE PERILOUS PATH TO THE FRONT

This chapter has offered Sho'aiyan's concept of the front through a close, context-specific reading that aims at rehabilitating his 'frontal thinking' from its shortcomings. Viewed from within his tripartite theory, the front appears as a necessary response to the internal plurality of the working class as represented by diverse *enlighteners*, these 'educator[s] of the class' (Rev 63). This plurality is owed to the proposition that 'rebellious spawning' takes place within multiple social watersheds. The party structure, therefore, is too restrictive for the revolutionary enlighteners' articulation of the working-class demands. Therefore, *the front provides an alternative but universal structure for a class that is internally diverse. The front's universal structure, however, always retains particular and historically bound content.* If the front succeeds in unifying the working class (particular unity) through the *co-articulation* of its multiple enlighteners, then, *contrary to the party*, it can encompass all anti-colonial militants (general unity). The latter is achieved by moving *from the few to the many*.

Sho'aiyan *falls short* in theoretically connecting the enlightener to the front: the leadership of the front can only be resolved through constant *articulation* of the people's demands by the enlighteners. But how exactly? His proposed content for the (unrealised) joint, frontal publication must be conceptualised as his way of bringing a vast array of demands under the frontal leadership that is *already established* through the militant *peratik* of Iranian communist guerrillas. Now, in the interest of reconstructing his thought, *here lies a great lesson for our time*. Had Sho'aiyan's experiments been successful, he would have been able to forge frontal *relations of equivalence* between heterogeneous social forces represented by militant Marxists and Muslims and later (non-militant) nationalists. In this context, targeting the Shah's regime in its entirety as the common enemy, the unified action of Fadaiyan and Mojahedin would have minimised the *relations of difference* between Marxist and Muslim militants and established *relations of equivalence* between them, thereby causing non-equivalential non-militants into an alliance with the hegemonic frontal vanguard—Fadaiyan—thus subsuming the plurality of demands of various classes under the strategic frontal demand of overthrowing the monarchy. This plan required the hegemonisation of the field of resistance against neo-colonial dictatorship by the militant communists.[27] The ultimate demand to overthrow the imperialist-backed monarchy—the common enemy, or more accurately, the 'constitutive outside' of the popular front—is arrived at through addressing the immediate demands of the diverse constituents of the front and achieved through the *articulatory practices* of the enlighteners or vanguards. The common enemy is key as it enables the creation of *regiments of signs* that cannot be assimilated or transmuted across *oppositional discursive divide*. Armed struggle is the *articulation of antagonistic relations* within a distinct and unassimilable political discourse. This enemy functions as a *frontal nodal point* that would allow the articulation of heterogeneous demands. But then we encounter one of the deepest prejudices of Marxist theory—the *stability of the proletarian identity* throughout the process of unification—that was perceived by neither Sho'aiyan nor Fadaiyan due to their essentialisms. Contrary to Marxism, *the identity of the groups within the front will be transformed due to their articulatory practices and through these groups' constructing a revolutionary*

197

discourse.[28] Had the PFG succeeded in leading the liberation front, its identity, as the hegemonic core of the projected front, would have been transformed beyond Fadaiyan's self-perception. For this to happen the discursive field must have been formed through the PFG articulation of the popular demands of the vast array of social classes and groups. Accordingly, *frontal politics is the politics proper of the Left and its transformative politics—internally and externally.* The doctrinal Left of the 1960s and 1970s was so preoccupied with (supposedly) representing the working class as the historically privileged agent that it failed to see its greater democratic function. Today, the Left would not be conceivable without a populist-democratic reach for a 'transversal project.'[29] This is precisely how the leftist-led front becomes popular and grows into a national force. In recent years, the political emergence of 'frontal' parties and alliances of the Left shows the merits of frontal politics through the 'enlighteners' as articulators of diverse grievances of multiple social forces and classes. Note the cases of People's Democratic Party (HDP) in Turkey (before the state's crackdown), as well as those of SYRIZA's rise to power in Greece, despite its failures, and the popularity of Podemos in Spain. None of them came to prominence under a dictatorship: the latter two did so within liberal democracies, while the former rose under a precarious parliamentary system. The hegemonic cores of these leftist frontal organisations have been key in their success but their leaders did not impose limitations on the identity of their alliance. This is precisely what Sho'aiyan *assumed* in his conceptualisation: that the Left was indispensable to the formation of the front (i.e. front as condition), and paradoxically, this is why he left the matter *untheorised*. This absence does not detract from the value of his *theory* of the front. Indeed, a careful reading of frontal theory of this marginalised Iranian theoretician proves that he was a forgotten precursor in the contemporary politics of the Left—one among many, of course, but within the Iranian case an important one, along with Jazani. His 'frontal thinking' anticipates today's frontal politics, arriving at his ideas mostly through experience and necessity.

Sho'aiyan's tripartite theory consists of the enlighteners and the front, but we still need to examine the one aspect he is best known for: his theory of *shuresh*, or rebellion, to which we now turn.

6

REBELLIOUS ESSENCE, REBELLIOUS ACTION

A theory and philosophy that does not guide the working class to the revolution and to the arms is not the working-class theory and philosophy, however filled with the working-class rhetoric. This is not the soul but only the corpse of Marxism.
Sho'aiyan, 'Some Hasty Glances', SW 33

Sho'aiyan's *oeuvre* grew out of his study of the Jangali movement. 'I can tell that this book [*A Review*] became a sort of life for me. Step-by-step with this book my eyes opened to new landscapes,' he reflects. 'It eventually led me to lose my faith in Leninism and reach the conclusion that Leninism itself is incorrect (*nadorost ast*). After turning and toying with these ideas and organising them for a while, I offered them in the book *Rebellion*' (SURMJ vi–vii). *Shuresh/Rebellion* stems from the concluding chapter of the Jangali book (originally titled 'October and Lenin's Ideas on the Revolution'), which Sho'aiyan took out for further elaboration.

201

He had realised that the roots of Lenin's betrayal of the Jangali movement was not merely political—i.e. out of the exigencies of a besieged revolution—but deeply theoretical (RRC 24). In 1971, the first version of *Rebellion* was prepared that, as Monajemi recollects, was basically an annotated table of contents (sent to Europe in 1972). In 1973, a second, extended version of *Shuresh* was typed and mimeographed in a few dozen copies. This is the version criticised by Momeni. The final, reworked and expanded manuscript, with reduced Kasravite prose, was ready in April 1974, and possibly in reaction to Momeni's criticisms Sho'aiyan changed its title to *Enqelab/ Revolution* (OLM 82, n. 6; Rev 12–14). It is worth noting that Sho'aiyan reportedly gave fifty copies of the second version of *Shuresh* to Mojahedin for distribution, but they refused to distribute it, claiming that the book 'would split Marxist forces.'[1] Momeni's (reportedly second version [IRJS 1]) rebuttal to the second version of *Rebellion*, titled *Not Rebellion, Judicious Steps Toward the Revolution*, was published by the PFG in 1974 (which Sho'aiyan received on 7 October 1974) to which Sho'aiyan wrote a rejoinder, *Injudicious Replies to 'Judicious Steps'* (dated January 1975). He admits that *Injudicious Replies* makes no new criticisms (IRJS 6) and is primarily an exposition of Momeni's Stalinist attitude.

Shuresh became Sho'aiyan's hallmark theory, an object of ruthless criticism by Momeni, and the subject of disregard by an entire generation of activists. Let us recall the anecdote related to me by the late Cosroe Chaqueri: he had published one thousand copies of *Revolution* in Florence, which was sold out within a year in Europe. But not a single review or even a mention of it appeared in any publication in the next three decades.

THE TURNING (AWAY)

Revolution begins, strangely, 'In the Name of Communism' and is dedicated to Nader Shayegan. The dedication, we might surmise, relates to Shayegan's analysis of the Bolshevik Revolution. Reportedly, in a pamphlet Shayegan had called Lenin a nationalist figure and the Russian Revolution a bourgeois-democratic one.[2] In any case, *Revolution* defies quick reading: with its complex arguments and unyielding prose compounded by polemical taunting, it begins by exposing—following the Jangali book—the Leninist cul-de-sac for revolutionary *praxis*, targeting the 'peaceful coexistence' with imperialism (Rev 10). Strangely, some chapters of the book are decorated with epigraphs not only from Marxist and western thinkers but also from the Quran and Shi'i figures, as well as other Iranian and non-Iranian writers. In order to present his arguments coherently here, I must glean the elements of his works in a categorical fashion.

(a) Refutation of Leninism and the Soviet Union. Sho'aiyan would not have been able to offer his own theory without debunking the *paradigmatic* Leninist model that dominated the Iranian Left. *Shuresh* therefore offers its contributions mainly through the critique of Leninism and colorful Soviet policies. Naturally, for the doctrinal thinking of Momeni, an attack on Leninism alone suffices to dismiss the book's entire argument: '*Shuresh*... is a book in negating Leninism and the October Revolution as well as an implicit negation of all other socialist revolutions that have taken place to this day.'[3] Momeni spends extensive pages distorting and detracting from Sho'aiyan's past activism (as shown in Chapter 4) and discrediting his ideas as unoriginal by attributing them to the works of 'counter-revolutionary' authors such as

Leon Trotsky and Isaac Deutscher that the Third Force-affiliate journal *Thought and Art* had promoted.[4] To add insult to injury, Momeni claims that 'most probably *Shuresh* would be publishable openly' due to its anti-Leninist content, if Sho'aiyan removed his attacks on SAVAK or the Shah![5] Momeni's resentful criticisms of Sho'aiyan are symptomatic of a theoretical suspicion shared by Jazani who clearly targets Sho'aiyan's 'radicalism' when he writes,

> The historical infiltration of nationalist bourgeoisie and its ideological traditions in the national liberation movement [and] the active role of petite bourgeoisie on the world scale from Trotskyism to the ideas of Marcuse and Fanon who mix a radical-revolutionary hue with the rejection of Marxism-Leninism constitute other elements that support the opportunistic leanings in different forms within our present movement and overall open the way for unhealthy understandings of armed struggle.[6]

This view, as I have argued elsewhere, blocks Jazani's opinion of the democratic core of his own theory.[7] Obviously, Momeni's standpoint is grounded in a theoretical suspicion nourished by a tenacious adherence to a dogma called 'Marxism-Leninism'—the target of Sho'aiyan's criticism. Such doctrinal understanding of the school of thought obfuscates that which is at the heart of Sho'aiyan's argument: *no idea is sacred,* and that which is held to be so only conceals a *radical negativity* through its positivist assertions.

In *Shuresh/Revolution,* avers Sho'aiyan, 'the flaw of *Leninism,* based on "revolution" [his thesis] and in the field of practice, [is] to be meticulously probed' (Rev 9; emphasis in the original). Building on his earlier thoughts and honing his earlier argument in 'The Life and Burial of a Theory' (1969), Sho'aiyan contends that Leninism offers only an impasse for revolutionary action because of its advocacy of 'peaceful coexistence' with imperialism (Rev 10), an utterly counter-revolutionary policy (Rev 24) and an idea for which Lenin sacrificed the Janganli movement. Note the way Sho'aiyan connects the Jangali affair to the foreign policy of the Soviet Union in his time, thus finding a theoretically nourished constant in history. To what extent this generalisation is sustainable will be for historians to examine. My concern here is to show the construction of a critique of Leninism by Sho'aiyan. Expanding on his articles in *Jahan-e Naw*—'The Life and Burial of a Theory' and 'The Words' (Chapter 2)—he debunks the Soviet policy of 'peaceful coexistence', pointing out that the word 'peace' here only means the 'absence of war' in a world of class conflicts (Rev 238–40, n. 74). The way Sho'aiyan approaches Lenin in light of the young Soviet Russia's betrayal of the Jangali movement is key to understanding his position: the October Revolution opened the possibility for a proletarian world revolution but the Bolsheviks decided to preserve themselves above the interests of the international proletariat and the internationalist essence of Marxism by making concessions with imperialism (Rev 125). This last assertion shows that he regarded the Jangali movement to be potentially a proletarian movement, which obviously it was not, although it entered into a short-lived alliance with the communists. But it also shows that, conceptually, for Sho'aiyan there was only a short distance between liberation and socialism—another assumption. In any case, the reason he offers for his argument is this: Lenin *assumed* that his 'theory of uprising' (*te'ori-ye qiyam*) was a universal model for revolutionary action, and insofar as workers in other countries did not stage revolts against their states the only triumphant proletarian state should preserve itself by forging a pact with imperialism based on the principle of peaceful coexistence (Rev

126, see also 151–7). In further probing the reason for such a turn in the Bolshevik Revolution, the fundamental question would be 'which necessities, in principle, drive the "proletariat of the victorious country" into a period of peaceful coexistence with the international counter-revolution?' (Rev 130). Sho'aiyan's answer is surgical: Lenin believed that the 'unequal development' of different countries only allows the proletariat of certain countries to revolt.[8] The idea originates with Leon Trotsky in his 'uneven and combined development' thesis. Because of this unevenness, the victorious proletariat must preserve its power, which in turn requires the victorious country to accelerate the rate of its development in order to resist the pressures of imperialism and supposedly prepare for the eventual confrontation with imperialism (Rev 141–2). Consequently, the victorious socialist state is now trapped in its national boundaries, isolated from liberation movements around the world (Rev 131). Sho'aiyan agrees that uneven development is a reality, but this unevenness is *economic*, not *political*. Separating unevenness from revolutionary action (or the lack thereof), he argues that the more economically developed country does not necessarily stand on a more advanced level politically (Rev 136). As such, he brilliantly demystifies the deeply rooted *assumption* that the political superstructure of advanced capitalist societies—i.e. liberal democracy—is the most advanced political configuration. Subsequently, the Soviet lack of commitment to world revolution allowed a turn toward statism that is also evident in China's foreign policy (Rev 130). In short, his argument continues, as a deviation in proletarian thinking, Leninism and especially Lenin and Stalin's policy of 'socialism in one country' mark off nationalist socialism from internationalist socialism (IRJS 146). If the conflict between labor and capital is global, then it must be resolved internationally, not in one country (Rev 152, 159). 'Socialism is a revolutionary-societal system—not a nationalistic society with its unworkerly (*nakar-gari*) meaning' (Rev 50). Thus, the October Revolution should have led to world revolution, had it not been for the treasonous theories of Lenin. Accordingly, the 'peaceful coexistence' is *essentially* counter-revolutionary. Still, Sho'aiyan pushes Lenin's ideas back to Marx and Engels to see if they shared such concepts: 'It seems that the criticism made of Lenin's thoughts on the party and the revolution are also pertinent to Marx himself... In any case, the basic reason why I could not analyse comrade Marx was because of my negligible knowledge of Marx and his ideas' (Rev 103). Likewise, he criticises Engels for confirming that the proletarian victory could be 'imaginable' through 'non-revolutionary and peaceful passages' in '"democratic" societies' (Rev 56). This line of thinking is bold and reveals an unrelenting critical mind. Although, unlike Lenin, Marx was not a 'nationalist' (Rev 104), for Sho'aiyan there is enough evidence, though not entirely solid at this time, to trace Lenin's misconceptions back to Marx. I am not sure how he would have applied his criticism to Marx, as his concept of revolution, tinted with anti-colonial national liberation, was clearly different from Marx's, thus rendering his potential critique of Marx and Engels untenable. All in all, though, debunking Leninist theory allows Sho'aiyan to search for new grounds for his own revolutionary theory.

Despite all these, he continues, the Iranian Left (Fadaiyan included) has 'made Lenin into a sacred and eternal statue and his thoughts—"incidentally" his most mistaken thoughts—into heavenly tablets upon which the sun will eternally shine' (RRC 13). Lenin was a great activist and theoretician of the working class, Sho'aiyan specifically points out, but in the eyes of Iranian Marxists he became 'sacred and eternal' (RRC 13) and 'the pure Lenin, the pure God!' (Rev 25). In Sho'aiyan's view, Leninism has shown its grave errors through the lived experience of his generation (Rev 129). He quotes Nader Shayegan who had reportedly averred, 'The very fact that I carry a weapon and live militantly means the rejection of Leninist methods' (quoted in Rev 116). That others in the militant ranks were willing to over-look their experiences and console themselves with imported theories is what baffled Mostafa. Sho'aiyan's criticism of Leninism now becomes clearer: he problematises certain aspects of Lenin's theory—preserving the Revolution at the cost of the Jangali movement and his 'uprising' theory—and ignores others— Lenin's vanguard theory to which he inevitably subscribed by virtue of being a militant. For him, *Leninism is a trope of the Iranian Left's uncreative and doctrinal adherence to an ideology that blocks the activists' view into their own experiences.*[9]

The theoretical roots of the pathology of Stalinism within the Iranian Left are now exposed by Sho'aiyan: he calls it 'Sovietism' (*Showravism*): Soviet Union to the North, Maoists to the East, Tudehists to the West and 'the judicious Fadaiyan' to the South— the 'natural-born communists' (*komonist-e madarzad*) (SOLF 7) who do not need critical thinking or reflection. The Fadai Guerrillas, in particular, ignore the contradiction between their theory and their practice—a contradiction they live every day. They simply follow ideological truisms and shut out criticism of doctrinal thinking.

(b) Collapsing self-acclaimed universal models. For most of the twen-tieth century, in the hands of uncreative revolutionaries Leninism had become a blueprint for proletarian movements—in many cases under the conditions that rendered Lenin's theories (at least in part) inapplicable. The Bolshevik Revolution was triumphant when, in the context of political and economic crisis exacerbated by war, through propaganda and agitation the Bolsheviks encour-aged the soldiers to turn their guns against their commanders

and eventually against the regime. According to Sho'aiyan, this means Lenin did not create a revolutionary army; he mobilised segments of the Tsarist counter-revolutionary army toward the revolution (Rev 187). Thus, in reality, the October Revolution was a 'coup d'état-revolution' (Rev 195). Obviously, reducing the Bolshevik Revolution to the moment of the putsch is reductive and unsound. This observation suffers from an anachronistic view: retrospectively, Sho'aiyan expects the Bolsheviks of the early twentieth century to have staged a revolution in the manner of the post-1950s anti-colonial wars of liberation in Africa and Asia. On the other hand, note that within the 1970s leftist world, calling the Bolshevik Revolution a coup was considered pure blasphemy for which Sho'aiyan was proverbially hit hard. For Sho'aiyan, even the Red Army—modeled after the Tsarist conscript army—was not a revolutionary army: 'It takes a great sense of humor to suppose the victories of such an army were the victories of the working class' (Rev 204). Writing elaborately on Lenin's errors (Rev 79–8, 107–9), Sho'aiyan argues that Lenin formulated his 'theory of uprising' (te'ori-ye qiyam)—cherished by Iranian Marxists—to masquerade the October putsch as a revolution. For Lenin, 'the revolution is fundamentally spontaneous and sudden' involving 'uninformed revolt' (khizesh-e na-agahaneh) (Rev 79). But he does not reject Lenin's theory entirely: 'uprising is the task of the masses' (Rev 82) achieved through prolonged class warfare. Thus, the so-called 'theory of uprising' does not train the workers for revolutionary practice and diverts the Party's energy toward propaganda and street protests. It is clear how Sho'aiyan imposes the expectations of his anti-colonial generation on the first socialist revolution in the world. The expectation that a revolution must train all workers to partake in revolutionary action was not just unrealistic: even Algerian or Cuban revolutionaries did not achieve such a task until after the victory of their movements.

His reading of Lenin and the Bolshevik Revolution, therefore, remains reductive and selective.

Interestingly, Sho'aiyan continues, Lenin calls political assassination 'terrorism' because it involves direct, armed action (Rev 115–16). This means that Lenin has indeed been against guerrilla warfare (IIME 16; Rev 101–2)—a fact the Iranian Left has been glossing over. But more importantly, conceptual myopia does not allow Lenin to understand revolution as processual (Rev 107, 109). In fact, borrowing from ophthalmological terminology, Sho'aiyan states that the Iranian militant Left cannot see that in practice it undermines Lenin's theory and yet advocates his theory, and this error reports the Left's suffering from squint-eye (*luchism*) (Rev 117). Clearly, Sho'aiyan concludes, 'Lenin's theory of uprising has never been the "main law" of revolution, it has never been, and it will never be' (RRC 13). Even the victorious outcome of the October Revolution does not mean that Lenin's theory was correct. This view of the Bolshevik Revolution, enabled by Sho'aiyan's studies in the 1960s (however reductive when it comes to the Bolshevik Revolution), illustrates that *the Iranian Left misconceives the absence of revolutionary theory in Lenin for its presence*. It is true that this observation was based on some problematic reading of Lenin's works available to Sho'aiyan in the 1960s and 1970s. But let us focus on what he wishes to say here: that *the Leninist model does not work for Iran*. And in reaching this conclusion he was not wrong.

Therefore, the Bolshevik Revolution is no 'model' to emulate, and Iranian Marxist militants err greatly in trying to attribute their armed struggle to Lenin's theory. It just won't fit. This is the contradiction between theory and practice to which I alluded earlier: Leninist theory was not compatible with the anti-colonial wars of liberation. Frantz Fanon also had the same suspicion. I am interested in *reconstructing* Sho'aiyan's theory, not defending all of his propositions, and to that end it is important to see how his rejection of the Leninist canon was meant to defend the *raison d'être* of Iranian Marxist revolutionaries whose *praxis* he regarded as authentic. As early as 1969, regarding the three successful communist revolutions of the twentieth century—the Soviet Union, China and Indochina, and Cuba—Sho'aiyan had submitted that 'the three had achieved victory through three different or relatively different methods, that is through three [distinct] innovations (*ebtekar*) and three [modes of] distinctness (*vizhegi*)' ('Party and Partisan' in SW 7). We have seen earlier that he also rejected Debray's *foco* theory, and the Cuban Revolution, as a model for Iran ('Party and Partisan' in SW 59). With remarkable precision, Sho'aiyan observes that the Chinese revolution was in fact the negation of Lenin's 'theory of uprising': it was rather more akin to Ahmadzadeh's 'small motor' theory (Rev 167–8). Moreover, that these revolutions were proletarian movements does not warrant their outcome as proletarian (RRC 38). 'One cannot unseeingly accept any theory that interprets the objective realities and offers a path toward the future—no matter how it is offered in a pure revolutionary, even communist, conscientious—unless its truth is proven in social action' (Rev 127). In other words, hitherto Marxist theories have only been *particular*—historically specific—theories and *not universal models*. Treating Marx, Lenin, and others in this way will prevent the activists from taking these revolutionary figures as gods and prophets: 'communism is a knowledge (*danesh*) not a religion (*kish*)' (Rev 17). Once these revolutions gave up their internationalist duties, they lost their proletarian essence. The evidence is in Vietnam's failure, as it abandoned war against imperialism to build its socialism (RRC 41).

In the Iranian case, the *praxis* of armed struggle has *in practice* debunked not only Leninism but also the approaches (e.g.

Engels) that consider the possibility of peaceful transition to socialism in democratic countries (Rev 56). For Sho'aiyan it is the lived experience that stands out as the primary guide, not imported theories: the Siahkal operation and the PFG action *in practice* radically question and refute Lenin's theory of revolution (RRC 16). Furthermore, he argues, there is an uncompromising division between the people and working class, on the one hand, and their imperialist enemies, on the other. This leads him to offer a new theory of *praxis*: revolutionary practice is the sole (*yeganeh*) measure of principles, he submits, and the works of 'Marx, Engels, Lenin, Mao and others... are merely cases that "probe the conditions of emancipation of the working class"' (Rev 17). His is evidently no ordinary theory. He confidently has global ambitions about it: '*Revolution* [his treatise] belongs to the working class in its world-historical dimension. Because *Revolution* is in fact the product of the proletarian life that the turn of fortune has given me the chance to harvest' (RRC 10).

Given that there are no universal revolutionary models to emulate, Sho'aiyan must now ambitiously aim at a universal theory of national liberation. He walks out of the Platonic cave to find the truth about his world. However, his comrades-in-arms in the cave were too accustomed to the seemingly animated images on the wall; they had forgotten there was a world out there to explore. So, our explorer would end up walking alone.

LIBERATION AND AGENCY: AN ONTOLOGY OF THE REVOLUTION

Revolution begins by drawing on the Marxian thesis that the objective, historical conditions of the proletariat (class-in-itself) have rendered it the universal, *historical* revolutionary agent.

When the workers' position within capitalism is energised by the revolutionary consciousness (class-for-itself) that is introduced to by the 'philosophers or enlightener layer' (Rev 38) of the working class, this world-historical class will be transformed into a revolutionary movement. The organisation that holds the two together—the locus of convergence of revolutionary consciousness (enlighteners) and the concrete class—is the Communist Party (Rev 39–40). But this is no 'Sovietist' communist party: for Sho'aiyan the party is a militant organisation (Rev 39): 'the working-class party is the *instigator* of the revolution' (Rev 40; emphasis in the original). Sho'aiyan's privileging *praxis* is clear in these lines: *he perceives Marxist militants* (the PFG in Iran) *as a de facto communist party*. As the 'guiding organisation of the class... the party is the field of organic solidarity of the [working-] class enlighteners with one another and with the class' (Rev 213, n. 6). 'The party and the revolution are the products and mutual outcome of one another' (SURMJ 109).

By offering this view, Sho'aiyan resolves two fundamental questions facing his generation. First, he resolves the issue of existence of the 'objective conditions of the revolution,' a requirement imposed by the Leninist revolutionary theory, which ironically caused a major disagreement among Fadaiyan's founders and their followers. Among the pro-Fadai prisoners in 1972 a prodigious majority defended Ahmadzadeh's theory that the objective conditions existed in Iran, isolating a handful that supported Jazani's thesis about the 'pivotal role of armed struggle.'[10] Ahmadzadeh concludes from the existing armed struggle that the objective conditions are ripe. His opponents confront him with the question, why then are there no mass movements, if the objective conditions are already in place? Ahmadzadeh's response is interesting: 'Should we conclude from the lack of spontaneous mass movements that the objective conditions of revolution are not ripe? ... In my opinion, no.'[11] He attributes the lack of movements to state repression. Jazani, *au contraire*, believed that the internal or domestic objective conditions did not exist, while simultaneously asserting that the objective conditions as such were not necessary for revolutionary action, and only three 'minimal conditions' (*sharayet-e haddeaqal*) were sufficient: the people's discontent, brutal dictatorship, and the presence of the militants.[12] However, he indicates the international conditions and experiences have rendered armed struggle possible and necessary.[13] Similarly, Zia Zarifi submits, 'In my opinion, the revolutionaries play a great role in completing and launching [*jahesh dadan*] the objective conditions of revolution. The objective conditions are not separated from the conscious revolutionaries by a Great Wall of China [in the sense that] the latter should wait until the former become ripe all by themselves. Selecting the violent path [*rah-e qahramiz*] gives the masses the hope for joining the struggle, but let us make no mistake, launching the violent path does not mean to stage the revolution.'[14]

For *self-declared* Leninists, both positions are problematic: the objective conditions must reveal themselves in mass movements (the lack of which causes a problem for Ahmadzadeh's theory), and the lack of these conditions renders armed struggle adventurist and voluntarist deviations (the problem with Jazani's theory). I submit that the abstract 'objective conditions of the revolution' is indeed the proverbial elephant in the room. Sho'aiyan rids himself of what he perceives as Leninist legacy and can therefore offer a *certain* combination of the two: like Jazani, Sho'aiyan argues that revolutionary conditions are absent in Iran, and one should not mistake urban guerrilla warfare for a war of liberation, although the former certainly moves in the direction of creating the latter.[15] In a way, he understands the necessity of armed struggle, although he does not extract the objective conditions from the de facto

214

existence of armed struggle, as does Ahmadzadeh. Sho'aiyan sides with Jazani's position (without knowing it; he had not read Jazani) that the international movements have made armed struggle possible. For Sho'aiyan, the enlighteners of the oppressed class teach it how to resist injustice and unify as a revolutionary agent. A new historical agent is therefore born out of the articulatory practices of the enlighteners. The objective conditions must therefore be *intelligible* (international conditions) and *practical* (internal conditions). In short, he *bypasses* the conceptual problem through his theory of rebellion. This bypassing, of course, gestures toward abandoning some fundamental principles associated with the then dominant revolutionary theories inspired by Marxism.

Second, Sho'aiyan resolves the problem of the Communist Party. The historical fiasco of the Tudeh Party has left Iran without a communist party, as the PFG founders believed, which imposed upon the militant generation the task of communist party refoundation. For Puyan, revolutionary action 'paves the way for the institution of the communist party,'[16] while Ahmadzadeh refers to Latin America where the Communist Party was not automatically the vanguard (as opposed to the Chinese–Vietnamese experience of the Communist Party leading the popular army) to echo Régis Debray that 'the guerrilla force is the embryo of the party; the guerrilla is the party.'[17] Realistically, Jazani perceives a distance between the guerrillas and the party: the national liberation front led by Fadaiyan will unify the plurality of militant vanguards and build the working-class party in the process of struggle.[18] Just like Ahmadzadeh and Jazani, Sho'aiyan believes that militant action will create the communist party; indeed being the enlighteners of the working class, the militant Marxists are already the communist party.

But this is specifically the communist party of a colonised country: as a universal signifier, the 'communist party' may encompass essentially different organisations—which serves the communists across the world to communicate their diverse experiences. But when it comes to the concrete task of building the communist party as the historical organisation to lead the universal agent of change, the working class, no two experiences are the same. This is where we encounter *particulars unified under a phantasmic universal*. So Sho'aiyan must now reconcile the essentially European-metropolitan Marxian theory with the realities of colonised nations, because, he argues, the pivot of the revolution has shifted to the East in the twentieth century (SURMJ 107). He submits that the party will stage '*any revolution* that eventually leads to the universal (*yekparcheh*, also meaning converged or all-encompassing) triumph of the working class; *any revolution* that contributes to the ultimate revolution of the working class' (Rev 40; emphasis added). In other words, he suggests, national liberation movements are *not* working-class revolutions but they *contribute* to the latter as they create revolutionary conditions. *Note how the concept of working class dangles from liberation movements, just because the working-class agency is sanctioned by a (presupposed) Marxist truism.* We do know that the historically privileged agency of the working class is a figment and product of Marxist theory—a false assumption in fact and indicative of class essentialism. Sho'aiyan's ruthless criticism does not go so far as questioning the working class as a theoretically privileged agent of history. He still adheres to class essentialism. In any case, with the 'objective' conditions of revolution being already ripe due to global capitalist domination, the 'subjective' conditions will be brought to the revolutionary agents by the working-class enlighteners. It is the vanguard's task to tie revolutionary consciousness to the spontaneous movements of the people (Rev 42–3).

Here is where he conceptually brings together postcolonial national liberation movements and the universal struggle of the proletariat. The time for 'patriotic' (*mihani*) revolutions is over (deriding the USSR); referring to the post-World War Two national liberation movements, he declares, 'the age of "patriotic" revolutions has passed. Now the age of "world" (*jahani*) revolutions arrives' (Rev 72). Since the conflict between labor and capital is international, it must also be resolved internationally (Rev 152, 159; SURMJ 101). This view allows Sho'aiyan to debunk 'regionalisations' of liberation movements (e.g. Africanisation) (Rev 233–5, n. 63; 246, n. 95) or the nationalisation of socialism (Rev 167). Indeed, his ideas resonate with Tricontinentalism. The First Tricontinental Conference, in Havana, Cuba, in 1966, was yet another step, and the most significant one, in the long series of anti-imperialist solidarity movements in Africa, Asia, and Latin America.[19] To this effect, Sho'aiyan certainly must have read Che Guevara's 'Message to the Tricontinental' (1967), where he declared,

What role shall we, the exploited people of the world, play? The peoples of the three continents focus their attention on Vietnam and learn their lesson. Since imperialists blackmail humanity by threatening it with war, the wise reaction is not to fear war. The general tactics of the people should be to launch a constant and a firm attack in all fronts where the confrontation is taking place.[20]

The solidarity between the Third World countries overrides their particularity and differences: they are all subject to imperialist aggression and exploitation, and if they resist they will be repressed. Vietnam signifies that.

In the national liberation age, therefore, the nature of (social-ist) revolution has changed: if Lenin's 'theory of uprising' ever had any currency, now is the time for 'enduring revolution' (*enqelab-e dirpai*) (Rev 107) hypostasised in the figure of Che Guevara who recognised the equally exploitative treatment of the Third World movements by the socialist camp and capital-ist countries (Rev 276–7, n. 204). This is where a liberationist socialism is launched by Che who declared, 'the autochthonous bourgeoisie have lost all their capacity to oppose imperialism... There are no other alternatives; either a socialist revolution or a make-believe revolution.'[21] Any revolution will inevitably begin within a country, but it must not devolve into a 'patri-otic revolution': it should become the springboard for 'global revolution' (*enqelab-e jahani*) until the last worker in the world is emancipated (Rev 45). In fact, triumphant socialism must serve the world liberation movement: 'Thus, the socialist system is a specific logistical system (*nezam-e vizheh-ye posht-e jebhe*) for the workers' revolution that becomes necessary in a par-ticular stage of expansion of the revolution. Then, socialism is installed not at the end of the revolution, but behind the frontline (*posht-e jebhe*) of the global revolution' (Rev 50). This is because, as mentioned, the gravity of revolution has shifted from the West to the East (SURMJ 107). His vision clearly entails 'war socialism' forced through by a dictatorship of the proletariat (Rev 54–5; SURMJ xii) to serve the international emancipation of the working class and by virtue of that the exploited people. How such a socialism is sustainable remains highly questionable. Interestingly, the idea resonates with the internationalist component of Marx's theory and the spirit of the Bolshevik Revolution before it was transformed into the Soviet Union.

SHURESH: WHAT IS IN A WORD?

I have already said that the Kasravite prose, for whatever reason Sho'aiyan employed it—he cites security reasons (Rev 11), a motive Momeni tauntingly questions[22]—actually granted him a singular language unadulterated by the common lexis that the New Communist Movement had unwittingly and uncritically inherited from the Tudeh Party, against whose legacy, ironically, it had emerged. These common idioms contain historically sanctioned significations that slip through the political intentions of their users and influence the leftist literature beyond its author's control. While these idioms allow for a discursive communication among the leftist activists, they also inescapably skew *semantically* that which is uttered. That is the effect of discourse: it sanctions significations and renders certain elements, as opposed to certain others, intelligible. We saw earlier (Chapter 2) that the first formulation of Sho'aiyan's theory of *shuresh* emerged in *What Is To Be Done?* (1968). A polysemic word, the Persian '*shuresh*' can be translated as 'rebellion,' 'revolt,' or 'uprising,' but in the context of Sho'aiyan's idiosyncratic conceptualisation I think 'rebellion' is the closest equivalent. I am aware that by preferring 'rebellion' to other seemingly interchangeable equivalents I, too, am sanctioning a certain hermeneutic direction in reconceptualising his theory for the English-speaking readers. But I think this direction is closest to the spirit of Sho'aiyan's concept. 'Rebellion' intends to capture the idea that 'the foundation and infrastructure of a rebel [*shureshi*] organisation is the masses and the masses alone' (WBD 1), and how the *heterogeneous masses*, converged within a *front*, are led by an already rebellious nucleus of *enlighteners* to a continuous revolutionary *armed struggle* that the forces of the status quo cannot defeat. The front unifies both the people's forces and the working-class forces 'from the few to the many' ('Half-a-Step' in 'HSW' 10).

The question is why, in transfiguring the common lexis of the Left, did Sho'aiyan choose to substitute *shuresh/rebellion* for *enqelab/revolution*? And where are his sources? I am inclined to make reasonable suggestions based on my intertextual reading of his work in the context of the shifting intellectual parlance of the 1960s. The one primary source I identify is Ahmad Kasravi, the very one that brought Sho'aiyan's idiosyncrasy under unrelenting criticism by Momeni.

The fact that Sho'aiyan deploys a Kasravite prose logically proves that he must have seriously read and internalised Kasravi, and, given his interest in Iranian history, Mostafa definitely must have read Kasravi's voluminous *History of Iranian Constitutionalism* (1940). *Shuresh* is a Persian term used by Kasravi in this work to signify armed resistance and popular armed uprising. When narrating pro-constitutionalist Sattar Khan and Baqer Khan's armed resistance in Tabriz against the coup by Mohammad Ali Shah, a period known as Minor Autocracy (*estebdad-e saghir*), and the prolonged siege of Tabriz by the army beginning on 20 June 1908, Kasravi observes: '"*shuresh*" itself grew stronger… and it was during these days that… [the revolutionaries] laid the foundations of Gilan's *shuresh*.'[23] Here, Kasravi suggests that *shuresh* moves not just from one place to another, but *from the few to the many* (Sho'aiyan's dictum): Sattar Khan's armed resistance in Amirkhiz district in Tabriz eventually grew into a nationwide armed uprising against the Shah.[24] Kasravi unwaveringly admires the persistence of armed people who risked everything for their rights.[25] He approves of the assassination of Premier Atabak (1858–1907) by Abbas Aqa Tabrizi (on 31 August 1907), a member of the Tabriz *anjoman* (grassroots council), on whose *anjoman* identity card were the words '*fadai-ye mellat*' (nation's

self-sacrificing [man]).[26] Kasravi clearly favored the idea that
the road to being a *fadai* was to continue with armed uprising.[27]
He praised the Social Democrats' clandestine Centre (*Markaz-e
Gheybi*) led by legendary communist agitator Heydar Amu Oghli,
endorsing his attempted assassination of Mohammad Ali Mirza.[28]
The concept of 'rebellion' therefore shows the reader striking
resemblances between the two authors from two different historical realities. Moreover, *shuresh* represents a term exclusively used
by the Fadai generation: it entered the armed guerrillas' lexicon
through the translation of the Latin American revolutionary
literature, in particular Che's *foco* that was translated as *kanun-e
shureshi*. Sho'aiyan's term *shuresh* brings these two signifieds across
two different experiences under one signifier.

In Iranian intellectual history, Kasravi primarily represents
a rationalist-modernist and nationalist figure who wrote volumes criticising religious beliefs from Shi'ism to Sufism and
Baha'ism and advocated a certain puritan-Persian belief system
named *Pakdini* (Purified Religion) that would resonate with both
pre-Islamic as well as modern Iran and become, he hoped, the
foundation of a new Iranian secular identity. The western reader
will find Kasravi's idea similar to those of the founders of sociology, Auguste Comte and Henri de Saint-Simon, who, against
the Catholic Church in France, respectively advocated 'positive
religion' and the 'New Christianity,' and shared the sociological
project of building a rational, modern France.

Kasravi's position and Sho'aiyan's adopting his prose, as we
saw in Chapter 4, did not sit well with Momeni who argued that
Sho'aiyan's Kasravite Persian was the very source of his problem.
In response, Sho'aiyan claims that his prose has nothing to do
with his thinking, asking Momeni to criticise his thought, not
his language. 'I can make up the words I want. This is not important. What is important is that what I think with help of this

word.'[29] Momeni is correct: the use of language does influence one's worldview, although he exploits this point to excommunicate Sho'aiyan. Kasravite prose unleashes a barrage of charges against Sho'aiyan based on guilt by association. Momeni draws on Sho'aiyan's 1960s intellectual excursions to show that his eclectic thought oscillates between the pro-Maleki, 'anti-international communist "socialists"' of the journal *Thought and Art* and Kasravi's bourgeois nationalism, which ultimately render his work, *Revolution*, to represent the interests of 'petite-bourgeois intellectuals.'[30] Sho'aiyan's deployment of 'a mechanistic and artificial language' is the source of his conceptual problems, Momeni submits. 'Firstly, the particular language of *Shuresh* has an organic relationship with the mode of thought of its author, and secondly, the issue of language is the first issue that is discussed in *Shuresh*.'[31] Kasravi is a poor choice: he is a 'bourgeois historian' with a 'progressive and benevolent' intention of purifying Persian for his 'aristocratic pleasure and amusement' against the 'Arab-strickenness of feudal intellectuals.' Kasravi's 'rationalisation' of language was erroneous because he forgot that the creators of language are the people.[32] In short, charges Momeni, Sho'aiyan misses the 'class character' of Kasravi's reforms and forgets that Kasravite esotericism is a poor choice for political writing, which should be understandable to people.[33]

Still Momeni's criticism continues: by adopting Kasravite prose, Sho'aiyan contracts a formalistic view that tends to distort concepts beyond recognition.[34] This choice forces Sho'aiyan into isolation as he steps out of the shared linguistic convention of the revolutionary-Marxist literature. He thus blocks off any chance of his ideas reaching the masses.[35] In the end, linguistic similarity produces intellectual similarity, and, since Kasravi was a bourgeois, idealist thinker, Sho'aiyan 'wishes to attain the hegemony of petite bourgeoisie in the revolution'; in fact, 'he specifically wants to maintain the hegemony of bourgeois intellectuals over the party and the revolution.'[36] Although achieved through logical fallacies like guilt by association and slippery slope, Momeni's verdict is nevertheless quite damning: by misrepresenting Sho'aiyan's work, Momeni portrays the man who relentlessly advocated the revolutionary action of the working class as the defender of that which he sought to destroy. Momeni presents Marx's complex theory of language (*inter alia* in *The German Ideology*) as simply instrumental, stating that for Marxism 'language is the tool for thinking.'[37] In this way of thinking, there is a certain populist view of language: that the activists should use established revolutionary parlance to reach out to the masses—as if the revolutionary lexicon were accessible to the masses at all and as if such has been the case in any Marxist tradition. To appreciate what I mean, just think of the convoluted and esoteric prose of *The Communist Manifesto*—a text addressing nineteenth-century workers![38] To summarise Momeni's point, Sho'aiyan's linguistic exclusiveness is the proof of his counter-revolutionary stance!

Admittedly, Sho'aiyan writes for leftist intellectuals and not for the masses, but in Momeni's criticising the inaccessibility of his works he finds that Iranian enlighteners 'do not like the challenge of thinking and cognitive inquiring' (Rev 13). This is why, according to Sho'aiyan, the Iranian anti-colonial movement has not produced 'a single revolutionary thinker or social researcher of equal weight to any other thinkers and innovators in the world.' Our best thinkers are still the Bàb (Seyed Ali Mohammad Shirazi [1819–50], founder of Babism from which Baha'ism split away), Aqa Khan Kermani, Kasravi and [Taqi] Erani (Rev 13). Against the intellectual ambiance of the uncreative application of dominant revolutionary models, Sho'aiyan regards his theory as a challenge to the 'tradition of killing thinking' of the Iranian Left (Rev 19). His writing style is necessary for challenging the 'quoting verses' (*ayeh avari*) tendency within leftist literature that loves to 'pull out a truckload of quotes from the corners of the books of this or that author and offer them as incontrovertible evidence to the courthouse of the reader's judgment' (Rev 15). In short, Sho'aiyan wishes to construct a revolutionary discourse on his own.

By attacking Sho'aiyan's specific prose, Momeni achieves a great deal: he conditions the reader, already challenged by Sho'aiyan's book, to dismiss his work altogether without serious engagement. Thus we can see how Sho'aiyan's work has never been given serious consideration, something this volume intends to address.

REBELLIOUS ACTION, REBELLIOUS THOUGHT

In Sho'aiyan's theory, *revolution constitutes a mode of existence* proper to the possibility of the historic transformation heralded by Marx and Engels' historical materialism, which constitutes the normative framework of Sho'aiyan's Marxist thinking, that which allows Sho'aiyan to share a theoretical foundation with his contemporary Marxists, those with whom, *paradoxically*, he engages in critical debate. For those of us who live in the postcommunist era, the historical determinism of Marx and Engels' Hegelian conception of history is just a figment of an age-old eschatological belief in the 'end of history,' a utopian promise of conflict-free, post-political life, a Eurocentric assumption that has been discredited and debunked for good. But Sho'aiyan belongs to another time. However radical his critique of various aspects of Marxism, he still upholds this old dogma. 'There is no doubt that this [the enemy's] domination will soon and inevitably be overthrown to the detriment of reaction and colonialism since not even all the accumulations of the world of colonialism can withstand the conscious and universal (*sarasari*) rebellion of the masses' (WBD 6–7). Historical determinism makes the revolution, and thereby his theory, *inevitable*. Without historical determinism, it appears, his theory would disintegrate, but as I shall show in the next chapter, his revolutionary theory would work even better without any theoretically sanctioned determinism.

Because it dismantles the reactionary-colonial systems world-wide, *revolution is life*: it contains the birth pangs of a new society. The organising concept here is 'rebellion' (*shuresh*). He refers to his own thinking as 'rebellious thought,' which signifies a mode of thinking attuned to *rebellion*—that is, uncompromising *revolutionary praxis* of global exploited masses spearheaded by their armed enlighteners (vanguards) until the world is free of capitalist-imperialist exploitation. Armed struggle stands out as the highest form of 'rebellious essence.' The *praxis* of Iranian militants and other revolutionaries in colonised societies across the world will be the true measure of their 'rebellious essence' (*gowhar-e shureshi*). *Rebellious essence*, enlivened by history, enables *rebellious thought* of the enlighteners of the working class, those who, through militant *praxis*, unleash volcanic eruption upon world exploiters through their unceasing *rebellious action*. This 'essence' (*gowhar*) is innate to the exploited classes, a position that is owed to the Marxian concept of the proletariat as the privileged agent of history. But the working class—and exploited and oppressed classes, for that matter—do not partake in rebellious action unless the element of revolutionary consciousness—rebellious thought—is brought to them by their enlighteners—that is, a plurality of vanguards. *Sensu stricto*, *shuresh* captures the condition in which social, political, and productive relations are repressive

225

and exploitive while popular resistances against such relations are not yet quite in place. *Rebellion* travels within the gap 'between the "happening" (*voqu'*) of revolution and its "victory" (*piruzi*),' a chasm as wide as the one 'between earth and heavens' (Rev 97). The preceding being the summary of his theory, we need to unpack it now.

(*a*) *The rebellious essence* is endowed within the agent of history, by virtue of the (presupposed) Marxian concept of agency, but like the 'diamond in the mine' (WBD 3) it needs to be extracted, purified, and polished. Here Sho'aiyan relies on Marxist essentialism as a springboard for his theory of agency and revolutionary *praxis*. His ruthless criticism of Marxian concepts, reviewed in previous chapters, stops here and he simply *assumes* the privileged stance of the proletarian agency by virtue of its constitution within the historical materialist conception of the development of mode of production. At the same time, presupposing a pre-endowed revolutionary agency provides Sho'aiyan with an opportunity to offer his unconventional understanding of revolutionary action. He declares cryptically:

> But all such *receiving existence* (*hastipaziri*)—from the embryo to birth—have been the spontaneous *acquiring existence* (*hastiyaftan*), indeed an inevitable (*jabri*) one. The working class had no role in its receiving an existence (*hastipaziri*)—as with other classes. The birth of the working class was beyond its will—as with other classes. But how about its [i.e. the working class] nurturing? Is the nurturing of the working class beyond its will, as was its birth? No. The working class is clearly involved in its own nurturing as well as [its] historical path-finding (*rahpui*). (Rev 60; emphasis added)

This passage constitutes the *ontology* of the proletariat. The working class is a product of capitalist class society (as with Marxian class-in-itself): like any child it had no say in its coming to existence. But its 'receiving its existence'—in its becoming a concrete, historic reality—in this determinate fashion does not automatically translate into a determinate course of action. The proletariat's 'acquiring existence' (as with Marxian class-for-itself) requires the working class to take charge of its own praxis through the education granted by Marxism, which for Sho'aiyan means that the working-class revolution is conceived in the womb of working-class *culture*, indeed a global culture (Rev 60–1). We can see where this line of argument leads: it highlights the key role of the enlighteners of the working class who bring to it revolutionary class consciousness. Expressed in conventional Marxist discourse, here we are dealing with how the vanguard connects the objective, concrete class with the subjective element of class consciousness that will bring the class to revolutionary action.

But, then, one is inclined to probe the essence of the working-class vanguard or enlighteners. Unlike the absolute majority of Marxist theories (including Jazani and Ahmadzadeh) who bypass this conceptual problem, Sho'aiyan offers a fascinating view of *class position* and *class belonging*. He asks, 'Members of the communist party that are not vocationally workers, and thus do not directly participate in the process of production, where do they stand in class division?' He replies, 'Undoubtedly, they belong in the ranks of "mental workers".' He asks again, 'But the mental workers of which class?' And he submits, 'Clearly, the working class's mental workers. For it has already been proved that all members of the communist party are among the best elements of the working class. Evidently, the best elements of a class belong to that class. And therefore members of the communist party belong socially to the working class' (IRJS 29). The *social and political existence* of the enlighteners, not their *economic position*, determines their belonging to the class they represent and educate. In short, *class position—a political position—determines class belonging, not vice versa.* Put differently, *revolutionary praxis— rebellious essence—transforms the actor's social existence in favor of (and always already to the detriment of) a certain class.* 'Merely being a worker' does not suffice for working-class consciousness (Rev 175), and it is the social life that defines class belonging, not vice versa (IRJS 60). Thus, while upholding the 'working class' as the historical revolutionary agent, due to Marxist theory, *he ends up*, willingly or otherwise, *de-essentialising the working class*: 'The thought (*pendar*) that just because someone is a worker or a peasant she or he will be in control of her or his political tongue (*zaban-e siyasi*) is just a figment (*pendar*). And a childish figment' (WBD 10). And the proletarian characteristics are not to be idealised; indeed, there are no individuals 'untainted [*paludeh*] by any impurities and unworkerly disease' (SOLI 32). While the working class, à la Marx, is economically constituted by a capitalist mode of production, it is class consciousness that constitutes its essence. Class, therefore, is not simply an economic category, but, rather, a social and political category (IRJS 34). This position is somewhat counterintuitive: the *antinomy* embedded in this brilliant argument is mindboggling. Sho'aiyan finds in the working class the masses, constituted by unjust class relations, that the revolutionary intellectual ought to mobilise and lead. To achieve that, he *displaces* the concept of agency from the objective realm of economy into the realm of revolutionary culture. He simultaneously remains caught in class essentialism and supersedes it. This is a *paradox*.

Expressed in post-Marxist terms, Sho'aiyan is challenging the *limits of social objectivity*.[39] Precisely because of that, his position infuriated Momeni who accuses Sho'aiyan of being a bourgeois thinker despite his advocacy of the working class. Against Momeni's position, Sho'aiyan declares that Momeni 'does not see a difference between "workers" and the working class. From the point of view of *Judicious Steps* [Momeni's rejoinder to Sho'aiyan], the working *class* is the same as the sum of all workers… And since a worker has a vocation as a worker, [Momeni's] *Judicious Steps* assesses the working class, which it believes to be the same as [the sum of] workers, as a vocational phenomenon' (IRJS 37; emphasis in the original). Rebellious essence conjoins the revolutionary enlightener with the class she represents and eliminates their distinction. The enlightener becomes the organic intellectual (Gramsci) of the class in that she shares the worldview of the class. The 'rebellious essence,' I conclude, is not a pre-ordained metaphysical substance: it is born out of the revolutionary *praxis*, which paradoxically was enabled by Marxist essentialism and determinism in the first place. Only those who have 'rebellious essence'—i.e. revolutionary consciousness—can join the transformative vanguard (WBD 2). And only the dissemination of the rebellious essence—i.e. the dissemination of revolutionary consciousness and its enactment through *polarising* action of armed struggle—can transform the status quo. Precisely because it polarises the populace, armed struggle begets revolutionary consciousness among the masses.

(b) *The rebellious thought* therefore signifies the process of bringing revolutionary consciousness to the class and the masses. Note that since the gravity of the revolution is moving from West to East, or, in other words, since the wars of liberation are taking precedence over working-class, socialist revolutions (e.g. the Bolshevik Revolution), and it is only through the former that the latter can unfold (e.g. Cuba and Vietnam), then rebellious thought is geared toward bringing *shuresh* to the vast array of exploited masses. The war of liberation, however, primarily involves the *liberation of consciousness*—indeed a complete *cultural deliverance*: 'To deliver the masses, the working class has to elevate the masses to the summit of its own culture and essence. And this is not doable unless in rebellion. A global rebellion! Rebellion is the best cultural school' ('Inquiry about a Critique,' in HSW 13). The subjective element, or consciousness (*agahi*), now weaves different loci of rebellion together and creates a front that aims for such global undertaking. This accentuates the presence of the rebellious enlighteners, these 'educators of the class,' and their revolutionary organisation. The rebellious thought, the revolutionary consciousness (*agahi*), will spread, once again, from the few to the many. Thus, it is the task of the vanguard (*pishahang*) to bring the masses to the revolution (WBD 1). Note how Sho'aiyan holds political education as the central mode of activism: because the revolutionary potential already and objectively exists within the exploited masses (Marxist essentialism), the subjective element, which is now lacking but needs to be brought to the people by the vanguard, will determine the future of revolution.

(c) Rebellious action arises where revolutionary consciousness and culture meet the agency it has created, or, put differently, where the abstract rebellious thought meets the concrete rebellious agency. But there is a gap between the two that corresponds to the Iranian reality.

> There are conditions in the life history of a class in which its vanguard neither has the freedom to deliver its message to the entire class and society nor can it submit to whining (*chosnaleh!*) and surrender. And this is a historical condition in which the class intends to militantly shake off its chains, but its organizational solidarity and

connections are so shattered that it must start the life-generating (*zendegibakhsh*) battle of armed movement using whatever number of the connecting cords [available]; and this is precisely the stage of rebellious spawning. ('Half-a-Step' in HSW 7–8)

This gap needs to be filled with the action of the rebellious organisation. Expectedly, the vanguard 'must be in *essence* (*gowhar*) worthy of the rebellious force' (WBD 2; emphasis added). 'No rebellious organisation can exist without being militant (*razmi*) and if an organisation wishes to be militant it must inevitably accept this aspect and continuously try to cultivate this [militant] aspect increasingly and radically' (WBD 4). Within the postcolonial movements we witness two tendencies: either the communist party leads the liberation movement (Vietnam) or the guerrillas do (Cuba). Like Ahmadzadeh,[40] Sho'aiyan prefers the latter, finding it compatible with the Iranian reality. The rebellious (*shureshi*) organisation undergoes two phases: (1) a preparatory phase, 'the period in which the organisation is not yet involved in open rebellious battle,' and (2) the operational phase, 'the period in which the organisation is fully engaged in a battle of death or rebellious life' (WBD 5). Evidently, Sho'aiyan writes from the experience of the first phase in Iran.

This is where the question of the masses is emphasised. But there is a dialectical relationship here. Sho'aiyan declares, 'although without the leadership of rebellious organisation the masses, separated from rebellion, are still an undefeatable force, they are nonetheless the subordinate and abject masses' (WBD 1). This overconfidence in the rather *idealised masses* guarantees, for Sho'aiyan, the vanguard's not relying on foreign powers—a conceptual safeguard against the Tudeh legacy reflective of the concerns of the Fadai generation. But this reliance also means that the entire theory of rebellion is about taking the armed struggle of revolutionary intellectuals to the people, the Gordian knot of urban guerrilla warfare theory, and the common concern of the three theorists of armed struggle in Iran—Jazani, Ahmadzadeh, and Sho'aiyan. Clearly, we are dealing with the question of *mobilisation* of the masses by the revolutionary intellectuals. Because, for Sho'aiyan, class position determines class belonging, the 'nominal' leadership of the working class through its vanguard enlighteners will *constitute* the 'people' (*khalq*) who will partake in the anti-reaction-colonialism struggle. This reveals a key theoretical aporia: on close inspection, then, the working class becomes the normative idea for liberation, but liberation involves the *eradication* of the class differences into *khalq*, a people that constitutes the force. This is the populist aspect of Sho'aiyan's theory. The fact of the matter is that it was the forging of the heterogeneous colonised masses into a new, unified 'people' (now named 'working class' because of the communist leadership) that constituted postcolonial Asian and African nations. For Sho'aiyan, this is how a unified people emerges out of the anti-colonial struggles, but, being an internationalist, Sho'aiyan still insists that yet another type of *people* must grow beyond national boundaries and cultures and into an internationalist movement until the capitalist world-system is diminished. He hopes the zeal for overthrowing the Shah will open a new front in the workers' international revolution, by 'international proletarian armies,'[41] and not succumb to 'right nationalism' (OLM 50). 'To reach communism there is no peaceful approach to imperialism. The only way is a series of revolutionary wars by the international working class, the world's masses against all imperialisms and reactionaries-colonialists until their defeat and the eradication of all imperialisms and reactionaries-colonialists upon the world's expanse! Workers of the World Revolt!' (SURMJ xii). The revolution is therefore a global phenomenon (SURMJ 101). The Iranian revolution is thus a reappearance of the world revolution ('Half-a-Step' in HSW 1).

This position strongly echoes Tricontinentalism and reminds us of ideas such as Frantz Fanon's advocacy for African liberation, indeed the 'endeavor to create a new man.'[42] Only a front, not a party, can contain the people's (*khalq*) demands due to the latter's plurality and its representatives. That is also why his proposed 'reaction-colonialism' captures the reality of colonised nations more accurately than the exhausted Marxist concept of class. This strategy unifies all. As mentioned (Chapter 3), the liberation movement and defeating imperialism is not the same as emancipation from capitalist exploitation. Recall that, in Sho'aiyan's view, the victory of the working class over capitalism is never conclusive, and capitalism can always return, as it did in the Soviet Union ('Some Pure Criticisms' in SW 17–18). Liberation is a key passageway to emancipation, but it requires *acting according to the essence of revolution* ('Some Pure Criticisms' in SW 27), a revolution that won't stop until the emancipation of the world's proletariat.[43] Armed struggle is therefore strategic in a world dominated by colonialist and imperialist military. National liberation will therefore lead to class warfare on national and later international levels (see Appendix). The internationalist tendency in Sho'aiyan's theory is reflective of the world in which he lived, but he falls short in theorising why the Iranian revolution should constitute a bastion for the global revolution. He simply makes the assertion and assumes the connection. And in reality we saw how the liberation movements in Africa and Asia failed to grow into international movements and instead ended up creating postcolonial, authoritarian, nationalistic states.

But back to Sho'aiyan: how does the revolutionary culture reach from the enlighteners to the masses? Unlike his contemporary Jazani, who offered a practical solution through organisation of labor, creation of a political wing, and increasingly shifting away from armed operations,[44] Sho'aiyan's theory, like Ahmadzadeh, relies on a *leap of faith*. 'The present frailty of an embryo to whom belongs the future due to its authenticity and purity should not motivate anxiety and confusion,' he declares. 'The strong phenomenon of tomorrow is weak today. But this frailty is transient and that strength will arrive when disbelievers do not expect it' ('Exposing' in SW 6). This optimism on his part is rather *unwarranted*. There is an element of will here, a volitionalism perhaps, the *belief* that 'the revolution imposes its necessity before the destruction of the old social order and before the establishment of the new one. A revolution's task is precisely this destruction and that establishment' (SURMJ 31). He wrote this last statement earlier in his thinking—late 1960s and early 1970s before Siahkal inspired a generation of dissenters, giving them hope. At this time, like Jazani and Ahmadzadeh, Sho'aiyan did not conceive of the possibility that armed struggle would be shunned by the very masses it tried to reach. And this is precisely what happened by 1976: the militant movement gradually began to shift toward other forms of struggle and abandon armed struggle. By 1974, Jazani had definitely shifted his focus to mobilising the masses through non-militant action. His proposed 'political wing' is an indication of that. As for Sho'aiyan, it seems that a similar doubt had blossomed in his thinking, too: toward the end of his life, sparks of doubt about the vanguard's armed struggle appear in his notes. He submits that the operations that do not directly and tangibly address the people's concrete concerns and experiences won't lead to mobilisation of the masses (see Appendix). This insinuates that *his last theoretical concern* was no longer about theorising the vanguard's armed struggle but, strictly, *about conceptualising how to instigate the people's war of liberation, in short, mass mobilisation.* He had clearly experienced, it appears, the limits of the intellectuals' armed struggle.

CONCLUSION: DISCOURSE AND REVOLUTIONARY ACTION

One cannot properly understand or appreciate Sho'aiyan's theory without decoding his distinct phraseology forming a set of relations between the (idiosyncratic and at times neologised) signifiers that produce a singular discourse that owes the identity of its various elements to diverse discursive sources—from Marxism to Latin American guerrilla theories, to postcolonial national liberation literature, and notably to Kasravi. Only by tracking his discourse back to these multiple sources and thereby gleaning and decoding his idioms will Sho'aiyan's work emerge as a coherent body of theory, but never without painstaking efforts at harmonising his original thoughts—at times paradoxical, essentialist, or naively assertive. Without trying to gloss over his errors, I argue that his theorising overshadows his conceptual problems. This is because he set the bar higher compared to Jazani or Ahmadzadeh: he wanted a fresh theory uncontaminated by the past. This book hopes to have achieved the demanding task of offering a *reconstructive interpretation* of Sho'aiyan by documenting the molecular formation of his ideas. The essential precondition for Sho'aiyan's attempt at constituting a *new revolutionary discourse* was refraining from the common idioms of the Left, and that was precisely the source of his being misunderstood and shunned by those he considered comrades-in-arms. He became an intellectual exile. *His theory of the revolution/rebellion could only have emerged from his new, intertextual and multiversal discourse.* For the doctrinal Left, still and unwittingly dominated by the theoretical discourse founded by the Tudeh Party, Sho'aiyan's concept of revolution/rebellion appears to be catachrestic, and that bewildered his critics, leading to his marginalisation to this day. Even as today's young savvy journalists try to reinvigorate his figure as the 'honourable rebel,'[45] they visibly fall short in articulating the theoretical significance of his work, let alone presenting a coherent summary of it.

Sho'aiyan's theory of revolution required from him the boldest task of all: while it is predicated upon two major metaphysical principles of Marxism—eschatological history and the conceptually privileged agency of the working class—he nevertheless had to radically question major assumptions and critically re-evaluate the contributions of Marxist (and Leninist) revolutionary theory from the pulpit of his concrete, lived experiences. He did not always succeed but managed to offer refreshing (and at times unreadable!) engagements. Above all, Sho'aiyan is confronted with the element of *contingency* in agency and action when he boldly admits that it is the intellectuals who bear the revolutionary action, albeit on behalf of and in the name of the working class (or the masses). This is because revolutionary class itself is not acting according to its historical agency. This lack of action, which problematises the presupposed agency of the working class, is then sidetracked in his work: he lets Marxist essentialism over-determine the concept. Consider it a metaphysical consolation! As for popularising armed struggle—which never happened in Iran—Sho'aiyan takes a leap of faith, simply because he belongs to the generation that has witnessed the heroic resistances or victories of popular liberation armies in Vietnam, Palestine, Algeria, and Cuba. Both of these positions hinder his theory in its attempt to reach its full potential. A contemporary reading of Sho'aiyan must therefore continue upon the path he opened, bring his ruthless critiques to fruition, and thus debunk his two assumptions as well, not to mention his naive belief in internationalist class war or his 'war socialism.' Having become privy to the *spirit* of his thought due to decades of scrutinising his works, I believe Mostafa would have done the same today (see Conclusion).

A number of his engagements assist us with this task: first, he demystifies the deeply rooted belief that there are universal models for revolution. On the contrary, he shows that all revolutions are particularistic. Revolutionary particularisms, nonetheless, are connected through unrelenting rebellious action. As such, his perceived 'world revolution' involves the confluence of particular rebellious forces in a voluntary and thus democratic—and therefore frontal—fashion, (counter-)hegemonically united against the conjoined twins, capitalism and imperialism. Accordingly, his concept of 'enduring revolution' (*enqelab-e dirpai*) has no resemblance to Trotsky's 'permanent revolution,' a resemblance that won him yet another label (Trotskyist) intended, in a Leninist-dominated Left in Iran, to humiliate him.[46] But the resemblance ends at the terminological level: for Trotsky, permanent revolution primarily meant to suggest that in 'backward' countries the bourgeois-democratic revolution would remain incomplete in terms of economic development and the revolutions must be made permanent, leading to workers' revolution. Since socialism in one country would not succeed because of capitalist pressure, workers in all countries should transform their bourgeois-democratic revolutions into socialist revolutions. Thus, following Marx and Engels, Trotsky's theory focuses on the international proletarian revolution. The foundations of Sho'aiyan's theory are different. His unrelenting revolutionary war is in fact inspired by Ernesto Che Guevara. This is why armed struggle, or *rebellion/shuresh*, is key: as an ultimate revolutionary action, it *polarises* society and thereby mobilises the exploited and colonised masses to stage revolutions against imperialism and colonialism. A certain, strong Fanonian streak links the liberationist pillar of his work to that of Che's unrelenting rebellion against imperialism. In this sense, socialism becomes the *telos* of all liberation movements, which in the end will unify the East and the West. Note that while Fanon was suspicious of western Marxism, Sho'aiyan offers his 'own' version of Marxism to reconcile the internationalist spirit of socialism with the national liberation movements. Hence, his approach to socialism is indeed liberatory. But he fails to *conceptually* attach telic socialism to liberation: he simply assumes one liberation will bring about socialism because that happened in Vietnam or Tanzania (and some other postcolonial nations), but that did not happen in so many other countries. In this sense, *shuresh* becomes a synecdochal term for all forms of rebellious actions against imperialism, colonialism, and capitalism. Sho'aiyan is correct in that a new humanity cannot emerge without a complete destruction of the existing world order. As such, his theory of revolution/rebellion, despite its problems, becomes an anti-systemic theory. He, therefore, envisioned a new world order that would end the existing unjust and exploitative relations. *Revolution* was tasked with preparing the way for such an ambitious vision for an entirely new humanity.

CONCLUSION

The Twenty-First-Century Revolutionary Theory

*Even though it may be interpreted as arrogance
and exhibitionism, let me add here that the
dragon has already been born. What is still left
[for us to do] is its support and cultivation and
growth. And this needs time. And... as long as
there is being, there is time.*

Sho'aiyan, IRJS 343

I did not write this book in order to condemn an original
thinker named Mostafa Sho'aiyan to the prison of historical particularities of a country named Iran that has been
marginalised by the orientalist epistemologies that reduce me
to the position of the 'native informant' whose task is to provide
'cases'—here Sho'aiyan—for the (apparently) universal theoretical and conceptual grand narratives of western historiography.
This book intends to rescue Sho'aiyan's work from the oblivion
imposed upon it both by two generations of Iranian intellectuals
and by scholarly research. When Sho'aiyan appears in the writings
of the aforesaid—if he does at all—both of these groups tend

to reduce him to a victim of Stalinism of the Left and his complex, maverick work to his encounters with the 'evil' Fadaiyan.[1] It is true that the extent of his marginalisation by the doctrinal Left can hardly be overstated. Yet, Sho'aiyan far surpasses these reductionisms, and, for the record, he is no victim at all and never felt like one: *he is marginal but singular*, and, as attested by his extensive writings, he was entirely capable of striking back at his critics and opponents through his own criticisms and open letters. Unconventional thinking, of course, has never been a matter of popular acclamation.

Contrary to the above, I submit, *Sho'aiyan was an international and internationalist thinker*, surpassing his Iranian particularity, although bound by Persian language that condemned his work to the margins. I know Mostafa would not feel at ease about my claim: in response to the late Cosroe Chaqueri (Edition Mazdak) who praised him as one of the originators of Iran's New Communist Movement, Mostafa replied that he rejected the claim that he was 'among the theoreticians and intellectual founders of the new movement in Iran' (RRC 10). This concluding chapter, therefore, draws on Sho'aiyan's conceptualisations for the purpose of rethinking today's struggles for social justice and democracy in this unjust human world by focusing on his contributions to rethinking a frontal and popular mobilisation of the masses. This task can only be achieved through a critical reappropriation of his concepts and propositions.

TERMINAL POINT: NATIONAL LIBERATION

Sho'aiyan lived in an age of heightened national liberation campaigns in Asia and Africa—a period in which former colonies were engaged in a battle of life and death for decolonisation and independence, from Vietnam to Angola, Cuba to Mozambique. Popular liberation fronts in these (former) colonies fought tooth and nail to oust foreign colonisers. Liberation from colonialism, however, produced mixed results. Grappling with the harsh realities of liberation on a planet run by the capitalist world-system, the emerging postcolonial nations went through the birth pangs of uneven development that forced them into the neo-colonial economies as peripheral players and suppliers of cash crops, cheap raw materials, and low-cost labor for the metropoles in the Global North that continued to flourish at the expense of the increasingly impoverished Global South. This trend, alas, continues to this day and has cast realistic doubts about the *global* future of human civilisations through massive impoverishment and imminent ecological collapse.

Che Guevara's death in Bolivia in 1967 symbolised the defeat of the idea of armed, peasant uprising. Situated within the three colonised continents, Algeria, Cuba, and Vietnam (among others) showed successfully how to resolve the problem of mass mobilisation for popular armed struggle. The problem was both theoretical and practical. Despite the early optimism of the originators of armed struggle in Iran, the urban guerrillas failed in achieving just that, and in response to the masses' indifference to guerrilla warfare, the guerrillas further theorised the problem, thus producing a rich body of theoretical literature. But the Iranian guerrillas were not alone in finding their objectives unrealised. In reaction to the harsh realities of peasant life, Latin American revolutionaries authored an urban guerrilla version of anti-colonial resistance by the mid-1960s, a model that quickly became universal as it inspired cohorts of young, educated seekers of social justice and advocates of emancipatory politics across the globe, from the Uruguayan Tupamaros (*Movimiento de Liberación*

Nacional-Tupamaros), to the German Red Army Faction (*Rote Armee Fraktion*), to the Italian *Brigate Rosse*, to the Japanese Red Army (*Nihon Sekigun*), to the Weather Underground in the United States, to the Popular Front for the Liberation of Palestine (*al-Jabhah al-Sha'biyyah li-Tahrir Filastin*). The list continues. The PFG emerged as a sister group in this global urban-militant, anti-imperialist, liberationist movement. Out of more than a decade of political experiences and experiments, Sho'aiyan shone as a distinctive theoretician in this movement.

This unique historical possibility of liberation appeared in the existential horizons of Iranian intellectuals as a possible way out of the country's seemingly endless nights of repression, and armed struggle offered them a choice between an enlivening possibility of realising a dynamic, participatory, just, and democratic Iran contrasted with the state-propagated notion of a functionary's stagnant, tedious life, rewarded with soulless middle-class existence but bereft of meaningful participation. To many of us today, such a binary may appear arbitrary, but it still resonates with a certain undiminishing truth. Sho'aiyan had made his choice but he entered the urban guerrilla *discursive field* as a theoretician with a critical rejection of Leninism (the way he understood it), which at the time functioned as the password to the revolutionary discourse. In refusing certain theoretical components attached to Leninism single-handedly, he left a legacy that is still valid in many of its aspects for today's postcommunist era, a time in which urban guerrilla movements no longer overdetermine revolutionary action.

That era has globally receded. The age of national liberation, as Fanon, Che, and Sho'aiyan had anticipated, produced for the most part nightmarish postcolonial dictatorships in Asia and Africa or military juntas in Latin America—all feeding a glutinous comprador elite, getting rich from the toil of hundreds of millions of workers and peasants, and selling national resources. Those countries, especially in Latin America, that later went through the process of democratisation, exceptions aside, found themselves caught in manipulated and feeble parliamentary systems that led the countries into being increasingly exploited by the capitalist metropoles. Che and Sho'aiyan were right, as was Fanon, that *national liberation was not sufficient*: the world needed an *international liberation*—a complete transformation of the capitalist world-system enabled by the rebellion of the people of the Global South (and the subaltern of the Global North). But then, although in many regions of the world (Colombia, India, Nepal, Kurdistan) popular armed militants continue to fight against their respective states, the age of armed struggle has come to an end. At least for now. Armed revolt no longer motivates the younger generations nor, for the most part, the people. In short, armed struggle is no longer deemed politically intelligible, much less desirable or practical in the face of militarised states—liberal democratic or not—aided by intrusive digital technologies that subject the citizens to constant surveillance, robbing them of privacy, conditioning them to be self-exhibitionist, and bombarding them with irrelevant information—the weapons of mass distraction. Today, there are still popular armed resistances of the poor and repressed—in Chiapas (Mexico), Rojava (West Kurdistan), or Naxalite-Maoist insurgency (India)—but these cases, their fantastic achievements duly noted, do not belong to a global trend. And, yes, there are still old-fashioned intellectual, armed groups such as *Türkiye Halk Kurtuluş Partisi-Cephesi*. The 'guerrilla warfare' of the *new generation* of intellectuals nowadays mostly consists of the acts of whistleblowers like Julian Assange, Edward Snowden, and Chelsea Manning, or rebellious groups such as Turkey's Marxist-Leninist Redhack.

Historically, *Sho'aiyan's work signifies the endpoint of an entire era of Iranian political theory.* I have previously proposed a tripartite theory of national self-assertion in Iran that I briefly reiterate here. National self-assertion and liberation in Iran was concomitant with the Constitutional Movement of 1906–11, which marks Iran's entry into political modernity characterised by demands for responsible government, constitutional rights, and the modern citizen. Constitutionalism begat institutional legalism that, in the context of the British and Russian imperialist encroachments at the time, aimed at enacting the right to national self-assertion and self-governance. But this first era of national self-assertion, already over within a decade, ended in Reza Shah's repressive modernisation that lasted until 1941. World War Two, ironically, brought Iran an era of relative political freedom, and, in the years that followed, the quintessence of national liberation and self-assertion returned in the shape of the oil nationalisation movement and constitutional limitation on the Shah's power. Led by Dr Mosaddeq, this movement sought national self-assertion in a democratic fashion. When the movement was overpowered by the direct intervention of American and English imperialisms in the 1953 coup, and the short-lived attempt at reviving the movement in the early 1960s failed in the face of the Shah's autocratic crackdown and social-legal reforms, the popular yearning for national self-assertion mutated into a last era of national liberation through armed struggle by the late 1960s. The era gradually withered in the wake of the 1979 Revolution, ironically an anti-imperialist, national self-assertion movement that, instead of liberating the Iranians and especially the poor, the toilers, and the vulnerable, allowed the Shi'i clerics to rise to power, move away from the promises of social justice and dignity embedded in the 1979 Revolution, and bring four decades of a turbulent, repressive, and crisis-ridden post-revolutionary period.[2]

Sho'aiyan came of age in the second era of Iran's seventy-year struggle for national self-assertion and became a prominent—albeit certainly maverick, marginal, and controversial—figure of the third era. As he personally and intellectually experienced the withering of national liberation, Sho'aiyan pushed for more radical views that culminated in one last theoretical attempt at resuscitating popular self-assertion. He tried to achieve this by reviving frontal politics reinforced by a preconceived and theoretically sanctioned revolutionary agency—but to no avail. It is no wonder that no political party has ever identified itself with his theories. It is equally unsurprising that, despite the recent attentions that tend to sanctify him by offering hollow narratives about his life and works, Sho'aiyan remains a forgotten figure: not only was he a terminal thinker, but indeed a thinker of a terminal point.

A THEORY FOR TODAY

If we take the last point seriously, we find ourselves confronted with a hermeneutic and moral choice (the two are not mutually exclusive): either we can condemn Sho'aiyan to a historiographical narrative about the past, a narrative bereft of life that treats him in the past tense, or we can reconstruct his work discursively, beyond his intentions, dogmas, and limitations, and bring him back to life. I have chosen to do the latter, which renders this work one of scholarly and critical advocacy.

I have shown in this book Sho'aiyan's intellectual and conceptual efforts in defining and theorising the experience of the rebellious generation of his time—a generation that ambitiously would not stop at anything short of a civilisational shift from (neo-)colonialism and capitalist world-system toward the floating signifier of 'socialism.' The path between the two was paved by revolutionary and militant action. To this global tendency, as it appeared theoretically and practically in Iran, Sho'aiyan brought a certain radicalism and eclecticism characterised by his idiosyncratic parlance that defied the common (Marxist-Leninist) idioms of the Iranian Left. Repudiating Leninism, as the common *master signifier* of his generation of activists, opened vast conceptual horizons to his inquisitive gaze and allowed him to become the marginal and inadvertent precursor of several ideas pertaining to discourse, hegemony, democratic organisational life, and liberation. But the pace of his thought was too fast for him to realise that the metaphysical assumptions which energised his theory—historical materialism and the privileged agency of the working class, above all—were in fact fetters. His death put an end to his boundless queries.

With the world of national liberation and wars of liberation in the former colonies closing on certain modalities of action, we need to rethink Sho'aiyan's contributions in light of the new conditions in this utterly unjust and oppressive world. Such rethinking is neither easy nor without controversies. In *my* reading, Sho'aiyan's theoretical legacy for today's world consists of the three pillars that this book discussed *in extenso*: the intellectuals, the front, and rebellion (or revolution). Living in the postcommunist world, it has become not only impractical but also unintelligible and theoretically unviable to think of a Marxist-leaning internationalist movement of global masses of the exploited. Nor is it possible to launch the armed struggles of the intellectuals with any meaningful effect. The exceptions to the latter involve the popular armed uprisings, not the intellectual ones. The theoretically determined agency of the working class as the champion of history (legacy of Marxism) has been shown conclusively to be just an abstract construct. These horizons of the possible have been diminishing for at least a couple of decades. The reasons for these shifts in our political and practical horizons exceed the focus of this book. The last claim does not mean the world has become a better place. We live in a world in which, in 2017, eight men owned as much as half of the rest of humanity. Inequality, oppression, and impoverishment on such a massive scale are unprecedented in history. The juggernaut of the capitalist world-system is taking the entire global civilisation to an ecological, economic, political, and social collapse with unprecedented velocity. Imperialist powers have hegemonised the world and numbed the collective consciousness of the masses through the globalisation of digital media. Reconstructing Sho'aiyan's revolutionary theory for today's realities therefore requires abandoning the elements in his thought that are no longer plausible for launching meaningful resistances against the world-system.

The enormous task of awareness raising, mobilisation of the populace, and giving vision and direction to the collective actions of different social groups still befalls the intellectuals. With higher, professional education now available in all four corners of the world, the rapidly increasing strata of intelligentsia have provided the social and cultural contexts for the growing strata of dissident intellectuals to rise. The intelligentsia nowadays do not simply refer to the highly educated class but generally to the professional groups also with the common denominator of their intellectual activity connecting them with the life of the class they more or less represent (Gramsci). This is where Sho'aiyan's concept of the 'enlighteners' of the people (of which his perceived 'enlighteners of the working class' remain a subsection) comes to the fore. Indeed, his concept of 'enlighteners' as opposed to the 'intellectuals' (which overlaps with 'intelligentsia') is useful here. The enlighteners are the group within the intelligentsia that by virtue of their social position, cultural and political awareness, education, and activism become the advocates of a social class or group or multiple classes or groups (due to intersectionality). And just as Sho'aiyan understood it, the enlighteners of each social class or group constitute many layers. There are indeed multiple representations of social constituencies. With the withering of the privileged agent of history, the multiple enlighteners of the subaltern and marginalised social groups enter the realm of politics with the multiplicity of demands. These demands are articulated by the enlighteners, the organic intellectuals, of the social groups. Thus, their perceived value and plausibility, and thus reception by the public, will be relative to the way these demands are *articulated*. Therefore, as with Sho'aiyan, *articulation is the essence of politics*. Politics becomes a contested discursive field between multiple actors from different subject positions and their adversaries, not necessarily one and the same for them all. Unless one movement wishes to *totalise* the contested field of politics *at the cost* of others (which is the case with fascism), these movements must create hegemonic alliances in order to challenge adversaries that wield the key political, economic, and social institutions. These alliances, therefore, are enabled and given solid shape by the mode of articulation of the multiple enlighteners of social groups.

The last point brings us to the second pillar of Sho'aiyan's theory: frontal thought. The front is the highest form of political organising where there is multiplicity of actors. Doing away with the privileged agent of history—which theoretically subsumed all identities and movements under the metanarrative of 'proletarian' world revolution—will open politics to the diversity of identities that together have the potential to construct the hegemonic front against a common enemy or adversary. Specifically, once we debunk the theoretically privileged agent of history as the central protagonist for systemic transformation, we can no longer presuppose the 'people' (*khalq*) as a pre-given and pre-defined entity of the oppressed and subaltern whose only, though transformative, task in history is to be mobilised by the action of the vanguard. This mechanistic view is best captured by Ahmadzadeh's theory that the small motor of the vanguard would ignite the larger motor of the masses, although this same idea continued to inform the Marxist revolutionary theory in more sophisticated ways (in the works of Jazani and Sho'aiyan in the Iranian case). Therefore, the hegemonic front is never pre-given and its content and contour will be contingent upon the specific co-articulations of demands of participating groups. Now we see that the aim of politics is revealed for what it really has been throughout: the *construction of the people*, as Ernesto Laclau would say.[3] A 'people' is a (counter-) hegemonic construct arising from contending and contested discourses across antagonistic political divisions and mobilised through the discursive articulation of concrete demands of heterogeneous social constituencies. A people, and thus society, does not pre-exist the hegemonic political formation. These are post-Marxist *extensions* arising from *my* reading of Sho'aiyan.

As such, expanding on the concept of the front, the irreducible multiplicity of social constituencies in a potential or future hegemonic front requires the multiplicity of ideological and theoretical stances of their enlighteners. And, as such, the theoretical postulates of the Left of today and tomorrow will arise from social movements. Today's frontal Left, as an umbrella group for hegemonic alliances, corresponds to the socialist, feminist, queer, ecological, aboriginal, and anarchistic components, among others, that define these movements and their demands. As a defender of the rights of the poor, marginalised, and vulnerable, this frontal Left insists on the dignity of the minorities. As such, this will be a *populist* Left due to its reach to the multiplicity of social constituencies. The activists of this frontal Left live through multiple subject positions and take the experiences from one movement to another. They are the builders of alliances across heterogeneous demands through the articulatory practices of enlighteners—the very alliances that make the front against a common adversary (or enemy) publicly intelligible and politically viable. Last but not least, although occupying the seat of state power, through electoral means or popular uprisings, always remains an important objective for the hegemonic front of the subaltern, the frontal Left and its constitutive movements engage in building political trenches that address the immediate demands of their constituents through social initiatives, cooperatives, mutual aid, and autonomous projects regardless of the state. That is why a programmatic conception of 'socialism' remains a superimposition and what remains 'socialist' in the hegemonic front of the Left will be the *socialisation* of demands.

The last component of Sho'aiyan's thought, rebellion, is the one which seems farthest from today's reality. With the age of liberation movements in visible retreat, the triumph of the capitalist world-system, structured around the core economies of the Global North and peripheral economies of the Global South, appears to be conclusive. In many cases, resistances against the Empire have arisen, in the past three decades, in the most reactionary and violent forms of militant, totalising, and terrorising fundamentalisms. As such, for my concluding theoretical reflections, the concept of rebellion seems hardest to connect to today's world. Therefore, some meticulous reconceptualisations are in order.

In the age of national liberation, the universal project of human emancipation from colonialism and (potentially) its concomitant imperialism and capitalist world-system enabled a solidarity across the decolonisation movements that were bound in their struggle to their national liberation but also to one another through struggles against common enemies—world colonial powers. This multilateral solidarity, the solidarity of the Global South, was rendered possible by the presence of *common enemies*, and it created the *internationalist* aspect of otherwise *national* liberation movements. To use contemporary terminology, world imperialism functioned as the 'constitutive outside' of the otherwise heterogeneous decolonisation movements that created a united front against their colonisers and oppressors. The attentive reader can see the resemblance of this observation with Sho'aiyan's worldview. But we must emphasise two important aspects. First, in the age of national liberation, an entire rebellious, anti-colonisation population is represented by the liberation movement(s) that lead it, while the 'new,' postcolonial people is represented by the postcolonial state. Pan-Africanism represents a continental manifestation of this solidarity of the oppressed while Tricontinentalism represents its global expression. Second, from a theoretical point of view, a nation's armed (concrete) uprising would function as the (abstract) epistemological marker of revolutionary transformation. Armed struggle, as pointed out, polarises society across an us-versus-them divide and leaves no room for political ambiguities. Armed struggle is incisive.

As mentioned, these last two components—representations of a supposedly unified popular movement by a liberation movement, and popular, armed uprising as the maker of postcoloniality—have significantly receded in our time and are certainly no longer the defining elements of liberation. The conditions of the people of the Global South, however, have indeed been exacerbated, the details of which I won't discuss here. Thus, two elements pertaining to the theory of *shuresh* still remain: first, the abject conditions intensified by political repression, conditions that are brought to the discursive field of politics thanks to the articulation of the enlighteners, and second, due to such articulations, solidarity among the subaltern—a solidarity that is both intra-national and inter-national. We have already seen that frontal politics is the organisational structure proper to this reality.

To these solidarities we must add solidarities across myriad subject positions that link the North and the South. We may say that the *rebellious subject positions* (not all subject positions are revolutionary) are formed against various structural, cultural, and political *discriminations*: gender inequality, discriminations based on sexuality and ethnicity/race, abuse and exploitation of the poor and vulnerable (low-income, elderly, children, disabled, immigrants, refugees), fighting for indigenous rights to land and way of life, challenging the continued ecological destruction by capitalism, to name but a few. These are rebellious movements, although they mostly partake in self-organisation from the bottom and often engage in legal battles and electoral politics. These two characteristics of contemporary movements clearly go against Sho'aiyan's conception of rebellious action as *anti-systemic*. The movements of our age do not engage in the subversion of the state, but they have the potential to transform society profoundly one battle at the time. Because these movements do not function on a pre-given, universal, and (monolithic) ideological roadmap, and must therefore incessantly function within the limits of the possible, they also run the risk of being co-opted by the powers that be and indeed in many cases movements end up in the reformist camps and function as an ancillary to the state. Yet, as I have said, the *solidarity* between these movements, due to overlapping and connecting subject positions, *articulated by the enlighteners*, both across the movements and across the globe, still holds the *potential solidarity* for a radical, albeit gradual, transformation that defines rebellious thought. Now, it seems, we have come full circle.

Of the three components of Sho'aiyan's theory discussed in this book, the concepts of the 'enlighteners' and 'frontal' politics and thought, with small modifications, appear to be not just compatible with, but in fact organic to, the essence of the social movements against the status quo in today's world. These two components can then be deployed to resuscitate the last pillar of his thought: rebellion, or *shuresh*. If we bracket the theoretical prerequisites for rebellious action (national liberation and revolutionary war spearheaded by the privileged agent), what remains will be the essence of 'rebellious thought': anti-systemic movements. In many respects, today's myriad social movements, each according to its own worldview and to varying degrees, do engage in an anti-systemic push for a better world.

In 1983, six activists from the city secretly entered the Mayan communities in the mountains of Chiapas in southern Mexico. On 1 January 1994, the Zapatista Army of National Liberation (EZLN) staged a popular armed uprising against the Mexican state, capturing six municipalities. In the twelve-day battle that ensued they were pushed back into the mountains and have been governing an autonomous rebel zone containing some quarter of a million indigenous peoples ever since. Their legacy is a mixture of success and failures. The Zapatistas succeeded in showing how, through patient community work, revolutionary intellectuals can be transformed into the organic intellectuals of the oppressed and mobilise them. The EZLN represents a movement that grew *from the few to the many*. They showed how to abandon the ideological dogmas that won't fit the concrete realities of their land, and created a bottom-up participatory, democratic structure in which the movement's military wing, far from leading the masses, is subordinate to popular, civil decision-making bodies, and every decision is put to democratic debate and vote. The Zapatistas proved that global solidarity, through vast international support networks in the early years of the internet, could protect a movement and impede a state from crushing the poorly armed rebel communities. The Zapatistas, however, failed to mobilise Mexican civil society for a new Mexico, although in recent years the momentum has been growing. I have had the good fortune of closely following the trajectory of the Zapatista movement since its inception. Unbeknownst to Sho'aiyan, the three pillars of his thought—revolutionary enlighteners, frontal politics, and rebellious thought—are all present in the Zapatistas that emerged twenty years after the death of Iran's lonesome guerrilla. This is not meant to falsely credit Sho'aiyan, but to point out that, *in essence*, he was a *global*, revolutionary thinker with a versatile theory beyond his own imangination.

From the popular, outstanding movement in Rojava (West Kurdistan)—which at present (early 2019) is governing about two million inhabitants under an outstanding system of democratic confederalism, which has done away with both the state and capitalism—to Turkey's People's Democratic Party (HDP), to the Greek government led by Coalition of the Radical Left (SYRIZA), to the populist, socialist party Podemos in Spain— creative resistances against capitalism, exploitative conditions, and oppressive states define a new age of frontal organisations engaged in global rebellion. Each of these movements suffers from serious shortcomings. For instance, SYRIZA suffers from a reformist naivety that caused it to retreat from its earlier revolutionary zeal. I understand that most of these exemplify the movement I have in mind. But my argument is that, at this point in history, these movements cannot be measured in terms of their successes or failures, as indeed they each bring to life a certain component of the rebellious front I advocate here. These are, I argue, dress rehearsals for moving toward a better world through the experiments that move, I hope, from the few to the many.

WE ALWAYS START AT THE END

This book set out to offer an intellectual biography of Sho'aiyan by showcasing the significance of his complex thought. I wanted to rescue Sho'aiyan from the prison of inept historical accounts—both in academic and journalistic publications—that lock his thought in an archaic and bygone past. The maverick thinker withstood unbearable state prosecution and crushing pressure by those he regarded as comrades-in-arms. He died as he had lived: alone and with honor. He left a legacy that was disowned by the leftist, revolutionary movement with which he deeply identified.

The age and the conditions in response to which Sho'aiyan wrote are long gone. The concerns, grievances, and inequalities that motivated him still remain, some perhaps in different shapes. He wrote until the end of an era. As such, we have to begin where he stopped. This book traced his thoughts from his formative years up to the last moment when his beautiful mind grew dim. I hope I have shone a new light on his unique thinking.

APPENDIX

The Question of the People: Synopsis of a Strategy[1]

MOSTAFA SHO'AIYAN

1. The question of the people (*khalq*) is the key question of the revolution (*enqelab*). Where the people stand is where victory will appear. If the people regard the revolution in a non-revolutionary and inactive way, the status quo will continue. And if the people pick up arms for the revolution, the counter-revolution[-ary forces] will be defeated. Therefore, the key question of the revolution is the question of the people.

2. But one cannot bring the people to the revolution overnight. Nor can one await the Leninist 'revolutionary conditions.' The armed vanguard is the armed nucleus of the people. But for the armed vanguard to be able to fulfill the duties of armed people, it must be able to concentrate its operations on those contemplated and known tactical lines that, in their strategic course, can bring the masses to the revolution.

3. The movement in Iran, as in many other regions in the world, does not enjoy the Leninist 'revolutionary conditions.' In

other words, spontaneous conditions and the predetermined course of events have not granted revolutionary conditions to the vanguard. In Iran, like many other countries, the people live under non-revolutionary conditions.

4. Our society's non-revolutionary conditions, among other things, do not mean that the people (*khalq*) is completely content with all of their relations and conditions and that they are spending happy days without any sorrow, trouble, or pain. On the contrary, old, accumulated, and endless oppression and suffering are tormenting the people. Nevertheless, there is one issue that, as an objective and tangible reality, leaves no room for doubting it, and that is, the Iranian people are not poised for revolutionary and armed approaches against the dominant, tormenting conditions. This may be due to the ancient tradition of tolerating domination (*setamkeshi*), or due to [the regime's] continued counter-revolutionary crackdowns, or due to the pessimistic attitudes caused by deviations and betrayals or confusions (*nadanamkariha*), or due to employing non-liberating methods by previous leaders or organisations that inevitably brought only defeat and failure, or due to reforms and transformations in the town and country implemented by the counter-revolution, or due to an absolute and violent police state whose shadow spreads all over society, or due to any other reason.

5. The vanguard cannot connect with the people unless it *simultaneously* addresses them. It cannot address the people unless it begins with [addressing] their tangible life, pains, and suffering, and the problems and abjections that are *directly* tangible for the people. Inattention (*biparvai*) to the objective life of the people, employing an image (*shamai*) that is not tangible for the people, engaging the

vanguard forces in a battle within the positions about which the masses do not have a deep and clear view, and have not, in their simple life, acquired a significant political awareness about them, practically separate the vanguard from the masses, despite the vanguard's dream (*shifteh*) to be close to the people with all its heart and emotions and sincere hopes and without hesitating in making courageous sacrifices.

6. Since its inceptive clash, the armed movement has generally faced two distinct but interconnected issues:

(a) The movement is unable to absorb the forces of the masses right away. This task requires a long process. But the movement can attract the enlightener (*rowshangari*) as well as conscious and semi-aware (*agah va nimeh-agah*) forces with a significant pace. In other words, for a while whose length cannot be determined with certainty in advance and whose length will vary depending on the various social and regional circumstances, yes for a long while, if a hand is stretched out to pick up the weapon [that was] dropped from the hand of a guerrilla fallen in his blood to defend the movement's trenches, this hand belongs to the enlighteners' forces, and in any case, not to the general masses (*tudehha-ye vasi'*) of society. And thus, the movement must inevitably arrange its directions (*khat-e harekat*) of military and political programs such that the latter would be compatible (*khanai*) with the characteristics and qualities of enlightener forces.

(b) At the same time, the vanguard neither could nor should restrict the source of its struggle and its support to such thin layers [i.e. intellectuals or enlighteners]. The vanguard is tasked with choosing such programs and military operations that are compatible with the needs and leanings of millions of the masses and propensities and pains of the people, so that it can gradually bring itself closer to the main source of the revolution—[that is,] to the masses—and take them step by step closer to the fateful battle.

Accordingly, firstly, the vanguard must contemplate this nearly dual condition [as mentioned above], and secondly, it must inevitably materialise the evolutionary process of the revolution through its studied and thoughtful programs and 'operations.'

IMAGES

Mostafa Sho'aiyan (1935–76)
(Courtesy of Asghar Monajemi)

Sho'aiyan and Jalal Al Ahmad, Asalem, 1969
(Courtesy of Asghar Monajemi)

From left, Parviz Sadri and Asghar Monajemi (the person to
the right is unidentified)
(Courtesy of Asghar Monajemi)

Marzieh Ahmadi Oskui (1945–74)

Nader Shayegan Shamasbi (1945–73)

Sho'aiyan and Monajemi on a trip to Khuzestan
(Courtesy of Asghar Monajemi)

The only poster commemorating Mostafa Sho'aiyan, 1980
(Courtesy of Anahita Shoaiyan)

BIBLIOGRAPHY

Abrahamian, Ervand. 1980. 'Structural Causes of the Iranian Revolution.' *MERIP Reports* (87): 21–6.

————. 1982. *Iran Between Two Revolutions* (Princeton, NJ: Princeton University Press).

————. 1989. *Radical Islam: The Iranian Mujahedin* (London: I. B. Tauris).

Afary, Janet. 1996. *The Iranian Constitutional Revolution, 1906–1911: Grassroots Democracy, Social Democracy, and the Origins of Feminism* (New York: Columbia University Press).

Ahmadzadeh, Massoud. 1976 [orig. 1970]. *Mobarezeh-ye Mosallahaneh: ham Estratezhi, ham Taktik* [*Armed Struggle: Both strategy and tactic*] (Umeä, Sweden: Organization of Iranian Students).

Al Ahmad, Jalal. 1964. *Yek Chah va Do Chaleh* [*One Well and Two Ditches*] (Tehran: Ravaq).

————. 1979a. *Dar Khedmat va Khiyanat-e Rowshanfekran, Jeld Avval* [*On the Services and Betrayals of the Intellectuals*, Vol. 1] (Tehran: Kharazmi).

————. 1979b. *Dar Khedmat va Khiyanat-e Rowshanfekran, Jeld Dovvom* [*On the Services and Betrayals of the Intellectuals*, Vol. 2] (Tehran: Kharazmi).

————. 2006 [orig. 1962]. *Gharbzadegi* [*Westoxification*] (Qom: Nashr-e Khorram).

Allamehzadeh, Reza. 2010. Interview by Peyman Vahabzadeh (Utrecht, 29 July 2010).

Anonymous. nd. '*Towzihati Piramun-e Davari-ye Eshtebahamiz Rafiq Sho'aiyan darbareh-ye Abdollah Anduri*' ['Explanations Regarding Comrade

Sho'aiyan's Erroneous Judgement about Abdollah Anduri'] (Unpublished letter to Edition Mazdak, nd).

———. 1976. '*Goruh-e Jazani-Zarifi Pishtaz-e Jonbesh-e Mosalahaneh-ye Iran*' ['The Jazani-Zarifi Group: Vanguard of Armed Movement in Iran']. *19 Bahman-e Te'orik* 4 (April 1976).

———. 1979. *Chand Maqaleh va Tahlil az Goruh-e Jaryan* [*Selected Articles and Analyses of the Jaryan Group*] (Tehran: not published).

———. *Jalal Al Ahmad beh Ravayet-e Asnad-e SAVAK* [*Jalal Al Ahmad According to SAVAK Documents*] (Tehran: Centre for Historical Documents, 2001).

Asgariyeh, Reza. nd. *Az Khaterat-e Zendan* [*Prison Memoirs*]. (Unpublished).

———. 2008. 'Letter to Cosroe Chaqueri' (11 August 2008).

———. 2016. '*Asabani Bud va Fohshha-ye Prolteri midad*' ['He Was Raging and Shouting Proletarian Curses']. *Nasim-e Bidari* 8, no. 74 (December 2016): 83–90.

Barahani, Reza. 1967. '*Qesseh-ye Enteshar-e* Jahan-e Naw *va Qesseh-ye Darmandegi-ye Rowshanfekran*' ['The Publication of *Jahan-e Naw* and the Story of Intellectuals' Desperation']. *Negin* 22: 8–10.

Béjar, Héctor. 1970. *Peru 1965: Notes on a Guerrilla Experience*, trans. William Rose (New York: Monthly Review Press).

Behrooz, Maziar. 1999. *Rebels with a Cause: The Failure of the Left in Iran* (London: I. B. Tauris).

———. 2004. 'The 1953 Coup in Iran and the Legacy of Tudeh,' in Mark Gasiorowski and Malcolm Byrne, *Mohammad Mosaddeq and the 1953 Coup in Iran* (Syracuse, NY: Syracuse University Press).

Behzadi, Manouchehr. 1974. '*Darbareh-ye Ravesh-e Taktiki-ye Hezb-e Tudeh Iran*' ['On the Tactical Methods of the Tudeh Party of Iran']. *Donya* 5 (November 1974): 8–15.

———. 1976. '*Jebheh-ye zedd-e Diktatori—Mokhalefatha va Porseshha*' ['The Anti-Dictatorship Front: Criticisms and Questions']. *Donya* 3, no. 10 (December 1976): 2–8.

Boggs, Carl. 1979. 'Marxism and the Role of Intellectuals.' *New Political Science* 1(2–3): 7–23.

Castañeda, Jorge G. 1993. *Utopia Unarmed: The Latin American Left After the Cold War* (New York: Vintage Books).

Chaqueri, Cosroe. 1995. *The Soviet Socialist Republic of Iran, 1920–1921: Birth of the Trauma* (Pittsburgh: Pittsburgh University Press).

———. 1999. 'Did the Soviets Play a Role in Founding the Tudeh Party in Iran?' *Cahiers du Monde russe* 40(3): 497–528.

———.2001. *The Russo-Caucasian Origins of the Iranian Left: Social Democracy in Modern Iran* (Richmond, Surrey: Curzon).

—, ed. 2007. *Mostafa Sho'aiyan, Hasht Nameh be Cherikha-ye Fadai-ye Khalq: Naqd-e Yek Manesh-e Fekri* [*Mostafa Sho'aiyan, Eight Letters to the People's Fadai Guerillas: Critique of an Intellectual Attitude*] (Tehran: Nashr-e Ney).

———.2010. 'Cherikha Jame'eh-ye Iran ra Nemishenakhtand' ['The Guerrillas Did Not Know Iranian Society']. *Mehrnameh* 6 (November 2010): 117–18.

Chehabi, H. E. 1990. *Iranian Politics and Religious Modernism: The Liberation Movement of Iran under the Shah and Khomeini* (Ithaca, NY: Cornell University Press).

Che Guevara, Ernesto. 1965. 'At the Afro-Asian Conference in Algeria.' *Marxists Internet Archive*. Available at: https://www.marxists.org/archive/guevara/1965/02/24.htm (accessed 9 November 2017).

———. 1967. 'Message to the Tricontinental.' *Marxists Internet Archive*. Available at: https://www.marxists.org/archive/guevara/1967/04/16.htm (accessed 7 April 2018).

CSHD (Centre for Study of Historical Documents). 2001. *Chap dar Iran beh Ravayat-e Asnad-e SAVAK: Sazman-e Cherikha-ye Fadai Khalq* [*The Left in Iran According to SAVAK Documents: Organization of People's Fadai Guerrillas*] (Tehran: Centre for Study of Historical Documents, Ministry of Intelligence).

Dabashi, Hamid. 2007. *Iran: A People Interrupted* (New York/London: The New Press).

———.2016. *Iran: The Rebirth of a Nation* (New York: Palgrave Macmillan).

Dangl, Benjamin. 2010. *Dancing with Dynamite: Social Movements and States in Latin America* (Oakland: AK Press).

Debray, Régis. 1967. *Revolution in the Revolution? Armed Struggle and Political Struggle in Latin America*, trans. Bobbye Ortiz (New York: Monthly Review Press).

Dussel, Enriqué. 1993. 'Eurocentrism and Modernity.' *Boundary* 2/20(3): 65–76.

Escobar, Arturo. 1995. *Encountering Development: The Making and Unmaking of the Third World* (Princeton: Princeton University Press).

—, and Sonia E. Alvarez (eds). 1992. *The Making of Social Movements in Latin America* (Boulder, CO: Westview Press).

Eskandari, Iraj. 1974. *'Chand Nokteh-ye Asasi Darbareh-ye Bonyadgozari-ye Hezb-e Tudeh-ye Iran va Tahavvol-e An'* ['Basic points on the foundation and development of the Tudeh Party of Iran']. *Donya* 3 (August–September 1974): 2–7.

Fanon, Frantz. 1994. *Toward the African Revolution*, trans. Haakin Chevalier (New York: Grove Press).

———. 2004. *The Wretched of the Earth*, trans. R. Philcox (New York: Grove Press).

Farrokhi, Foruzandeh. 2005. *'Mahmoud Tavakkoli Keh Bud va Cheh Goft?'* ['Who Was Mahmoud Tavakkoli and What Did He Say?']. *Jahan-e Ketab* 10(3) (June 2005): 28–9.

———. 2007. *'Taz'if-e Hakemiyyat-e Melli Khiyanat Ast'* ['Weakening the National Government Is Betrayal']. *Aftab Online*, 24 June 2007. Available at: https://goo.gl/k55tGf (accessed 30 July 2017).

Fatapour, Mehdi. 2001. Interview by Peyman Vahabzadeh. 24 November.

Fayaz, Ali. n.d. *'Tasahol-e Marksisti? 1'* ['Marxist Tolerance? Part 1'], not published.

———. 2003. *'Tasahol-e Marksisti? 2'* ['Marxist Tolerance? Part 2']. *Kargah Andisheh va* Peykar, 18 February 2003. Available at: http://kargari.de/?page_id=209 (accessed 24 July 2017).

Forutan Fumani (Gh. Farahang Forutan). n.d. *'Seyr-e Nazariyeh Andisheha-ye Farhangi'* ['The Process of the Theory of Cultural Thoughts'] (Unpublished manuscript).

Forutan, Gh. Farhang (Abbas). 2017. Telephone conversation with Peyman Vahabzadeh. 13 September.

———. 2018. Telegram messaging with Peyman Vahabzadeh. 6 April.

Foucault, Michel. 1992. 'Preface,' in Gilles Deleuze and Félix Guattari, *Anti-Oedipus: Capitalism and Schizophrenia* (Minneapolis: University of Minnesota Press): xi–xiv.

Golesorkhi, Ali. 2009. Telephone interview by Peyman Vahabzadeh. 11 March.

Gott, Richard. 2008. *Guerrilla Movements in Latin America* (New York: Seagull Books).

Gramsci, Antonio. 1968a. *'Peydayesh-e Rowshanfekran'* ['The Formation of Intellectuals'], trans. M. Hezarkhani. *Arash* 15 (February–March 1968): 27–36.

———. 1968b. *'Moze'-e Mokhtalef-e Rowshanfekran: No'-e Shahri va No'-e Rustai'* ['Positions of Intellectuals: Urban and Rural'], trans. M. Hezarkhani. *Arash* 16 (April 1968): 17–28.

———. 1969a. '*Me'yarha-ye Enteqad-e Adabi*' ['Criteria for Literary Criticism'], trans. M. Hezarkhani. *Arash* 19 (January–February 1969): 17–21.

———. 1969b. '*Chand Noqteh Atf-e Moqadamati*' ['Introductory Remarks'], trans. M. Hezarkhani. *Arash* 20 (April 1969): 63–93.

———. 1971. *Selections from the Prison Notebooks*, ed. & trans. Q. Hoare & G. Nowell Smith (New York: International Publishers).

———. 1995. *Further Selections from the Prison Notebooks*, ed. & trans. D. Boothman (Minneapolis: Minnesota University Press).

Heydar (Mohammad Dabirifard). 1999. '*Rafi q Bizhan Jazani va Sazman-e Cherikha-ye Fadai Khalq Iran*' ['Comrade Bizhan Jazani and the OIPFG'], in *Jong-i Darbareh-ye Zendegi va Asar-e Bizhan Jazani* [*A Collection on the Life and Works of Bizhan Jazani*], ed. Centre for Collection and Publication of Bizhan Jazani's Works (Paris: Khavaran): 245–68.

Jahani Asl, Mohammad Nasser. 2017. *Identity, Politics, Organization: A Historical Sociology of the Democratic Party of Iranian Kurdistan and the Kurdish Nationalist Movement*. Ph.D. Dissertation, University of Victoria.

Jameson, Fredric. 1988. *The Ideologies of Theory: Essays 1971–1986*. Vol. 2 (Minneapolis: University of Minnesota Press).

Javan, F. M. 1972. *Cherikha-ye Khalq Cheh Miguyand?* [*What Do the People's Guerrillas Say?*] (Germany: Tudeh Press).

Jazani, Bizhan. nd. *Tarikh-e Si Saleh-ye Siyasi* [*The Thirty-Year Political History*] (GDR: OIPFG).

———. 1976a. *Jam'bandi-ye Mobarezat-e Si Saleh-ye Akhir dar Iran* [*Summation of the Struggles of the Past Thirty Years in Iran*]. *19 Bahman-e Te'orik* 5–6.

———. 1976b. *Cheguneh Mobarezeh-ye Mosallahaneh Tudehi Mishavad* [*How Armed Struggle Becomes a Mass Movement*] (Germany: OIPFG).

———. 1976c. '*Vahdat va Naqsh-e Estratezhik-e Cherikha-ye Fadai-e Khalq*' ['Unification and the Strategic Role of the People's Fadai Guerrillas']. *19 Bahman-e Te'orik* 1 (December 1976): 1–9.

———. 1976d. '*Hezb-e Tabaqeh-ye Kargar dar Iran*' ['The Working-Class Party in Iran']. *19 Bahman-e Te'orik* 1 (December 1976): 30–56.

———. 1976e. *Panj Resaleh* [*Five Essays*]. *19 Bahman-e Te'orik* 8 (December 1976).

———. 1978. *Nabard ba Diktatori-ye Shah* [*War against the Shah's Dictatorship*] (np: OIPFG).

———. 1979. *Tahlil-e Moqe'iyat-e Niruha-ye Enqelabi dar Iran* [*An analysis of the position of revolutionary forces in Iran*] (np: OIPFG).

————.2009. *Enqelab-e Mashrutiyyat-e Iran: Niruha va Hadafha* [*The Iranian Constitutional Revolution: Forces and Objectives*] (Paris: The Union of People's Fadaiyan of Iran).

————, and Hassan Zia Zarifi. 1976 [orig. 1967]. *Tez-e Goruh-e Jazani: Masa'el-e Jonbesh-e Zedd-e Este'mari va Azadibakhsh-e Khalq-e Iran va Omdehtarin Vazayef-e Komonistha-ye Iran dar Sharayet-e Konuni* [Thesis of Jazani's Group: *Issues Pertaining to the Anti-Colonial and Liberation Movement of Iran and the Main Duties of Iranian Communists in Present Conditions*] (np: 19 Bahman Publisher).

Jazani, Mihan. 1999. '*Bizhan: Ma'shuq, Rafiq, Hamsar*' ['Bizhan: Lover, Comrade, Spouse'], in *Jong-i darbareh-ye Zendegi va Asar-e Bizhan Jazani* [*A Collection on the Life and Works of Bizhan Jazani*], ed. Centre for Collection and Publication of Bizhan Jazani's Works (Paris: Khavaran): 15–92.

Kar (Organ of the Iranian People's Fadai Guerrillas) 1, no. 30 (3 September 1979).

Kasravi, Ahmad. 2013. *Tarikh-e Mashruteh-ye Iran* [*History of Iranian Constitutionalism*] (Tehran: Negah).

Katouzian, Homa. 2004. 'The Strange Politics of Khalil Maleki,' in S. Cronin (ed.), *Reformers and Revolutionaries in Modern Iran: New Perspectives on the Iranian Left* (London/New York: Routledge): 165–88.

————.2018. *Khalil Maleki: The Human Face of Iranian Socialism* (London: Oneworld Publications).

Katsiaficas, George. 1987. *The Imagination of the New Left: A Global Analysis of 1968* (Boston: South End Press).

Kaveh. 1984. '*Yadi az Mostafa Sho'aiyan*' ['*Remembering Mostafa Sho'aiyan*']. *Iranshahr* V(49), 24 February 1984: 8, 11.

Keddie, Nikki R. 1981. *Roots of Revolution: An Interpretive History of Modern Iran.* (New Haven: Yale University Press).

Keshavarz Sadr, Houshang. 2012. '*Pas-e Dusti: beh Monasebat-e Salmarg-e Mahmoud Tavakkoli, Rowshanfekr-e Tanha*' ['Guarding a Friendship: on the Anniversary of Passing of Mahmoud Tavakkoli, the Lonely Intellectual']. *Asre Nou*, 30 May 2012. Available at: http://asre-nou.net/php/view_print_version.php?objnr=21215 (accessed 29 July 2017).

Khrushchev, Nikita. 1956. 'Speech to 20th Congress of the C.P.S.U.' *Marxists Internet Archive*. Available at: https://www.marxists.org/archive/khrushchev/1956/02/24.htm (accessed 9 November 2017).

————.1959. 'On Peaceful Coexistence.' *Foreign Affairs* 38, no. 1: 1–18.

Kianuri, N. 1976. '*Hezb-e Tabaqeh-ye Kargar va Mobarezan-e dara-ye E'teqadat-e Mazhabi*' ['The Working-Class Party and the Activists of Religious Beliefs']. *Donya* 3, no. 9 (December 1976): 2–7.

Laclau, Ernesto. 2005. *On Populist Reason* (London: Verso).

———, and Chantal Mouffe. 1985. *Hegemony and Socialist Strategy: Toward a Radical Democratic Politics* (London: Verso).

Lefort, Claude. 1988. *Democracy and Political Theory* (Cambridge, UK: Polity Press, 1988).

Lenin. V. I. 1902. 'Revolutionary Adventurism.' *Marxists Internet Archive*. Available at: https://www.marxists.org/archive/lenin/works/1902/sep/01.htm (accessed 21 July 2018).

———. 1974. 'On the Slogan for a United States of Europe,' in *Collected Works of Lenin*, Vol. 21 (Moscow: Progress Publishers): 339–43.

———. 1989. *Two Tactics of Social-Democracy in the Democratic Revolution* (New York: International Publishers).

———. 1992. *What Is To Be Done?* (New York: International Publishers).

Lievesley, Geraldine, and Steve Ludlam, eds. 2009. *Reclaiming Latin America: Experiments in Radical Social Democarcy* (London: Zed Books).

Mahrooyan, Houshang. 2005. *Mostafa Sho'aiyan: Motefakker-e Yeganeh-ye Tanha* [*Mostafa Sho'aiyan: The Lonely Singular Thinker*] (Tehran: Nashr-e Baztab Negar).

Mahdavi, Mojtaba. 2017. 'Iran: Multiple Sources of Grassroots Social Democracy?' in *Iran's Struggles for Social Justice: Economics, Agency, Justice, Activism*, ed. P. Vahabzadeh (New York: Palgrave MacMillan): 271–88.

Maleki, Khalil. 1998. *Nehzat-e Melli-ye Iran va Edalat-e Ejtema'i* [*Nationalist Movement of Iran and Social Justice*], ed. Abdollah Borhan (Tehran: Nashr-e Markaz).

Mannheim, Karl. 1969. *Ideology and Utopia* (London: Routledge & Kegan Paul).

Marcos (Subcomandante Insurgente). 2001. *Our Word Is Our Weapon* (New York: Seven Stories Press).

Marx, Karl, and Friedrich Engels. 1970. *The German Ideology*, ed. C. J. Arthur (New York: International Publishers).

Massoud (alias). 1966. '*Arzyabi-ye Barkhi Javaneb-e Roshd-e Eqtesadi-ye Iran pas az Kudeta*' ['An Assessment of Certain Aspects of Economic Growth in Iran After the Coup']. *Donya* 7, no. 3 (Fall 1946): 8–23.

———. 1974. '*Az Harf ta Amal: Natayej-e Vagozari-e Saham beh Kargaran*' ['From Words to Action: The Outcome of Distributing Shares to the Workers']. *Donya* 3 (September 1974): 16–18.

Matin[-asgari], Afshin. 1999. *Konfedrasion: Tarikh-e Jonbesh-e Daneshjuyan-e Irani dar Kharj az Keshvar 1332–57* [*Confederation: The History of the Iranian Student Movement Abroad 1953–1979*], trans. Arastu Azari (Tehran: Shirazeh).

———. 2018. *Both Eastern and Western: An Intellectual History of Iranian Modernity* (London/New York: Cambridge University Press).

Meijer, Jan M., ed. 1971. *The Trotsky Papers 1917–1922*, Vol. II (The Hague: Mouton).

Mignolo, Walter D. 2009. 'Epistemic Disobedience, Independent Thought and Decolonial Freedom'. *Theory, Culture & Society* 26(7–8): 159–181.

Mikailian, Vartan. 2007. '*Shahed-e Eyni*' ['The Eyewitness'], in Mostafa Sho'aiyan and Hamid Momeni, *Darbareh-ye Rowshanfekr: Yek Bahs-e Qalami* [*On Intellectuals: A Debate in Writing*], ed. Nasser Pakdaman (Köln, Germany: Forough Verlag): 146–53.

Mohajer, Nasser, and Mehrdad Baba Ali. 2016. *Beh Zaban-e Qanun: Bizhan Jazani va Hassan Zia Zarifi dar Dadgah-e Nezami* [*In the Language of Law: Bizhan Jazani and Hassan Zia Zarifi in the Military Court*] (Berkeley, CA: Nashr-e Noghteh).

Monajemi, Asghar. 2018. 'In-Person Communication with Peyman Vahabzadeh'. Irvine, CA, 19 August.

Momeni, Hamid. nd. *Shuresh na, Qadamha-ye Sanjideh dar Rah-e Rnqelab* [*Not Rebellion: Judicious Steps Towards the Revolution*] (np: Support Committee for the New Revolutionary Movement of Iranian People).

Momeni, Hamid. 1979. *Pasokh beh Forsattalaban darmored-e '*Mobarezeh-yi Mosalahaneh, ham Stratezhi, ham Taktik' [*A Rejoinder to the Opportunists on* Armed Struggle: Both Strategy and Tactic] (Tehran: Entesharat-i M. Bidsorkhi).

———, and Mostafa Sho'aiyan. nd. *Juyeshi Piraumun-e Rowshanfekr ya Rowshangar-e Tabaqeh-ye Kargar* [*An Inquiry into the Intellectual or the Enlightener of the Working Class*] (np: Enqelab Publishers).

———.1975. *Shuresh Na, Qadamha-yi Sanjideh dar Rah-e Enqelab; Pasokhha-ye Nasanjideh beh Qadamha-yi Sanjideh* [*Not Rebellion, Judicious Steps on the Path to the Revolution; Injudicious Replies to Judicious Steps*] (Florence: Edition Mazdak).

Moradi Ghiyasabadi, Reza. 2007. '*Matn-e Kamel-e Defa'iyyat-e Khosrow Golesorkhi va Karamatollah Daneshian*' ['Complete Defense Statements of Khosrow Golesorkhi and Karamatollah Daneshian']. *Persian Studies* (11 February 2007). Available at: http://ghiasabadi.com/golesorkhi.html (accessed 26 January 2018).

Mouffe, Chantal. 2017. 'We urgently need to promote a left-populism.' *Verso Books* (4 August 2017). Available at: https://www.versobooks.com/blogs/3341-chantal-mouffe-we-urgently-need-to-promote-a-left-populism (accessed 27 January 2018).

Nabard-e Khalq (Organ of the Organisation of Iranian People's Fadai Guerrillas), no. 1 (February 1974).

Nabard-e Khalq (Organ of the Organisation of Iranian People's Fadai Guerrillas), no. 2 (April 1974).

Nabard-e Khalq (Organ of the Organisation of Iranian People's Fadai Guerrillas), no. 3 (May 1974).

Nabard-e Khalq (Organ of the Organisation of Iranian People's Fadai Guerrillas), no. 4 (August 1974).

Nabard-e Khalq (Organ of the Organisation of Iranian People's Fadai Guerrillas), no. 5 (January 1975).

Nabard-e Khalq (Organ of the Organisation of Iranian People's Fadai Guerrillas), no. 6 (April 1975).

Nabard-e Khalq (Organ of the Organisation of Iranian People's Fadai Guerrillas), no. 7 (May–June 1976).

Nabavi, Behzad. 2002. '*Razha-ye Behzad Nabavi*' ['The Secrets of Behzad Nabavi']. *Hamshahri*, no. 2706 (27 April 2002).

———.2011. '*Kuler-e khaneh-ye Mahasti ra man nasb kardam*' ['I Installed the AC in Mahasti's House']. *Parsineh Website* (12 September 2011). Available at: https://goo.gl/xy72Pi (accessed 9 September 2017).

———.2016. '*Goruh-e Khun-e Rajavi ba Digaran Farq Darad*' ['Rajavi's Blood Type Is Different From That of Others']. *Sobh-e Naw* 128 (21 November 2016): 8–11.

Naderi, Mahmoud. 2008. *Cherikha-ye Fadai-ye Khalq: az Nokhostin Konesh ta Bahman-e 1357, Jeld-e Avval* [*People's Fadai Guerrillas: From their first acts until February 1979*, Vol. 1] (Tehran: Political Studies and Research Institutes).

Negahdar, Farrokh. 2008. Interview by Peyman Vahabzadeh. London, 7–8 December.

Nejat Hosseini, Mohsen. 2001. *Bar Faraz-e Khalij-e Fars* [*Over the Persian Gulf*] (Tehran: Nashr-e Ney).

Nejati, Gholam Reza. 1992. *Tarikh-e Siyasi-ye Bistopanj Saleh-ye Iran* [*The Twenty-Five Year Political History of Iran*] (Tehran: Rasa Cultural Services).

Nili, Ali, ed. 2016. 'Shureshi-ye Sharif ['The Honourable Rebel']. *Nasim-e Bidari* 8, no. 74 (December 2016): 55–108.

Novak, George. 1935. George Novak, 'Marxism and the Intellectuals.' *The New International* II:7 (December 1935): 227–32. Available at: http://www.marxistsfr.org/archive/novack/1935/12/x01.htm (accessed 19 December 2017).

OIPFG. 1974. *Nabard-e Khalq* [*People's Combat*] no. 4 (July 1974).

OIPFG. 1975a. *Edam-e Enqelabi-ye Abbas Shahriyari, Mard-e Hezar Chehreh* [*The Revolutionary Execution of Abbas Shahriyari, a Man with a Thousand Faces*] (np: OIPFG).

OIPFG. 1975b. *Nashriyeh-ye Dakheli* [*The Internal Bulletin*], no. 14 (August–September 1975).

OIPFG. 1977. *Chahar Resaleh az Sazman-e Cherkha-ye Fadai-ye Khalq-e Iran* [*Four Essays by the Organization of Iranian People's Fadai Guerrillas*] (Germany: Support Committee of Iranian Peoples New Revolutionary Movement).

Oskui, Marziyeh Ahmadi. 1974. *Khaterati az Yek Rafiq* [*Memoirs of a Comrade*] (np: OIPFG).

Peykar, ed. 2014. *Ketab-e Goftogu-ye Sazman-e Cherikha-ye Fadai-ye Khalq-e Iran va Sazman-e Mojahedin-e Khalq-e Iran* [*The Dialogue of OIPFG and OIPM*] (Frankfurt: Andeesheh va Peykar Publications).

Pitman, Thea, and Andy Stafford. 2009. 'Introduction: Transatlanticism and Tricontinentalism.' *Journal of Transatlantic Studies* 7(3): 197–207.

PSRI (Political Studies and Research Institute). 2005. *Sazman-e Mojahedin-e Khalq: az Peydai ta Farjam (1344–1384)*, [*The People's Mojahedin Organisation: from its Origins to its Demise (1965–2005)*, Vol. 1] (Tehran: PSRI).

———.2006. *Sazman-e Mojahedin-e Khalq: az Peydai ta Farjam (1344–1384)*, [*The People's Mojahedin Organisation: from its Origins to its Demise (1965–2005)*, Vol. 2] (Tehran: PSRI).

Puriya, Arsalan. 1976 [orig. 1973]. *Karnameh-ye Mosaddeq* [*The Record of Mosaddeq*], ed. Mostafa Sho'aiyan (Florence: Edition Mazdak).

Puyan, Amir Parviz. 1979 [orig. 1970]. *Zarurat-e Mobarezeh-ye Mosallahaneh va Radd-e Te`ori-ye Baqa* [The Necessity of Armed Struggle and the Refutation of the Theory of Survival] (Tehran: Gam Publishers).

Raf'at. 2001. Telephone interview by Peyman Vahabzadeh. 6 and 9 November, 3 December.

Razavi Faqih, Massoud. 2017. '*Mostafa Sho'aiyan: Maqzub-e Cherikha-ye Khalq va Matlub-e Mojahedin-e Khalq*' ['Mostafa Sho'aiyan: Damned by People's Guerrillas and Favourite of the People's Mojahedin'] *Tarikh-e Irani* (18 May 2012). Available at: https://goo.gl/TQCNfG (accessed 18 October 2017).

Rejali, Darius M. 1994. *Torture and Modernity: Self, Society, and State in Modern Iran.* (Boulder, CO: Westview Press).

Reza`i, Ahmad. 1975 [orig. 1972]. *Tahlili az Nehzat-e Hosseini* [*An Analysis of Hossein's Movement*] (Springfield, MO: Liberation of Movement of Iran-Abroad).

———. 2012. '*Dar Rasa-ye Mahmoud Tavakkoli*' ['Mourning Mahmoud Tavakkoli']. *Enqelab-e Eslami* (February 2014). Available at: https://www.enghelabe-eslami.com/tamas/21-didgagha/tarikhi/7751-2014-03-13-20-30-16.html (accessed 30 July 2017).

Sadri, Hossein. 2008. 'Letter to Peyman Vahabzadeh.' 25 December.

Sa'idi, Fatemeh. 2012. '*Gushehhai az Shekanjeh dar SAVAK*' ['Being Tortured by SAVAK']. *Jahan-e Zan* (27 July 2012). Available at: https://jahanezan.wordpress.com/2012/07/27/18916/ (accessed 2 December 2017).

Salehi, Anush. 2002. *Ravi-ye Baharan: Mobarezat va Zendegi-ye Karamatollah Daneshian* [*The Spring's Narrator: The Life and Struggles of Karamatollah Daneshian*] (Tehran: Nashr-e Qatre).

———. 2010. *Mostafa Sho'aiyan va Romantism Enqelabi* [*Mostafa Sho'aiyan and Revolutionary Romanticism*] (Spånga, Sweden: Baran).

Samakar, Abbas. 2001. *Man yek Shureshi Hastam* [*I Am a Rebel*] (Los Angeles: Sherkat-e Ketab).

Sarabi, Sam, ed. 2012. '*Parvandeh-i Bara-ye Mostafa Sho'aiyan*' ['A Mostafa Sho'aiyan File']. *Shargh Newspaper* 1526 (12 May 2012): 19–32.

Serafat, Sediqeh. 2005. '*Amuzgari va Mobarezeh-ye Cheriki*' ['Being a teacher and guerrilla warfare']. *Asr-e Nou* (15 October). Available at: http://asre-nou.net/1348/mehr/24/m-6.html (accessed 19 July 2017).

Sho'aiyan, Anahita. 2012. Facebook correspondence with author (12 February 2012).

————. 2017. Email correspondence with author (10 October 2017).

Sho'aiyan, Mostafa. nd-a. *Chand She'r az Pahneh-ey Nabard* [*Poems from the Battlefield*] (Florence: Edition Mazdak).

————. nd-b. *Tezi Baray-e Taharrok va Nimgami dar Rah: Jebheh-ye Enqelab-e Rahaibakhsh-e Khalq* [*A Thesis for Mobilisation and Half-a-Step on the Way: the National Liberation Revolution Front*] (Tehran: Nashr-e Olduz).

————.nd-c. [*'Mas'aleh-ye Khalq'*] ['The Question of the People'] (Unpublished).

————. nd-d. [*'Sazman-e Pishtaz'*] ['The Vanguard Organisation'] (Unpublished).

————. 1960. *'Khiyanat'* ['Betrayal']. (Unpublished).

————. 1968. *'Cheh Bayad Kard?'* [*What Is To Be Done?*]. Mimeographed monograph.

Sho'aiyan, Mostafa. 1972. *Nimgami dar Rah: Jebheh-ye Rahaibakhsh-e Khalq* [*Half-a-Step on the Way: The People's Liberation Front*] (np: Enqelab Publishers).

————. 1973. *'Kalanjari ba Qoqnus'* ['An Encounter with Sphinx'] (Unpublished).

————. 1975. ['Letter to Mazdak'] (November 1975, unpublished).

————. 1976a. *Chand Neveshteh* [*Selected writings*] (Florence: Edition Mazdak).

————. 1976b. *Enqelab* [*Revolution*] (Florence: Edition Mazdak).

————. 1976c. *Sheshomin Nameh-ye Sargoshadeh be Cherikha-ye Fadai* [*The Sixth Open Letter to the Fadai Guerrillas*] (Florence: Edition Mazdak).

————. 1976d. *Jang-s Sazesh* [*A War to Compromise*] (Florence: Edition Mazdak).

————. 1976e. *Negah-i beh Ravabet-e Showravi va Nehzat-e Enqelabi-ye Jangal* [*A Review of the Relations Between the Soviet Union and the Revolutionary Movement of Jungle*] (Florence: Edition Mazdak).

————. 1976f. *Pasokhha-ye Nasanjideh be 'Qadamha-ye Sanjideh'* [*Injudicious Replies to 'Judicious Steps'*] (Florence: Edition Mazdak).

————. 1976g. *Do enteqad beh Cherikha-ye Fadai Khalq* [*Two Critical Essays on the People's Fadai Guerrillas*] (Florence: Edition Mazdak).

————. 1976h. *'Pasokh-e Rafiq Sorkh'* ['Response of Red Comrade']. *Problems of Revolution and Socialism* 6 (Spring 1976): 10–43.

————. 1976i. *'Nameh-ye Sargoshadeh be Mazdak'* ['Open Letter to Mazdak']. *Problems of Revolution and Socialism* 6 (Spring 1976): 49–92.

————. 1977. *Naqsh-e Esrail va Rezhim-e Pahlavi dar Khavar-e Miyaneh* [*On the Role of Israeli and Iranian Regimes in the Middle East*] (Florence: Edition Mazdak).

————. 1980a. '*Chehelomin Ruz-e Dargozasht-e Mosaddeq dar Ahmadabad*' ['The Fortieth Day of Mosaddeq's Passing in Ahmadabad']. *Ketab-e Jom'eh* 29 (6 March 1980): 4–10.

————. 1980b. *Shesh Nameh-ye Sargoshadeh beh Sazman-e Charikha-ye Fadai-e Khalq-e Iran* [*Six Open Letters to the Organization of Iranian People's Fadai Guerrillas*] (Tehran: Edition Mazdak).

————, and Marzieh Ahmadi Oskui. 1973a. '*Darbareh-ye She'r-e "Cheshm beh Rah"*' ['On the Poem "Awaiting"'] (Unpublished).

————. 1973b. '*Kalanjari ba Qoqnus*' ['An Encounter with Sphinx'] (Unpublished).

Sho'aiyan, Mostafa, and Hamid Momeni. 2007. *Darbareh-ye Rowshanfekr: yek Bahs-e Qalami* [*On Intellectuals: A Debate in Writing*], ed. Nasser Pakdaman (Köln, Germany: Forough Verlag).

Siavoshi, Sussan. 1990. *Liberal Nationalism in Iran* (Boulder, CO: Westview Press).

Strangers in a Tangled Wilderness, ed. 2015. *A Small Key Can Open a Large Door* (np: Combustion Books).

Tavakkoli, Mahmoud. 1975 [orig. 1959]. *Tahlili az Khat-e Mashy-e Siasi-ye Hezb-e Tudeh-ye Iran* [*An Analysis of the Political Directions of the Tudeh Party of Iran*], in *Historical Documents: The Workers', Social-Democratic, and Communist Movement in Iran* V, ed. C. Chaqueri (Florence: Mazdak).

————. 1983 [orig. 1964]. *Tahlili az Jame'eh-ye Sosiyalistha-ye Iran* [*An Analysis of the Socialist League of Iran*], in *Historical Documents: The Workers', Social-Democratic, and Communist Movement in Iran* X, ed. C. Chaqueri (Tehran: Antidote Publications).

Torkman, Mohammad. 1995. *Namehha-ye Doktor Mosaddeq* [*Letters of Dr Mosaddeq*] (Tehran: Hazaran).

Trotsky, Leon. 1939. 'The Three Conceptions of the Russian Revolution.' *Marxist Readings*. Available at: http://www.internationalist.org/three.html (accessed 6 February 2018).

Trotsky, Leon. 1968. '*Chekideh-ye Te|ori-ye Enqelab-e Modavem*' ['A Synopsis of the Theory of Permanent Revolution']. *Jahan-e Naw* 23(7–8–9) (Autumn 1968): 171–5.

Tudeh Party of Iran-Central Committee. 1976. '*Komiteh Markazi-ye Hezb-e Tudeh-ye Iran az Hameh-ye Mokhalefan-e Rezhim-e Teror va Ekhtenaq-e Konuni-ye Iran Da'vat Mikonad*' ['The Central Committee of Tudeh Party of Iran Invites All Those Opposing the Present Terror and Repression Regime in Iran']. *Donya* 3, no. 4 (June 1976): 3–5.

Ulyanovsky, R., and V. Pavlov. 1973. 'The Non-capitalist Path as a Historical Reality,' in *Asian Dilemma: A Soviet View and Myrdal's Concept* (Moscow: Progress Publishers): 152–69.

Vahabzadeh, Peyman. 2003. *Articulated Experiences: Toward A Radical Phenomenology of Contemporary Social Movements* (Albany, NY: State University of New York Press).

———. 2005. 'Bizhan Jazani and the Problems of Historiography of the Iranian Left'. *Iranian Studies* 38:1 (March 2005): 167–78.

———. 2007a. 'Mostafa Sho'aiyan: The Maverick Theorist of the Revolution and the Failure of Frontal Politics in Iran'. *Iranian Studies* 40:3 (June 2007): 405–25.

———. 2007b. 'Mustafa Shu'a'iyan and *Fada`iyan-i Khalq*: Frontal Politics, Stalinism, and the Role of Intellectuals in Iran'. *British Journal of Middle Eastern Studies* 34:1 (April 2007): 43–61.

———. 2007c. '*Pishvazheh: Takandishi-ye Sho'aiyan va barkhord-e Chap-e A'ini*' ['Foreword: Sho'aiyan's Singular Thought and the Reaction of the Doctrinal Left'], in Cosroe Chaqueri, ed., *Mostafa Sho'aiyan, Hasht Nameh beh Cherikha-ye Fadai Khalq: Naqd-e yek Manesh-e Fekri* [*Mostafa Sho'aiyan, Eight Letters to the People's Fadai Guerrillas: Critique of An Approach*] (Tehran: Nashr-e Ney): iv–xix.

———. 2010a. *A Guerrilla Odyssey: Modernization, Secularism, Democracy, and the Fadai Period of National Liberation in Iran, 1971–1979* (Syracuse, NY: Syracuse University Press).

———. 2010b. '*Tajrobeh-ey Kuba Dast-e Avval beh Iran Naresid*' ['The Cuban Experience Did Not Come to Iran First Hand']. *Mehrnameh* 6 (November 2010): 117–18.

———. 2011a. 'SAKA: Iran's Grassroots Revolutionary Workers' Organisation'. *Revolutionary History* 10:3 (Spring 2011): 348–59.

———. 2011b. 'Mostafa Sho'a'iyan: An Iranian Leftist Political Thinker Unlike His Peers'. *Revolutionary History* 10:3 (Spring 2011): 360–75.

———. 2011c. 'Secularism and the Iranian Militant Left: Cultural Issues or Political Misconception?' *Comparative Studies of South Asia, Africa, and the Middle East* 31:1 (March 2011): 85–93.

————. 2012. *Exilic Meditations: Essays on a Displaced Life* (London: H&S Media).

————. 2015a. 'Rebellious Action and the "Guerrilla Poetry": Dialectics of Art and Life in the 1970s Iran,' in K. Talattof, ed., *Persian Language, Literature and Culture: New Leaves, Fresh Looks; In Honor of Ahmad Karimi-Hakkak* (London/New York: Routledge): 103–22.

————. 2015b. 'A Generation's Myth: Armed Struggle and the Creation of Social Epic in the 1970s Iran,' in Houchang Chehabi, Peyman Jafari, and Maral Jefroudi (eds), *Iran in the Middle East: Transnational Encounters and Social History* (London: I. B. Tauris): 183–98.

————. 2015c. *Parviz Sadri: Namai az yek Zendegi-ye Siyasi* [*Parviz Sadri: A Political Biography*] (Vancouver: Shahrgon Books).

————. 2015d. 'Fadā'iān-e Ḵalq.' *Encyclopaedia Iranica*, online edition, 2015, available at: http://www.iranicaonline.org/articles/fadaian-e-khalq (accessed 7 December 2015).

————. 2017. 'Historical and Conceptual Preparations for a Multidisciplinary Study of Social Justice in Iran,' in *Iran's Struggles for Social Justice: Economics, Agency, Justice, Activism*, ed. P. Vahabzadeh (New York: Palgrave Macmillan): 9–27.

————. 2019. *Violence and Nonviolence: Conceptual Excursions into Phantom Opposite* (Toronto: University of Toronto Press).

Varon, Jeremy. 2004. *Bringing the War Home: The Weather Underground, the Red Army Faction, and Revolutionary Violence in the Sixties and Seventies* (Berkeley: University of California Press).

Wallerstein, Immanuel. 1989. '1968, Revolution in the World-System: Theses and Queries.' *Theory and Society* 18: 431–49.

White, Paul. 2015. *The PKK: Coming Down from the Mountains* (London: Zed Books).

Zia Zarifi, Hassan. 1996. '*Enqelabiyyun Naqsh-e Bozorgi dar Takmil-e Sharayet-e Eini-ye Enqelab Darand*' ['Revolutionaries Play a Significant Role in Completing the Objective Conditions of the Revolution']. *Rah-e Azadi* 47: 30.

NOTES

INTRODUCTION: REACTIVATING DISTORTED HISTORIES

1   A recent intellectual biography of the leftist thinkers of Iran is Homa
    Katouzian, *Khalil Maleki: The Human Face of Iranian Socialism* (London:
    Oneworld Publications, 2018). While many biographies of leftist
    thinkers are available in the market, researched *intellectual* biographies
    that try to *reconstruct* Iranian leftist thinkers' thoughts and approaches
    for today's debates and reflections are indeed few and far between and
    only recently emerging. This book identifies itself with this new trend.

2   See, for example and among recent publications and attending different
    subjects, Arturo Escobar and Sonia E. Alvarez (eds), *The Making of Social
    Movements in Latin America* (Boulder: Westview Press, 1992); Jorge G.
    Castañeda, *Utopia Unarmed: The Latin American Left After the Cold War*
    (New York: Vintage Books, 1993); Richard Gott, *Guerrilla Movements
    in Latin America* (New York: Seagull Books, 2008); Benjamin Dangl,
    Dancing with Dynamite: Social Movements and States in Latin America
    (Oakland: AK Press, 2010).

3   Peyman Vahabzadeh, 'Mostafa Sho'aiyan: The Maverick Theorist
    of the Revolution and the Failure of Frontal Politics in Iran'. *Iranian
    Studies* 40:3 (June 2007), pp. 405–25; Peyman Vahabzadeh, 'Mustafa
    Shu'a'iyan and *Fada`iyan-I Khalq*: Frontal Politics, Stalinism, and the
    Role of Intellectuals in Iran'. *British Journal of Middle Eastern Studies* 34:1
    (April 2007), pp. 43–61; Peyman Vahabzadeh, '*Pishvazheh: Takandishi-ye
    Sho'aiyan va Barkhord-e Chap-e A`ini*' ['Foreword: Sho'aiyan's Singular

Thought and the Reaction of the Doctrinal Left'], in Cosroe Chaqueri, ed., *Mostafa Sho'aiyan, Hasht Nameh beh Cherikha-ye Fadai Khalq: Naqd-e Yek Manesh-e Fekri* [*Mostafa Sho'aiyan, Eight Letters to the People's Fadai Guerrillas: Critique of An Approach*] (Tehran: Nashr-e Ney), pp. x–xix; Peyman Vahabzadeh, *A Guerrilla Odyssey: Modernization, Secularism, Democracy, and the Fadai Period of National Liberation in Iran, 1971–1979* (Syracuse, NY: Syracuse University Press, 2010), Ch. 6; Peyman Vahabzadeh, 'Mostafa Sho'a'iyan: An Iranian Leftist Political Thinker Unlike His Peers'. *Revolutionary History* 10:3 (Spring 2011), pp. 360–75.

4   See Walter D. Mignolo, 'Epistemic Disobedience, Independent Thought and Decolonial Freedom.' *Theory, Culture & Society* 26:7–8 (2009): 159–81.

5   Vahabzadeh, *A Guerrilla Odyssey*, p. xviii.

6   Hamid Momeni, *Shuresh Na, Qadamha-ye Sanjideh dar Rah-e Enqelab* [*Not Rebellion: Judicious Steps Towards the Revolution*] (np: Support Committee for the New Revolutionary Movement of Iranian People, nd); Hamid Momeni and Mostafa Sho'aiyan, *Juyeshi Piraumun-e Rowshanfekr ya Rowshangar-e Tabaqeh-ye Kargar* [*An Inquiry into the Intellectual or the Enlightener of the Working Class*] (np: Enqelab Publishers, nd); Mostafa Sho'aiyan and Hamid Momeni, *Darbareh-ye Rowshanfekr: Yek Bahs-e Qalami* [*On Intellectuals: A Debate in Writing*], ed. Nasser Pakdaman (Köln, Germany: Forough Verlag, 2007).

7   Kaveh, 'Yadi az Mostafa Sho'aiyan' ['Remembering Mostafa Sho'aiyan']. *Iranshahr* V(49), 24 February 1984, pp. 8, 11; Ali Fayaz, 'Tasahol-e Marksisti? 1' ['Marxist Tolerance? Part 1'], np. Ali Fayaz, 'Tasahol-e Marksisti? 2' ['Marxist Tolerance? Part 2']; *Kargah Andisheh va Peykar*, 18 February 2003. Available at: *http://kargari.de/?page_id=209* (accessed 24 July 2017).

8   Houshang Mahrooyan, *Mostafa Sho'aiyan: Motefakker-e Yeganeh-ye Tanha* [*Mostafa Sho'aiyan: The Lonely Singular Thinker*] (Tehran: Nashr-e Baztab Negar, 2005).

9   Chaqueri, ed., *Mostafa Sho'aiyan, Eight Letters*.

10   The term 'yellow journalism' refers to pseudo-intellectual or pseudo-critical journals and journalists in Iran who, with critical-intellectual gestures, try to advance the cultural agendas of the state, both before and after the 1979 Revolution, by offering distorted accounts of historical events or intellectual positions. In relation to our discussion, in today's

Iran, a distinct project has been launched to discredit the past struggles of the Left, not by ignoring it, but instead by bringing it to light through distortions, omissions, and reappropriation.

11   Anush Salehi, *Mostafa Sho'aiyan va Romantism Enqelabi* [*Mostafa Sho'aiyan and Revolutionary Romanticism*] (Spånga, Sweden: Baran, 2010).

12   Sam Sarabi, ed., 2012. '*Parvandeh-i bara-ye Mostafa Sho'aiyan*' ['A Mostafa Sho'aiyan File']. *Shargh Newspaper* 1526 (12 May 2012): 19–32.

13   Ali Nili, ed., '*Shureshi-ye Sharif*' ['The Honourable Rebel']. *Nasim-e Bidari* 8:74 (December 2016): 55–108.

14   Peyman Vahabzadeh, *Parviz Sadri: Namai az Yek Zendegi-ye Siyasi* [*Parviz Sadri: A Political Biography*] (Vancouver: Shahrgon Books, 2015).

1. THE MAKING OF A SINGULAR REVOLUTIONARY

1   Representing this generation's turning point in political views are the defense statements of Bizhan Jazani and Hassan Zia Zarifi, founders of the armed group the surviving members of which staged the legendary attack on the Siahkal gendarmerie post in February 1971—an operation that inaugurated urban guerrilla warfare that lasted until the 1979 Revolution. See Nasser Mohajer and Mehrdad Baba Ali, *Beh Zaban-e Qanun: Bizhan Jazani va Hassan Zia Zarifi dar Dadgah-e Nezami* [*In the Language of Law: Bizhan Jazani and Hassan Zia Zarifi in the Military Court*] (Berkeley, CA: Nashr-e Noghteh, 2016).

2   'Repressive development' captures my characterisation of the Pahlavi era: economic *development* through *peripheral* participation in world capitalism and political *repression*. See: Vahabzadeh, *A Guerrilla Odyssey* (op. cit.), pp. 1–5.

3   Salehi, *Mostafa Sho'aiyan* (op. cit.), pp. 20–22.

4   Anahita Sho'aiyan, email correspondence with author (10 October 2017).

5   Anahita Sho'aiyan, Facebook correspondence with author (12 February 2012).

6   Cosroe Chaqueri, 'Did the Soviets Play a Role in Founding the Tudeh Party in Iran?' *Cahiers du Monde russe* 40(3) (July–September 1999): 497–528; Ervand Abrahamian, *Iran Between Two Revolutions* (Princeton, NJ: Princeton University Press, 1982), pp. 281–446; Maziar Behrooz,

Rebels with a Cause: The Failure of the Left in Iran (London: I. B. Tauris, 1999), pp. 1–42; Maziar Behrooz, 'The 1953 Coup in Iran and the Legacy of Tudeh,' in Mark Gasiorowski and Malcolm Byrne, *Mohammad Mosaddeq and the 1953 Coup in Iran* (Syracuse, NY: Syracuse University Press, 2004), pp. 102–25.

7   Abrahamian, *Iran Between Two Revolutions*, pp. 188–92; 257–8.

8   Mojtaba Mahdavi, 'Iran: Multiple Sources of Grassroots Social Democracy?' in *Iran's Struggles for Social Justice: Economics, Agency, Justice, Activism*, ed. P. Vahabzadeh (New York: Palgrave MacMillan, 2017), pp. 271–88.

9   Abrahamian, *Iran Between Two Revolutions*, pp. 258–9; Nikki R. Keddie, *The Roots of the Revolution: An Interpretive History of Modern Iran* (New Haven and London: Yale University Press, 1981), pp. 129–30.

10   Abrahamian, *Iran Between Two Revolutions*, pp. 257–8.

11   See Salehi, *Mostafa Sho'aiyan*, pp. 33–5.

12   Mostafa Sho'aiyan and Marzieh Ahmadi Oskui, *'Darbareh-ey she'r-e "Cheshm beh rah"'* ['On the Poem "Awaiting"'], (unpublished typed carbon copy, 1973), pp. 9–10 (letters in this volume are individually paginated).

13   Vahabzadeh, *Parviz Sadri* (op. cit.), p. 18.

14   Hossein Sadri, Letter to Peyman Vahabzadeh (25 December 2008).

15   Anonymous, *Chand Maqaleh va Tahlil az Goruh-e Jaryan* [*Selected Articles and Analyses of the Jaryan Group*] (Tehran: np, 1979), p. 6; see also: Houshang Keshavarz Sadr, *'Pas-e Dusti: beh Monasebat-e Salmarg-e Mahmoud Tavakkoli, Rowshanfekr-e Tanha'* ['Guarding a Friendship: on the Anniversary of Passing of Mahmoud Tavakkoli, the Lonely Intellectual']. *Asre Nou*, 30 May 2012. Available at: http://asre-nou.net/php/view_print_version.php?objnr=21215 (accessed 29 July 2017).

16   Anonymous, *Selected Articles and Analyses of the Jaryan Group*, pp. 19–22, 182–3.

17   Ahmad Ronasi, *'Dar Rasa-ye Mahmoud Tavakkoli'* ['Mourning Mahmoud Tavakkoli']. *Enqelab-e Eslami* (February 2014). Available at: https://www.enghelabe-eslami.com/tamas/21-didgagha/tarik hi/7751-2014-03-13-20-30-16.html (accessed 30 July 2017). See also Bizhan Jazani, *Tarikh-e Si Saleh-ye Siyasi* [*The Thirty-Year Political History*] (GDR: OIPFG, nd), p. 106. Jazani's account must be read with caution, as his historiography shows distortions and misinformation.

18 Keshavarz Sadr, 'Guarding a Friendship'; Foruzandeh Farrokhi, *'Taz'if-e Hakemiyyat-e Melli Khiyanat Ast'* ['Weaking National Government Is Betrayal']. *Aftab Online*, 24 June 2007. Available at: https://goo.gl/k55tGf (accessed 30 July 2017); Salehi, *Mostafa Sho'a'iyan*, pp. 47–8. Foruzandeh Farrokhi, *'Mahmoud Tavakkoli Keh Bud va Cheh Goft?'* ['Who Was Mahmoud Tavakkoli and What Did He Say?']. *Jahan-e Ketab* 10:3 (June 2005), p. 29.

19 Mahmoud Tavakkoli, *Tahlili az Khat-e Mashy-e Siasi-ye Hezb-e Tudeh-ye Iran* [*An Analysis of the Political Directions of the Tudeh Party of Iran*], in *Historical Documents: The Workers', Social-democratic, and Communist Movement in Iran V*, ed. C. Chaqueri (Florence: Mazdak, 1975 [orig. 1959]).

20 See 'Biography' in Mostafa Sho'aiyan, *Tezi Baray-e Taharrok va Nimgami dar Rah: Jebheh-ye Enqelab-e Rahaibakhsh-e Khalq* [*A Thesis for Mobilisation and Half-a-Step on the Way: the People's National Liberation Revolution Front*] (Tehran: Nashr-e Olduz, nd), p. 11.

21 Sho'aiyan's letter to Mazdak. June 1975. Unpublished.

22 Jalal Al Ahmad, *Dar Khedmat va Khiyanat-e Rowshanfekran, Jeld Dovvom* [*On the Services and Betrayals of the Intellectuals*, Vol. 2] (Tehran: Kharazmi, 1979), p. 208.

23 Homa Katouzian, 'The Strange Politics of Khalil Maleki,' in S. Cronin (ed.), *Reformers and Revolutionaries in Modern Iran: New Perspectives on the Iranian Left* (London/New York: Routledge, 2004), pp. 166–8.

24 For an insider's account see Al Ahmad, *On the Services and Betrayals of the Intellectuals*, Vol. 2, pp. 161–215; Jalal Al Ahmad, *Yek Chah va Do Chaleh* [*One Well and Two Ditches*] (Tehran: Ravaq, 1964), pp. 33–44, 49–51.

25 Katouzian, 'The Strange Politics of Khalil Maleki', p. 168.

26 See Khalil Maleki, *Nehzat-e Melli-ye Iran va Edalat-e Ejtema'i* [*Nationalist Movement of Iran and Social Justice*], ed. Abdollah Borhan (Tehran: Nashr-e Markaz, 1998), pp. 28–9, 36–7. The article cited here is a reprint of the editorial of *Elm va Zendegi* (*Science and Life*), Vol. 1, no. 7 (September 1952) written by Maleki.

27 See Abrahamian, *Iran Between Two Revolutions*, pp. 421–3; Keddie, *Roots of Revolution*, pp. 150–60.

28 See Sussan Siavoshi, *Liberal Nationalism in Iran* (Boulder, CO: Westview Press, 1990), pp. 89–127; H. E. Chehabi, *Iranian Politics and Religious*

Modernism: The Liberation Movement of Iran under the Shah and Khomeini (Ithaca, NY: Cornell University Press, 1990), pp. 143–54.

29 See Keddie, *Roots of Revolution*, p. 159.

30 Nabavi as quoted in Salehi, *Mostafa Sho'aiyan*, p. 52.

31 Vahabzadeh, *A Guerrilla Odyssey*, pp. 30–34.

32 Mihan Jazani, 'Bizhan: *Ma'shuq, Rafiq, Hamsar*' ['Bizhan: Lover, Comrade, Spouse'], in *Jong-i Darbareh-ye Zendegi va Asar-e Bizhan Jazani* [*A Collection on the Life and Works of Bizhan Jazani*], ed. Centre for Collection and Publication of Bizhan Jazani's Works (Paris: Khavaran, 1999), p. 37.

33 Ibid.

34 Salehi, *Mostafa Sho'aiyan*, pp. 52–4.

35 Anonymous, *Jalal Al Ahmad beh Ravayet-e Asnad-e SAVAK* [Jalal Al Ahmad According to SAVAK Documents] (Tehran: Centre for Historical Documents, 2001), p. 20. In this report, Sho'aiyan's name is reported as 'Sho'ai'.

36 See Chehabi, *Iranian Politics and Religious Modernism*; Keddie, *Roots of Revolution*, p. 156; Abrahamian, *Iran Between Two Revolutions*, p. 460.

37 Bazargan as quoted in Gholam Reza Nejati, *Tarikh-e Siyasi-ye Bistopanj Saleh-ye Iran* [*The Twenty-Five Year Political History of Iran*] (Tehran: Rasa Cultural Services, 1992), p. 373. This statement is apocryphal: while widely quoted, it does not appear in the transcripts of the trial statements.

38 Jazani, *The Thirty-Year Political History*, p. 86.

39 One source (SOLI 22, n. 2) credits Sho'aiyan for having co-authored two extensive critical essays, published anonymously, on the Tudeh Party of Iran (Tavakkoli, *An Analysis of the Political Directions of the Tudeh Party of Iran* [1975, orig. 1959]) and Khalil Maleki's Socialist League of Iran's Nationalist Movement (*Jame'eh-ye Sosiyalistha-ye Nehzat-e Melli-ye Iran*) founded in 1960 (Tavakkoli, *An Analysis of the Socialist League of Iran* [1983, orig. 1964]). This account is certainly incorrect. Tavakkoli was the sole writer of both treatises.

40 These include his romantic novella *Akhtar and Homayun* (1960, unpublished) and several poems published in Salehi, *Mostafa Sho'aiyan*, pp. 32–7.

41 Salehi, *Mostafa Sho'aiyan*, p. 54.

42   See the 1963 reports of student protests in the Appendix in Chaqueri, ed., *Mostafa Sho'aiyan, Eight Letters* (op. cit.), p. 189.

43   Salehi, *Mostafa Sho'aiyan*, p. 74.

44   In *Mostafa Sho'aiyan*, Salehi provides a long fictionalised account of Sho'aiyan's 'depression' by conjuring up images of this period of his life based on his personal letters and notes as well as the memories of his friends, which leave the impression that Sho'aiyan had indeed had mental illness (pp. 76–94). While mental illness is not a stigma and some of Sho'aiyan's writings indicate emotional ups and downs, Salehi's account is not based on facts. Collapsing the genres of fiction and historiography and posing it as biography has been pointed out by Sho'aiyan's close comrade, Asghar Monajemi, who expressly refutes Salehi's depiction. See Asghar Monajemi, '*Nokati Chand Piramun-e Ketab-e Mostafa Sho'aiyan va Romantism-e Enqelabi*' ['Remarks About the Book, Mostafa Sho'aiyan and Revolutionary Romanticism']. *Asre-nou.net* (9 January 2011). Available at: http://asre-nou.net/php/view.php?objnr=13080 (accessed 10 January 2011).

45   See Vahabzadeh, *Parviz Sadri*, p. 24.

46   Vahabzadeh, *A Guerrilla Odyssey*, p. 4.

47   Ibid., pp. 7–13.

48   See Mohammad Nasser Jahani Asl, *Identity, Politics, Organization: A Historical Sociology of the Democratic Party of Iranian Kurdistan and the Kurdish Nationalist Movement*. Ph.D. Dissertation (University of Victoria, 2017), pp. 191–200.

49   In 1953, 14,500 students were enrolled in four universities and 2,538 in technical training schools. In 1977, 154,315 undergraduate students were enrolled in sixteen universities and 227,507 in eight hundred technical training schools (Ervand Abrahamian, 'Structural Causes of the Iranian Revolution.' *MERIP Reports* 87 [May 1980], p. 22).

50   See Ervand Abrahamian, *Radical Islam: The Iranian Mujahedin* (London: I. B. Tauris, 1989), pp. 85–92.

51   It is worth noting, for the record, that the OIPM leadership fled to Europe in 1981 and then moved to Iraq (at war with Iran at the time), refashioning itself as a 'liberation army,' but in fact it emerged as a violent and secretive cult of a few thousands, the surviving members of which are now aging in exile.

52   See Vahabzadeh, *A Guerrilla Odyssey*, Ch. 2.

53   Ibid., pp. xxi, 22–3; Behrooz, *Rebels with a Cause* (op. cit.), p. 50.

54   George Katsiaficas, *The Imagination of the New Left: A Global Analysis of 1968* (Boston: South End Press, 1987).

55   See Héctor Béjar, *Peru 1965: Notes on a Guerrilla Experience*, trans. William Rose (New York: Monthly Review Press, 1970).

56   Afshin Matin[-asgari], *Konfedrasion: Tarikh-e Jonbesh-e Daneshjuyan-e Irani dar Kharj az Keshvar 1332–57* [*Confederation: The History of the Iranian Student Movement Abroad 1953–1979*], trans. Arastu Azari (Tehran: Shirazeh, 1999), p. 183.

57   Cosroe Chaqueri, '*Cherikha Jame'eh-ye Iran ra Nemishenakhtand*' ['The Guerrillas Did Not Know Iranian Society']. *Mehrnameh* 6 (November 2010), p. 118.

58   See Bizhan Jazani and Hassan Zia Zarifi, *Tez-e Goruh-e Jazani: Masa'el-e Jonbesh-e Zedd-e Este'mari va Azadibakhsh-e Khalq-e Iran va Omdehtarin Vazayef-e Komonistha-ye Iran dar Sharayet-e Konuni* [*Thesis of Jazani's Group: Issues Pertaining to the Anti-Colonial and Liberation Movement of Iran and the Main Duties of Iranian Communists in Present Conditions*] (np: 19 Bahman Publisher, 1976 [orig. 1967]).

59   See Peyman Vahabzadeh, '*Tajrobeh-ey Kuba Dast-e Avval beh Iran Naresid*' ['The Cuban Experience Did Not Come to Iran First Hand']. *Mehrnameh* 6 (November 2010): 117–18.

60   Vahabzadeh, *Parviz Sadri*, pp. 25–6.

61   Salehi, *Mostafa Sho'aiyan*, pp. 103–4.

62   Mostafa Sho'aiyan. '*Chehelomin Ruz-e Dargozasht-e Mosaddeq dar Ahmadabad*' ['The Fortieth Day of Mosaddeq's Passing in Ahmadabad']. *Ketab-e Jom'eh* 29 (6 March 1980), p. 10.

63   And Iranian newspapers, in reaction to the public perception of SAVAK's involvement in Takhti's death, made every effort to link the champion's suicide to his depression and domestic conflict with his wife. Takhti's chronicles were also published. The reportage made no mention of the protest component in reporting the mass rallies to Takhti's resting place in Ibn Babuyeh Cemetery. See *Kayhan Havai* 2853 (8 January 1968), pp. 1–3; 2854 (9 January 1968), pp. 1–3; 2857 (13 January 1968), p. 3. See also Salehi, *Mostafa Sho'aiyan*, p. 106.

64   Salehi, *Mostafa Sho'aiyan*, pp. 108–10. Salehi reports Ehsan Naraqi's statement that Parviz Sabeti, Head of Internal Security Division of SAVAK, had phoned him and inquired about Sho'aiyan. Upon this

contact, having taken place circa 1969–70, Naraqi asked Sho'aiyan to leave the Institute (Salehi, *Mostafa Sho'aiyan*, p. 194).

65   Asghar Monahemi, telephone conversation with Peyman Vahabzadeh (24 September 2017).

66   Hossein Sadri, letter to Peyman Vahabzadeh (25 December 2008).

67   The story of the grenade shells has been mystified beyond imagination. Nabavi claims that the pieces for the shells were separately ordered from different metalwork shops. No other account confirms this claim, which implies that Sho'aiyan and Sadri actually kept Nabavi in the dark. Nabavi talks about 3,000 shells, which sounds rather extravagant. He also claims that the shells were supposed to be filled with dynamite (Behzad Nabavi, *'Kuler-e Khaneh-ye Mahasti ra Man Nasb Kardam'* ['I Installed the Air Conditioner in Mahasti's Home']. *Parsine.* 12 September 2011. Available at: https://goo.gl/xy72Pi [accessed 10 July 2017]). See also: Salehi, *Mostafa Sho'aiyan*, pp. 230–31. In its reportage on the raid on the Sho'aiyan–Shayegan group, the daily newspaper *Kayhan* reports the recovery of seven hundred handmade grenades, attested by the photo, that resemble a crude prototype of today's stainless steel coffee mugs with lids. For my account of these events see Vahabzadeh, *Parviz Sadri*, pp. 28–35.

68   Ali Golesorkhi, telephone interview by Peyman Vahabzadeh (11 March 2009).

69   Reza Barahani, *'Qesseh-ye Enteshar-e* Jahan-e Naw *va Qesseh-ye Darmandegi-ye Rowshanfekran'* ['The Publication of *Jahan-e Naw* and the Story of Intellectuals' Desperation']. *Negin* 22 (1967): 8–10. See also the editorial to the first issue of the new series: Raza Barahani, *'Chand Harf Beja-ye Moqaddameh'* ['A Few Words in Lieu of Introduction']. *Jahan-e Naw* 1, no. 1 (June 1966): i–ix.

70   Mostafa Sho'aiyan, *'Bazjui'* ['Interrogation']. *Jahan-e Naw* 24, no. 1 (April 1969): 160.

71   In two earlier articles on Sho'aiyan I had mentioned that Mofidian had taken two of Sho'aiyan's books to Europe, which is not accurate. I hereby correct these statements (Vahabzadeh, 'Mostafa Sho'aiyan: The Maverick Theorist of the Revolution' [op. cit.]; Vahabzadeh, 'Mustafa Shu'a'iyan and *Fada`iyan-i Khalq'* [op. cit.]).

72   See the Appendix in Chaqueri, ed., *Mostafa Sho'aiyan, Eight Letters*, pp. 190–93.

73   Salehi, *Mostafa Sho'aiyan*, pp. 130–40; Anonymous, *Jalal Al Ahmad According to SAVAK Documents*, p. 242.

74   Nabavi, 'I Installed the Air Conditioner.'

75   Salehi, *Mostafa Sho'aiyan*, p. 233.

76   Chaqueri, ed., *Mostafa Sho'aiyan, Eight Letters*, p. 192; PSRI (Political Studies and Research Institute), *Sazman-e Mojahedin-e Khalq: az Peydai ta Farjam (1344–1384) 1 [The People's Mojahedin Organisation: from its Origins to its Demise (1965–2005)*, Vol. 1] (Tehran: PSRI, 2005), p. 583.

77   Behzad Nabavi as quoted in PSRI, *The People's Mojahedin*, Vol. 1, p. 567, n. 2; Vahabzadeh, *Parviz Sadri*, p. 42. See also Behzad Nabavi, '*Razha-ye Behzad Nabavi*' ['The Secrets of Behzad Nabavi']. *Hamshahri*, no. 2706 (27 April 2002); Salehi, *Mostafa Sho'a'iyan*, p. 187.

78   Vahabzadeh, *Parviz Sadri*, pp. 37–60.

79   Reza Allamehzadeh, interview by Peyman Vahabzadeh (Utrecht, 29 July 2010).

80   See also Salehi, *Mostafa Sho'aiyan*, pp. 208–10; Anush Salehi, *Ravi-ye Baharan: Mobarezat va Zendegi-ye Karamatollah Daneshian* [The Spring's Narrator: The Life and Struggles of Karamatollah Daneshian] (Tehran: Nashr-e Qatre, 2002); Abbas Samakar, *Man Yek Shureshi Hastam* [I Am a Rebel] (Los Angeles: Sherkat-e Ketab, 2001). For a succinct account of the trial of this group of writers and graduates of the Superior Institute of Television and Cinema (founded in 1969) see Vahabzadeh, *A Guerrilla Odyssey*, pp. 218–19, n. 1.

81   Mahmoud Naderi, *Cherikha-ye Fadai-ye Khalq: az Nokhostin Konesh ta Bahman-e 1357, Jeld-e Avval* [People's Fadai Guerrillas: From Their First Acts until February 1979, Vol. 1] (Tehran: Political Studies and Research Institutes, 2008), p. 198; PSRI, *The People's Mojahedin*, Vol. 1, p. 583.

82   See Vahabzadeh, *A Guerrilla Odyssey*, pp. 25–30.

83   Salehi, *Mostafa Sho'aiyan*, p. 196.

84   Reza Asgariyeh, '*Asabani Bud va Fohshha-ye Prolteri Midad*' ['He Was Raging and Shouting Proletarian Curses']. *Nasim-e Bidari* 8, no. 74 (December 2016), pp. 85–6.

85   Salehi, *Mostafa Sho'aiyan*, pp. 214–15.

86   Vahabzadeh, *Parviz Sadri*, p. 53.

87   See Asgariyeh, 'He Was Raging and Shouting Proletarian Curses.' Asgariyeh also wrote a letter to Nashr-e Ney, publisher of *Mostafa Sho'aiyan, Eight Letters* (2007), edited by C. Chaqueri, and affixed a

fifteen-page typed 'Prison Memoir' to it, recounting the disputed events, arguing that Sho'aiyan committed an error in his judgment about him (Reza Asgariyeh, *Az Khaterat-e Zendan* [*Prison Memoirs*] [Unpublished, nd]).

88   According to Salehi, pictures of Sho'aiyan were posted on inter-city gendarmerie posts by 1972 (Salehi, *Mostafa Sho'aiyan*, p. 227). This claim remains unconfirmed.

89   See also Salehi, *Mostafa Sho'aiyan*, p. 227.

90   Asghar Monajemi, telephone conversation with Peyman Vahabzadeh (24 September 2017).

91   Raf'at, telephone interview by Peyman Vahabzadeh (6 November 2001).

92   See also Salehi, *Mostafa Sho'aiyan*, pp. 234–5.

93   See Forutan Fumani, '*Seyr-e Nazariyeh Andisheha-ye Farhangi*' ['The Process of the Theory of Cultural Thoughts'] (unpublished manuscript, nd), p. 1; Gh. Farhang Forutan (Abbas), telephone interview by Peyman Vahabzadeh (13 September 2017). Reza`i pretended to collaborate with his interrogators and was taken out of prison, accompanied by security teams, to identify the places and peoples that might lead SAVAK to the rest of Mojahedin cadres. Tipped off by his family (during a prison visit) on where to go (arranged by his comrades), on one of these trips, as Forutan recalls, either Nasser or Arzhang (around seven and ten years old at the time) posed as a shoeshine boy who, by insisting on polishing Reza`i's shoes, inserted the message containing instructions in his shoes (ibid.). See also Nabavi's narrative (what he heard in prison) and Serafat's recollection (Sediqeh Serafat, '*Amuzgari va Mobarezeh-ye Cheriki*' ['Being a teacher and guerrilla warfare']. *Asr-e Nou* [15 October 2005]. Available at: http://asre-nou.net/1348/mehr/24/m-6.html [accessed 19 July 2017]).

94   See Massoud Razavi Faqih, '*Mostafa Sho'aiyan: Maqzub-e Cherikha-ye Khalq va Matlub-e Mojahedin-e Khalq*' ['Mostafa Sho'aiyan: Damned by People's Guerrillas and Favourite of the People's Mojahedin'] *Tarikh-e Irani* (18 May 2012). Available at: https://goo.gl/TQCNfG (accessed 18 October 2017). The book in question is Ahmad Reza`i, *Tahlili az Nehzat-e Hosseini* [*An Analysis of Hossein's Movement*] (Springfield, MO: Liberation of Movement of Iran-Abroad, 1975 [orig. 1972]).

95   Salehi, *Mostafa Sho'aiyan*, p. 235.

96   See PSRI (Political Studies and Research Institute), *Sazman-e Mojahedin-e Khalq: az peydai ta farjam (1344–1384) 2* [*The People's Mojahedin Organisation: from its Origins to its Demise (1965–2005)*, Vol. 2] (Tehran: PSRI, 2006), pp. 3–18. See also Mohsen Nejat Hosseini, *Bar Faraz-e Khalij-e Fars* [*Over the Persian Gulf*] (Tehran: Nashr-e Ney, 2001), p. 361.

97   PSRI, *The People's Mojahedin*, Vol. 1, pp. 628–30.

98   See ibid, pp. 554–5.

99   Behzad Nabavi, '*Goruh-e Khun-e Rajavi ba Digaran Farq Darad*' ['Rajavi's Blood Type Is Different From That of Others']. *Sobh-e Naw* 128 (21 November 2016), p. 11.

100   Cosroe Chaqueri, '*Sargozasht-e Mostafa Sho'aiyan*' ['Biography of Mostafa Sho'aiyan'], in Chaqueri, ed., *Mostafa Sho'aiyan, Eight Letters*, pp. xxxiii–xxxvi; Salehi, *Mostafa Sho'aiyan*, pp. 260–3, 266.

101   Gh. Farhang Forutan (Abbas), telephone conversation with Peyman Vahabzadeh (4 October 2017). Forutan recalls that there had been a debate within the group about choosing either 'People's Democratic Front' or 'People's Democratic Rebellious Front.'

102   Serafat, 'Being a Teacher and Guerrilla Warfare.'

103   Raf'at, telephone interview by Peyman Vahabzadeh (6 November 2001); Serafat, 'Being a Teacher and Guerrilla Warfare.' Sho'aiyan makes a brief reference to this in SOLI 143.

104   Serafat, 'Being a Teacher and Guerrilla Warfare.'

105   Raf'at, telephone interview by Peyman Vahabzadeh (6 November 2001); see also: Chaqueri, ed., *Mostafa Sho'aiyan, Eight Letters*, pp. 8, 64–8.

106   Raf'at, telephone interview by Peyman Vahabzadeh (6 November 2001); see also Vahabzadeh, *A Guerrilla Odyssey*, pp. 189–90.

107   See also Serafat, 'Being a Teacher and Guerrilla Warfare'; Chaqueri, 'Biography of Mostafa Sho'aiyan,' in Chaqueri, ed., *Mostafa Sho'aiyan, Eight Letters*, p. xxxv.

108   Anonymous, '*Towzihati Piramun-e Davari-ye Eshtebahamiz Rafiq Sho'aiyan Darbareh-ye Abdollah Anduri*' ['Explanations Regarding Comrade Sho'aiyan's Erroneous Judgement about Abdollah Anduri'] (Unpublished letter to Edition Mazdak, nd).

109   Serafat, 'Being a Teacher and Guerrilla Warfare.'

110   Nejat Hosseini, *Over the Persian Gulf*, p. 309.

111 Marziyeh Ahmadi Oskui, *Khaterati az Yek Rafiq* [*Memoirs of a Comrade*] (np: OIPFG, 1974).

112 I am grateful to the late Cosroe Chaqueri and Gh. Farhang Forutan for sending me these exchanges. These include '*Kalanjari ba Qoqnus*' ['An Encounter with Sphinx'] (unpublished, October 1973), which is an engagement with Oskui's short story, 'Hello Teacher' ('*Salam Aqa Mo'alem*) as well as 'On the Poem "Awaiting"' ['*Darbareh-ey she'r-e "Cheshm beh rah"*'] (unpublished, 1973).

113 Salehi, *Mostafa Sho'aiyan*, p. 140.

114 Sadri in Vahabzadeh, *Parviz Sadri*, p. 54.

115 Amir Parviz Puyan, *Zarurat-e Mobarezeh-ye Mosallahaneh va Radd-e Te'ori-ye Baqa`* [*The Necessity of Armed Struggle and the Refutation of the Theory of Survival*] (Tehran: Gam Publishers, 1979 [orig. 1970]). See Sho'aiyan's '*Cheh nabayad kard?*' ['What Is Not To Be Done?'] in SW and his 1974 preface to it (SW 1) (articles in this volume are individually paginated). See also Vahabzadeh, *A Guerrilla Odyssey*, pp. 134–8.

116 Massoud Ahmadzadeh, *Mobarezeh-ye Mosallahaneh: ham Estratezhi, ham Taktik* [*Armed Struggle: Both Strategy and Tactic*] (Umeä, Sweden: Organisation of Iranian Students, 1976 [orig. 1970]). See Sho'aiyan's '*Chand Khordehgiri-ye Nab*' ['Some Pure Criticisms'] in SW 2–3, and his 1974 preface to it (SW 1) (articles in this volume are individually paginated).

117 The letters in these two volumes (SOLI and SOLF) were gathered and published in: Chaqueri, ed., *Mostafa Sho'aiyan, Eight Letters*.

118 Esma'il Khakpur and Jalal Fattahi were arrested in this incident. See Naderi, *People's Fadai Guerrillas*, pp. 471–5; Salehi, *Mostafa Sho'aiyan*, p. 338.

119 Vahabzadeh, *A Guerrilla Odyssey*, p. 192. Sho'aiyan reports a threat made against him by Ashraf, which he reciprocates (SOLF 5). That said, the claim that the Fadai leaders planned to assassinate Sho'aiyan remains unreasonable: Sho'aiyan was not considered a security risk and Fadaiyan had never purged members based on ideological disagreements.

120 Salehi, *Mostafa Sho'a'iyan*, pp. 390–1, 393, 403.

121 Ibid., p. 404.

122 Ibid., pp. 414–15.

123 See Vartan Mikailian, '*Shahed-e Eyni*' ['The Eyewitness'], in Sho'aiyan and Momeni, *On Intellectuals: A Debate in Writing* (op. cit.), pp. 146–53;

security report in PSRI, *The People's Mojahedin*, Vol. 1, p. 566; Reza Asgariyeh, 'Letter to Cosroe Chaqueri' (11 August 2008). Constable Yunesi was executed after the 1979 Revolution by the Revolutionary Tribunal for his role in Sho'aiyan's death.

124   Mikailian, 'The Eyewitness,' p. 151.

125   Ibid., pp. 149–50.

126   Salehi, *Mostafa Sho'aiyan*, p. 425.

127   Asghar Monajemi, 'In-Person Communication with Peyman Vahabzadeh' (Irvine, CA, 19 August 2018).

128   Gh. Farhang Forutan (Abbas), 'Telephone Conversation with Peyman Vahabzadeh' (25 September 2017).

2. EXPERIENCES AND EXPERIMENTS IN THE 1960S

1   Hamid Dabashi, *Iran: A People Interrupted* (New York/London: The New Press, 2007).

2   Fredric Jameson, *The Ideologies of Theory: Essays 1971–1986*, Vol. 2 (Minneapolis: University of Minnesota Press, 1988), p. 207.

3   Immanuel Wallerstein, '1968, Revolution in the World-System: Theses and Queries.' *Theory and Society* 18 (1989): 431–49.

4   See Al Ahmad's account about the schemes to humiliate him and followers of Maleki: Al Ahmad, *On the Services and Betrayals of the Intellectuals*, Vol. 2 (op. cit.), pp. 216–31.

5   Maleki, *Nationalist Movement of Iran and Social Justice* (op. cit.), pp. 29, 126. This edited volume provides key writings by Maleki from 1952 and 1963.

6   Ibid., pp. 13–29.

7   Ibid., p. 127.

8   Ibid., p. 160.

9   See Manifesto of the Socialist League of Iran's Nationalist Movement (September 1960) in ibid., pp. 196–246.

10   Ibid., pp. 9–10.

11   Ibid., pp. 56, 102.

12   Ibid., p. 57.

13   Ibid., pp. 79, 85, 93.

14   Ibid., p. 111.

15   Ibid., pp. 145–6.

16   Ibid., pp. 208–9.

17   Tavakkoli, *An Analysis of the Political Directions of the Tudeh Party of Iran*
       (op. cit.). This book comes in two consecutive parts (111 and 279 pages
       respectively), each of which is paginated separately.

18   Tavakkoli, *An Analysis*, Part 2, pp. 26, 76.

19   Tavakkoli, *An Analysis*, Part 1, p. 2.

20   See Cosroe Chaqueri, *The Russo-Caucasian Origins of the Iranian Left:
       Social Democracy in Modern Iran* (Richmond, Surrey: Curzon, 2001), esp.
       chs 4–8; Janet Afary, *The Iranian Constitutional Revolution, 1906–1911:
       Grassroots Democracy, Social Democracy, and the Origins of Feminism* (New
       York: Columbia University Press, 1996), pp. 81–8, 255–83.

21   Tavakkoli as quoted in Farrokhi, 'Who Was Mahmoud Tavakkoli?' (op.
       cit.), pp. 28–9.

22   Tavakkoli, *An Analysis*, Part 1, p. 3.

23   Ibid., pp. 19, 20–22.

24   Anonymous, *Selected Articles and Analyses of the Jaryan Group* (op. cit.),
       pp. 16–17.

25   Ibid., pp. 68–9.

26   Tavakkoli, *An Analysis*, Part 2, p. 94; Part 1, pp. 90, 95.

27   Tavakkoli, *An Analysis*, Part 1, p. 4.

28   Ibid., pp. 30–7.

29   Ibid., p. 7.

30   Ibid., p. 44. Whether Tavakkoli actually coined this term is not known
       although the term was not used (widely) in prior literature (e.g. Maleki's
       writings).

31   See Béjar, *Peru 1965* (op. cit.), p. 11.

32   Bizhan Jazani, *Enqelab-e Mashrutiyyat-e Iran: Niruha va Hadafha* [*The
       Iranian Constitutional Revolution: Forces and Objectives*] (Paris: The
       Union of People's Fadaiyan of Iran, 2009).

33   See Bizhan Jazani, *Jam'bandi-ye Mobarezat-e Si Saleh-ye Akhir dar
       Iran* [Summation of the Struggles of the Past Thirty Years in Iran]. *19
       Bahman-e Te`orik*, 5-6 (1976), p. 12. See also Vahabzadeh, *A Guerrilla
       Odyssey*, p. 81.

34   Bizhan Jazani, *Cheguneh Mobarezeh-ye Mosallahaneh Tudehi Mishavad*
       [*How Armed Struggle Becomes a Mass Movement*] (Germany: OIPFG,
       1976), p. 39.

35   See Vahabzadeh, *A Guerrilla Odyssey*, pp. 255–6.

36   Mostafa Sho'aiyan, 'Khiyanat' ['Betrayal']. Unpublished, 1960. The first
     seven pages of the total of twenty-seven pages are missing in my typed
     version.

37   Jazani and Zia Zarifi, Thesis of Jazani's Group (op. cit.), p. 2; original
     emphasis. Although the original publication credited the group for
     authorship and the next publication has Jazani as the author, I argue
     that this analysis was co-authored by Jazani and Zia Zarifi as a summary
     of Group One's internal discussions. The misleading title 'Thesis of
     Jazani's Group' was given to the work by Manouchehr Kalanatri, Bizhan's
     maternal uncle and an original member of Group One, who functioned
     as the group's publisher and logistical member in London, UK.

38   Ibid., p. 2.

39   Ibid., p. 4.

40   Hassan Zia Zarifi, Hezb-e Tudeh va Kudeta-ye 28 Mordad 32 [The Tudeh
     Party and the 19 August 1953 Coup] (Tehran: np, 1979), p. 33; my
     emphasis. See also Vahabzadeh, A Guerrilla Odyssey, p. 197.

41   Jazani and Zarifi, Thesis of Jazani's Group, p. 4.

42   Sho'aiyan's Preface to Arsalan Puriya, Karnameh-ye Mosaddeq [The
     Record of Mosaddeq], ed. Mostafa Sho'aiyan (Florence: Mazdak, 1976
     [orig. 1973]), p. ii; my emphasis. He applies the same critique to the
     Azerbaijan Democratic Party (ibid.) and states that 'This book is very
     useful for those in Fadaiyan's ranks who are not familiar with the events
     of this period [the 1950s] as they are too young and have no access to
     the sources' (ibid., v). Here Sho'aiyan rises as a scholar who spends his
     underground life to construct an edited, abridged version (199 pages)
     of Puriya's 769-page treatise (first published underground and later by
     Mazdak).

43   OIPFG, Edam-e Enghelabi-ye Abbas Shahriyari, Mard-e Hezar Chehreh
     [The Revolutionary Execution of Abbas Shahriyari, a Man with a Thousand
     Faces] (np: OIPFG, 1975).

44   Puyan, The Necessity of Armed Struggle (op. cit.), p. 15; see also
     Vahabzadeh, A Guerrilla Odyssey, p. 136.

45   Ahmadzadeh, Armed Struggle: Both Strategy and Tactic (op. cit.), pp. 19,
     20.

46   F. M. Javan, Cherikha-ye Khalq Cheh Miguyand? [What Do the People's
     Guerrillas Say?] (Germany: Tudeh Press, 1972).

47 Whether the PFG ever publicised this article remains unknown. The article's tone did not adhere to the norms of polemics. Signed Serteq, it was first published by Mazdak in Europe in *Manifestus: Problems of Revolution and Socialism* (Winter 1975), pp. 62–7, and later anthologised in *Selected Writings* (1976).

48 This work has not yet been published. The copy used is a typed manuscript.

49 Salehi, *Mostafa Sho'aiyan* (op. cit.), p. 54.

50 Mohammad Torkman (ed.), *Namehha-ye Doktor Mosaddeq* [*Letters of Dr Mosaddeq*] (Tehran: Hazaran, 1995), p. 303.

51 Torkman (ed.), *Letters of Dr Mosaddeq*, p. 303.

52 Jazani, *The Thirty-Year Political History* (op. cit.), p. 105. On Jazani's distortions, see Peyman Vahabzadeh, 'Bizhan Jazani and the Problems of Historiography of the Iranian Left.' *Iranian Studies* 38:1 (March 2005): 167–78.

53 Tavakkoli as quoted in Farrokhi, 'Who Was Mahmoud Tavakkoli?', p. 29. Unfortunately, I could not obtain a copy of *What Is To Be Done?*

54 Tavakkoli as quoted in Farrokhi, 'Who Was Mahmoud Tavakkoli?', p. 28. This idea runs through the entire Jaryan analyses (see Anonymous, *Selected Articles and Analyses of the Jaryan Group*, p. 128).

55 Maleki, *Nationalist Movement of Iran and Social Justice*, pp. 145–7.

56 Ibid., pp. 231–4.

57 Jazani, *The Thirty-Year Political History*, pp. 105–6.

58 Jaryan's review of the Second National Front, dated 1964, contains the elements discussed in Sho'aiyan's treatise. Jaryan regards political alliances as the prerequisite for ending despotism, arguing that national unity (*ettehad-e melli*) is not simply the unity of political parties (Anonymous, *Selected Articles and Analyses of the Jaryan Group*, pp. 57–9). The article takes time to show why a front is superior to a party (ibid., pp. 60–2).

59 See Antonio Gramsci, *Selections from the Prison Notebooks*, ed. & trans. Q. Hoare & G. Nowell Smith (New York: International Publishers, 1971), p. 194.

60 Salehi, *Mostafa Sho'aiyan*, p. 66.

61 Sadri, letter to the Peyman Vahabzadeh (25 December 2008).

62 New scholarship questions whether Shirazi had ever issued a tobacco boycott *fatwa*, thus suggesting that the whole boycott affair was the handiwork of Iranian merchants and masses, aided by rumour of clerical

support (Hamid Dabashi, *Iran: The Rebirth of a Nation* [New York: Palgrave Macmillan, 2016], pp. 77, 187).

63   Salehi, *Mostafa Sho'aiyan*, p. 66.

64   Also in Chaqueri, *Mostafa Sho'aiyan, Eight Letters* (op. cit.), pp. 123–4, n. 18.

65   Mostafa Sho'aiyan, '*Bazjui*' ['Interrogation'], *Jahan-e Naw* 24, no. 1 (April 1969): 160; Mostafa Sho'aiyan, '*Vazhehha*' ['The Words'], *Jahan-e Naw* 24, no. 3 (August–September 1969): 91–102; Mostafa Sho'aiyan, '*Sargozasht va Dafn-e Yek Te'ori*' ['The Life and Burial of a Theory'], *Jahan-e Naw* 23, nos 10–12 (Winter 1969): 26–35; Mostafa Sho'aiyan, '*Negahi beh Towte'h-ye Khal'-e Selah-e Omumi.' Faslha-ye Sabz* ['A Glance at the General Disarmament Conspiracy'] (unpublished); Mostafa Sho'aiyan, '*Khordehgirihai az Amuzgaran*' ['Review of *The Teachers*'] (unpublished). The latter is a review of *Amuzgaran*, a play written by Mohsen Yalfani and staged in 1970 with collaboration of Said Soltanpour. SAVAK banned the play after ten shows and imprisoned Yalfani and Soltanpour for three months. Sho'aiyan's review therefore was not publishable, for obvious reasons.

66   Nikita Khrushchev, 'Speech to 20th Congress of the C.P.S.U.' *Marxists Internet Archives*. Available at: https://www.marxists.org/archive/khrushchev/1956/02/24.htm (accessed 9 November 2017).

67   Nikita Khrushchev, 'On Peaceful Coexistence.' *Foreign Affairs* 38, no. 1 (1959), p. 3.

68   Ernesto Che Guevara, 'At the Afro-Asian Conference in Algeria.' *Marxists Internet Archive*. Available at: https://www.marxists.org/archive/guevara/1965/02/24.htm (accessed 9 November 2017).

69   Norman Fairclough, *Critical Discourse Analysis: The Critical Study of Language* (London: Routledge, 2010).

70   See Arturo Escobar, *Encountering Development: The Making and Unmaking of the Third World* (Princeton: Princeton University Press, 1995).

71   This article was sent to the National Front in Europe but was not published (Chapter 1).

72   Salehi, *Mostafa Sho'aiyan*, p. 101.

73   See Massoud (alias), '*Az Harf ta Amal: Natayej-e Vagozari-e Saham beh Kargaran*' ['From Words to Action: The Outcome of Distributing Shares to the Workers']. *Donya* 3 (September 1974). This article shows that Tudeh regarded the reform as demagogical, interestingly, because it

was only implemented in a small fraction of factories and because Iran's comprador capitalist economy would not allow a genuine program. It was therefore the regime's ploy to win the workers' support. Overall, the Tudeh Party's approach to the Shah's reforms was confused, even opportunistic. Since Tudeh followed the Soviet Union foreign policy, the Party could not demand the overthrow of the regime: the strategic objective of Tudeh was the realisation of Iran's national-democratic struggle but tactically this did not mean overthrowing the regime. In justifying why it had abandoned the strategic slogan of overthrowing the monarchy, the Party announced, 'To destroy the autocratic rule and the existing regime of terror and repression *may not mean* the destruction of monarchy and the establishment' of a republic, which is one of the demands of the people and our Party' (Manouchehr Behzadi, '*Darbareh-ye Ravesh-e Taktiki-ye Hezb-e Tudeh Iran*' ['On the Tactical Methods of the Tudeh Party of Iran']. *Donya* 5 [November 1974], p. 12 [emphasis added]). Stated differently, although Tudeh demanded a republic in its platform, it would accept being legal opposition under a reformed monarchy. Expectedly, Tudeh implicitly relates its new policy to the international influence of the Soviet Union (ibid., p. 14).

74   According to the Tudeh Party, the regime followed a 'capitalist path to development' as opposed to the Soviet prescription for developing countries, the 'non-capitalist path,' meant to support postcolonial societies through their economic dependence upon the Soviet Union (see Massoud [alias], '*Arzyabi-ye Barkhi Javaneb-e Roshd-e Eqtesadi-ye Iran pas az Kudeta*' ['An Assessment of Certain Aspects of Economic Growth in Iran After the Coup']. *Donya* 7, no. 3 [Fall 1966]: 8–23). This means the 'socialist' measures, such as those of the Shah, could not bear fruit under dependent capitalism. For the Soviet model see R. Ulyanovsky and V. Pavlov, 'The Non-capitalist Path as a Historical Reality,' in *Asian Dilemma: A Soviet View and Myrdal's Concept* (Moscow: Progress Publishers, 1973): 152–69.

75   See Antonio Gramsci, '*Peydayesh-e Rowshanfekran*' ['The Formation of Intellectuals'], trans. M. Hezarkhani. *Arash* 15 (February–March 1968): 27–36; Antonio Gramsci, '*Moze'-e Mokhtalef-e Rowshanfekran: No'-e Shahri va No'-e Rustai*' ['Positions of Intellectuals: Urban and Rural'], trans. M. Hezarkhani. *Arash* 16 (April 1968): 17–28; Antonio Gramsci, '*Me'yarha-ye Enteqad-e Adabi*' ['Criteria for Literary Criticism'], trans.

M. Hezarkhani. *Arash* 19 (January–February 1969): 17–21; Antonio Gramsci, '*Chand Noqteh Atf-e Moqadamati*' ['Introcutory Remarks'], trans. M. Hezarkhani. *Arash* 20 (April 1969): 63–93. The first two articles are the two parts of Gramsci's famous essay on intellectuals (Antonio Gramsci, *Selections from the Prison Notebooks*, ed. & trans. Q. Hoare & G. Nowell Smith [New York: International Publishers, 1971], pp. 5–22.

76   Gramsci, *Selections from the Prison Notebooks*, pp. 106–14, 118–22, 58, n. 8.

77   Vahabzadeh, *A Guerrilla Odyssey*, p. 85.

78   Jazani and Zia Zarifi, *Thesis of Jazani's Group*, p. 8.

79   Jazani, *The Thirty-Year Political History*, p. 113.

80   Bizhan Jazani, *Nabard ba Diktatori-ye Shah* [*War against the Shah's Dictatorship*] (np: OIPFG, 1978), pp. 11–13. See also Vahabzadeh, *A Guerrilla Odyssey*, p. 87.

81   See Gramsci, *Selections from the Prison Notebooks*, pp. 106–14, 229–38, 245–6.

82   See Afshin Matin-asgari, *Both Eastern and Western: An Intellectual History of Iranian Modernity* (London/New York: Cambridge University Press, 2018).

83   Gramsci, *Selections from the Prison Notebooks*, pp. 106–14, 229–39.

84   Mostafa Sho'aiyan, '*Nameh-ye Sargoshadeh beh Rafiq Majid darbareh-ye "Darbreh-ye Rowshanfekr-2"*' ['Open Letter to Comrade Majid on "On Intellectuals-2"'], in Momeni and Sho'aiyan, *An Inquiry into the Intellectual or Enlightener* (op. cit.), p. 34.

85   Vahabzadeh, *A Guerrilla Odyssey*, pp. 245–6.

86   Cosroe Chaqueri, *The Soviet Socialist Republic of Iran, 1920–1921: Birth of the Trauma* (Pittsburgh: University of Pittsburgh Press, 1995), p. xix.

87   Let us not forget that in reaction to the 1919 agreement the movement led by Sheikh Mohammad Khiabani (1880–1920) in Azerbaijan led to the establishment of short-lived Azadisetan (April–September 1920).

88   Chaqueri, *The Soviet Socialist Republic of Iran*, p. 283.

89   Jan M. Meijer (ed.), *The Trotsky Papers 1917–1922*, Vol. II (The Hague: Mouton, 1971), p. 209; emphasis added. This 'top-secret' telegram (dated 4 June 1920) by Trotsky was addressed to Čičerin and copied to Lenin, Kamenev, Krestinskij, and Bucharin.

90   Chaqueri, *The Soviet Socialist Republic of Iran*, p. 450.

91   Ibid., p. 288.

92   Frantz Fanon, *The Wretched of the Earth*, trans. R. Philcox (New York: Grove Press, 2004), p. 239.

93   See Vahabzadeh, *A Guerrilla Odyssey*, pp. 13, 20.

94   On the cosmopolitan character of Iranian culture see Hamid Dabashi, *Iran: A People Interrupted* (New York/London: The New Press, 2007).

95   See Ernesto Laclau and Chantal Mouffe, *Hegemony and Socialist Strategy: Toward a Radical Democratic Politics* (London: Verso, 1985).

96   For discussion about signs, their motility, and a radical critique of Saussurian linguistics see Hamid Dabashi, *Iran: The Rebirth of a Nation* (New York: Palgrave MacMillan, 2016), pp. 147–72.

3. FACING THE FADAIYAN

1   See Vahabzadeh, *A Guerrilla Odyssey* (op. cit.), p. 133.

2   Ahmadzadeh, *Armed Struggle: Both Strategy and Tactic* (op. cit.), p. 19; see also p. 20.

3   Régis Debray, *Revolution in the Revolution? Armed Struggle and Political Struggle in Latin America*, trans. Bobbye Ortiz (New York: Monthly Review Press, 1967).

4   Ibid., p. 96.

5   Ahmadzadeh, *Armed struggle: Both Strategy and Tactic* (op. cit.), pp. 136, 133.

6   For an account of Ahmadzadeh's theory see Vahabzadeh, *A Guerrilla Odyssey*, pp. 138–46.

7   V. I. Lenin, 'Revolutionary Adventurism' (1902). *Marxists Internet Archives*. Available at: https://www.marxists.org/archive/lenin/works/1902/sep/01.htm (accessed 21 July 2018).

8   Vahabzadeh, *A Guerrilla Odyssey*, p. 19; Farrokh Negahdar, interview by Peyman Vahabzadeh (London, 7–8 December 2008).

9   Puyan, *The Necessity of Armed Struggle* (op. cit.). For a review of Puyan's work see Vahabzadeh, *A Guerrilla Odyssey*, pp. 134–8.

10   Sho'aiyan's largely polemical defense of Puyan is a response to a critical essay that, contra Puyan, suggests ways of organising the working class other than those deemed possible by Puyan.

11   Naderi, *People's Fadai Guerrillas* (op. cit.), p. 397.

12   Ahmadzadeh, *Armed struggle: Both Strategy and Tactic*, p. 133.

13   Ibid., p. 96.

14   V. I. Lenin, *What Is To Be Done?* (New York: International Publishers, 1992), p. 25.

15   Raf'at, telephone interview by Peyman Vahabzadeh (6 November 2001) (op. cit.). On Yusef Keshizadeh (killed in the summary executions in Kurdistan, August 1979), see *Kar* (Organ of the Iranian People's Fadai Guerrillas) 1, no. 30 (3 September 1979), p. 2.

16   See also Salehi, *Mostafa Sho'aiyan* (op. cit.), p. 358.

17   According to Momeni, Sho'aiyan advocated blowing up the Tehran oil refinery in order to cause fuel shortages that would lead the people into conflict with the state (Hamid Momeni, 'Darbareh-ye Rowshanfekr-2' ['On Intellectuals-2'], in Momeni and Sho'aiyan, *An Inquiry into the Intellectual or Enlightener* [op. cit.], p. 25).

18   See also Raf'at, telephone interview by Peyman Vahabzadeh (6 November 2001); Serafat, 'Being a Teacher and Guerrilla Warfare' (op. cit.); Salehi, *Mostafa Sho'aiyan*, pp. 266–7; Chaqueri, ed., *Mostafa Sho'aiyan, Eight Letters* (op. cit.), pp. 123–4, n. 18.

19   See Naderi, *People's Fadai Guerrillas*, p. 476.

20   Heydar (Mohammad Dabirifard), 'Rafiq Bizhan Jazani va Sazman-e Cherikha-ye Fadai Khalq Iran' ['Comrade Bizhan Jazani and the OIPFG'], in *A Collection on the Life and Works of Bizhan Jazani* (op. cit.), p. 250.

21   Mehdi Fatapour, interview by Peyman Vahabzadeh (24 November 2001).

22   Naderi, *People's Fadai Guerrillas*, pp. 477–8.

23   Fatemeh Sa'idi, 'Gushehhai az Shekanjeh dar SAVAK' ['Being Tortured by SAVAK']. *Jahan-e Zan* (27 July 2012). Available at: https://jahanezan. wordpress.com/2012/07/27/18916/ (accessed 2 December 2017).

24   Raf'at, telephone interview by Peyman Vahabzadeh (6 November 2001); Mahin Mohtaj, *Sa'at-e Chahar-e An Ruz* [*Four O'Clock on That Day*] (Tehran: Qasidehsara, 1999), pp. 258–9. Sa'idi's interrogation documents deny Sho'aiyan's version of the events and place the responsibility on Sho'aiyan instead of Ja'fari (Naderi, *People's Fadai Guerrillas*, pp. 477–8). She was severely tortured because SAVAK knew about her connection with two of Iran's most wanted dissidents, Sho'aiyan and Ja'fari, but she managed to withhold essential information (SOLF 29).

25   CSHD (Centre for Study of Historical Documents), *Chap dar Iran beh Ravayat-e Asnad-e SAVAK: Sazman-e Cherikha-ye Fadai Khalq* [*The*

Left in Iran According to SAVAK Documents: Organization of People's Fadai Guerrillas] (Tehran: Centre for Study of Historical Documents, Ministry of Intelligence, 2001), pp. 101–2, 104; *Nabard-e Khalq*, no. 7 (May–June 1976), pp. 180–7. For a discussion about this subject see: Vahabzadeh, *A Guerrilla Odyssey*, pp. 64–5.

26   Vahabzadeh, *A Guerrilla Odyssey*, pp. 226–43.

27   The first extensive letter is dated 21 April 1974 and followed by four shorter letters, with the fifth one dated 23 August 1974. These include a letter to Saba Bizhanzadeh and another to Arzhang and Nasser, in which Mostafa intentionally speaks to the children in a harsh, militaristic language (SOLI 128, 135). The shorter letters were intended to clarify misunderstandings about him. The last letter is dated 1974–5 and exclusively documents his last meeting with Ashraf.

28   Despite Oskui's charges, confirmed by Ashraf, Sho'aiyan maintained his comradely demeanor toward her while she was in the PFG ranks: there are surviving written exchanges between the two over a poem by Sho'aiyan and a short story by Oskui. See Mostafa Sho'aiyan and Marzieh Ahmadi Oskui, *'Darbareh-ey she'r-e "Cheshm beh rah"'* ['On the Poem "Awaiting"'] (unpublished, 1973); Mostafa Sho'aiyan and Marzieh Ahmadi Oskui, *'Kalanjari ba Qoqnus'* ['An Encounter with Sphinx'] (unpublished, October 1973). See also Oskui's response to Sho'aiyan's in 'An Outline on How to Study' (June 1973) in SW.

29   In fact, Sho'aiyan failed to deliver the one rather unchallenging task (blowing up a power line) assigned to him by Ashraf, and, despite his excuses, he agreed that he deserved to be criticised for his failure (SOLF 14).

30   OIPFG, *Nabard-e Khalq* 4 (July 1974), p. 8.

31   On these cases, respectively, see Vahabzadeh, *A Guerrilla Odyssey*, pp. 32–3, 48–9, 41–2, 157–66.

32   OIPFG, *Nashriyeh-ye Dakheli* [*The Internal Bulletin*], no. 14 (August–September 1975), p. 37.

33   *Nabard-e Khalq*, no. 1 (February 1974) was the last publication that consistently uses the designation 'PFG.' Changes to designation and emblem began emerging from no. 2 (April 1974) and no. 3 (June 1974). In 1975–6 the name of the group changed to the Organisation of Iranian People's Fadai Guerrillas (OIPFG).

34   See Vahabzadeh, *A Guerrilla Odyssey*, p. 47.

35 In the history of the PFG there are two confirmed (and two unconfirmed) cases of purges. One is related to a 'security' case when Asad (alias) left his base without notice, while the other (Abdollah Panjehshahi), strangely, pertained to a love affair. No purges within the PFG had any ideological basis (contrary to the claim in Behrooz, *Rebels with a Cause* [op. cit.], pp. 66–7). On the PFG purges see Vahabzadeh, *A Guerrilla Odyssey*, pp. 60–5.

36 Karl Mannheim, *Ideology and Utopia* (London: Routledge & Kegan Paul, 1969), p. 36.

37 Jazani, *War Against the Shah's Dictatorship* (op. cit.), p. 39.

38 See Vahabzadeh, *A Guerrilla Odyssey*, pp. 177–84.

39 Chaqueri, 'Did the Soviets Play a Role in Founding the Tudeh Party in Iran?' (op. cit.).

40 Iraj Eskandari, '*Chand Nokteh-ye Asasi Darbareh-ye Bonyadgozari-ye Hezb-e Tudeh-ye Iran va Tahavvol-e An*' ['Basic points on the foundation and development of the Tudeh Party of Iran']. *Donya* 3 (August–September 1974), p. 4.

41 See Vahabzadeh, *A Guerrilla Odyssey*, pp. 181–2.

42 For some cases of factional purges, smear campaigns, and manipulations within various Fadai splinter groups see Vahabzadeh, *A Guerrilla Odyssey*, pp. 70–4.

4. ON INTELLECTUALS

1   See Al Ahmad, *On the Services and Betrayals of the Intellectuals*, Vol. 1 (op. cit.), pp. 89–109.

2   Persian translations of Gramsci at this time were 'The Formation of Intellectuals' (op. cit.); 'Positions of Intellectuals: Urban and Rural' (op. cit.); 'Criteria for Literary Criticism' (op. cit.); 'Introductory Remarks' (op. cit.).

3   Gramsci, *Selections from the Prison Notebooks* (op. cit.), p. 5; Gramsci, 'The Formation of Intellectuals' (Persian), p. 27.

4   See Darius M. Rejali, *Torture and Modernity: Self, Society, and State in Modern Iran* (Boulder, CO: Westview Press, 1994). In particular, see my discussion on 'Technologies of Resistance' in Vahabzadeh, *A Guerrilla Odyssey* (op. cit.), pp. 226–43.

5   Vahabzadeh, *A Guerrilla Odyssey*, pp. 226–43.

6   For my extensive reflections on acting and liberation see Peyman Vahabzadeh, *Violence and Nonviolence: Conceptual Excursions into Phantom Opposites* (Toronto: University of Toronto Press, 2019), chs 3 and 4.

7   OIPFG, *Chahar Resaleh az Sazman-e Cherkha-ye Fadai-ye Khalq-e Iran* [*Four Essays by the Organization of Iranian People's Fadai Guerrillas*] (Germany: Support Committee of Iranian Peoples New Revolutionary Movement, 1977).

8   In his book-length rejoinder to Sho'aiyan's *Revolution*, Momeni offers an extensive summary of the objections to Sho'aiyan's *rowshangar* (enlightener). See Momeni and Sho'aiyan, *An Inquiry into the Intellectual or Enlightener* (op. cit.). For Momeni's additional objections see Momeni *Not Rebellion* (op. cit.), pp. 102–19.

9   Salehi, *Mostafa Sho'aiyan* (op. cit.), p. 313.

10   Mostafa Sho'aiyan, 'Negahi beh Darbareh-ye Rowshanfekr-1' ['A Glance at On Intellectuals-1'], in Momeni and Sho'aiyan, *An Inquiry into the Intellectual or Enlightener*, p. 10.

11   Hamid Momeni, 'Darbareh-ye Rowshanfekr-2' ['On Intellectuals-2'], in Momeni and Sho'aiyan, *An Inquiry into the Intellectual or Enlightener*, p. 25.

12   Momeni, 'On Intellectuals-2,' p. 32.

13   Ibid., p. 25.

14   Mostafa Sho'aiyan, 'Nameh-ye Sargoshadeh beh Rafiq Majid darbareh-ye "Darbreh-ye Rowshanfekr-2"' ['Open Letter to Comrade Majid on "On Intellectuals-2"'], in Momeni and Sho'aiyan, *An Inquiry into the Intellectual or Enlightener*, p. 42.

15   Naderi, *People's Fadai Guerrillas* (op. cit.), p. 505.

16   Namely, Momeni, *Not Rebellion*, and Sho'aiyan, IRJS.

17   Momeni, 'On Intellectuals-2,' p. 25.

18   Sho'aiyan, 'A Glance,' p. 11.

19   Momeni, 'On Intellectuals-2,' p. 26.

20   Gramsci, *Selections from the Prison Notebooks*, p. 5.

21   Ibid.

22   Ibid., p. 8.

23   Ibid.

24   Ibid., p. 9.

25   Ibid.

26   Ibid., p. 12.

27   Ibid., p. 15.

28   Gramsci, 'The Formation of Intellectuals' (Persian in *Jahan-e Naw*), p. 31. Sho'aiyan makes the silly remarks that this distinction does not apply to the wrestler (IRJS 348, n. 4).

29   Karl Marx and Friedrich Engels, *The German Ideology*, ed. C. J. Arthur (New York: International Publishers, 1970), p. 53.

30   George Novak, 'Marxism and the Intellectuals.' *The New International* II:7 (December 1935). Available at: http://www.marxistsfr.org/archive/novack/1935/12/x01.htm (accessed 19 December 2017).

31   Carl Boggs, 'Marxism and the Role of Intellectuals.' *New Political Science* 1:2–3 (1979), p. 9.

32   Ibid., p. 7.

33   Hamid Momeni, *'Darbareh-ye Rowshanfekr-1'* ['On Intellectuals-1'], in Momeni and Sho'aiyan, *An Inquiry into the Intellectual or Enlightener*, pp. 1–2.

34   Ibid., p. 3.

35   Mostafa Sho'aiyan, *'Yek Layeh'* ['A Stratum'], in Momeni and Sho'aiyan, *An Inquiry into the Intellectual or Enlightener*, p. 5.

36   Sho'aiyan, 'A Stratum,' pp. 5–9, 12.

37   Sho'aiyan, 'A Glance,' p. 16.

38   Ibid., pp. 16–17.

39   Ibid., p. 18.

40   Ibid., pp. 19–20.

41   Momeni, 'On Intellectuals-2,' p. 23.

42   Ibid., p. 26.

43   Ibid., p. 29.

44   Ibid., pp. 30–31.

45   Ibid., p. 31.

46   Hamid Momeni, *Pasokh beh Forsattalaban darmored-e* 'Mobarezeh-yi Mosalahaneh, ham Stratezhi, ham Taktik' [*A Rejoinder to the Opportunists on* Armed Struggle: Both Strategy and Tactic] (Tehran: Entesharat-i M. Bidsorkhi, 1979), p. 28.

47   Momeni, 'On Intellectuals-2,' pp. 32–3.

48   Momeni, *Not Rebellion*, pp. 110–11.

49   Sho'aiyan, 'Open Letter,' pp. 54–5.

50   Ibid., p. 36.

51   Ibid., p. 39.

52   Ibid., p. 44.

53   Ibid., p. 54.

54   Ibid., p. 46.

55   Ibid., p. 51.

56   Ibid., p. 52.

57   Gramsci, *Selections from the Prison Notebooks*, p. 12.

58   'It always happens that individuals belong to more than one private association, and often to associations which are objectively in contradiction to one another' (Gramsci, *Selections from the Prison Notebooks*, p. 265).

59   Jazani, *The Thirty-Year Political History* (op. cit.), pp. 104–6, 168; see also Anonymous, '*Goruh-e Jazani-Zarifi Pishtaz-e Mobarezeh-yi Mosallahani dar Iran*' ['The Jazani–Zarifi Group: Vanguard of Armed Movement in Iran']. *19 Bahman Te`orik*, no. 4 (April 1976), p. 9.

60   Momeni, *Not Rebellion*, p. 37; Momeni's rejoinder was originally published in Hamid Momeni and Mostafa Sho'aiyan, *Shuresh Na, Qadamha-yi Sanjideh dar Rah-e Enqelab; Pasokhha-ye Nasanjideh beh Qadamha-yi Sanjideh* [*Not Rebellion, Judicious Steps on the Path to the Revolution; Injudicious Replies to Judicious Steps*] (Florence: Edition Mazdak, 1975). This volume contains Momeni's *Not Rebellion* and Sho'aiyan's rebuttal, *Injudicious Replies*. However, all references to Momeni's rejoinder in this book are taken from the version of *Not Rebellion* published separately by the PFG.

61   Momeni, *Not Rebellion*, pp. 6, 15–17, 31–3.

62   Ibid., pp. 34–5, 37.

63   Ibid., p. 12.

64   Ibid., pp. 122, 71–2, 77.

65   Ibid., p. 103.

66   Ibid.

67   Ibid., pp. 105–6.

68   Ibid., p. 107.

69   Ibid., p. 110.

70   Ibid., p. 119.

71   Ibid., p. 111.

72   Ibid., p. 122.

73   Ibid., p. 108.

74 Ibid., p. 123.

75 Nasser Pakdaman, *'Darbareh-ye Yek Bahs-e Qalami'* ['On a Debate in Writing'], in Sho'aiyan and Momeni, *On Intellectuals: A Debate in Writing* (op. cit.), pp. 75–145.

76 Farzin Vahdat, *God and Juggernaut: Iran's Intellectual Encounter with Modernity* (Syracuse, NY: Syracuse University Press, 2002).

77 Ibid., p. 108.

78 Ali Mersepassi, *Intellectual Discourse and the Politics of Modernization: Negotiating Modernity in Iran* (Cambridge/New York: Cambridge University Press, 2000), p. 1.

79 Ibid., p. 8.

80 Ibid., pp. 160, 171.

81 Ibid., p. 159.

82 Ibid., p. 166.

83 Vahabzadeh, *A Guerrilla Odyssey*, pp. 1–5.

84 Ibid., pp. 79, 94.

85 Ernesto Che Guevara, *Guerrilla Warfare* (Lincoln: University of Nebraska Press), p. 143.

86 Richard Gott, *Guerrilla Movements in Latin America* (New York: Seagull Books, 2008), p. xxvi.

87 Jeremy Varon, *Bringing the War Home: The Weather Underground, the Red Army Faction, and Revolutionary Violence in the Sixties and Seventies* (Berkeley: University of California Press, 2004); George Katsiaficas, *The Imagination of the New Left: A Global Analysis of 1968* (Boston: South End Press, 1987); Matin, *Confederation* (op. cit.), pp. 213, 243, 260–1.

88 Ernesto Laclau and Chantal Mouffe, *Hegemony and Socialist Strategy: Toward a Radical Democratic Politics* (London: Verso, 1985), p. 4.

5. FRONTAL POLITICS, FRONTAL THINKING

1 On Jazani's theoretical novelty in deploying the Latin American concept of 'armed propaganda' in a different and creative way see Vahabzadeh, *A Guerrilla Odyssey*, pp. 38–41.

2 Mostafa Sho'aiyan, ['*Sazman-e Pishtaz*'] ('The Vanguard Organisation') (nd: unpublished).

3 The only Persian publication of Foucault prior to this time was an interview about his then recently published book *Les mots et les choses*

(1966; English, *The Order of Things* [1970]). The interview was published in *Jahan-e Naw* (23, nos 4–6 [Summer 1968]: 40–47) as '*Strukturalism-e Fuko*' ('Foucault's Structuralism') trans. Mohammad Qazi. The interview contains no significant reference to Foucault's theory of discourse, although this is the book where he developed the concept. Laclau's first book was published in 1977. My point? Neither theorist could have inspired Sho'aiyan's approach. His theory is his own.

4   Laclau and Mouffe, *Hegemony and Socialist Strategy* (op. cit.), p. 96; emphasis added.

5   Gramsci, *Selections from the Prison Notebooks*, p. 57.

6   Ibid., pp. 57–8; emphasis added.

7   In regard to epistemic and linguistic imperialisms see Mignolo, 'Epistemic Disobedience, Independent Thought and Decolonial Freedom' (op. cit.); Enriqué Dussel, 'Eurocentrism and Modernity,' *Boundary* 2/20:3 (1993): 65–76.

8   PSRI, *The People's Mojahedin Organisation*, Vol. 1 (op. cit.), p. 583.

9   Ibid.

10   The volume *Half-a-Step on the Way: The People's Liberation Front*, contains three pieces: an article by Sho'aiyan under the same title, a rejoinder by PFG titled (by publisher) '*Naqd-e Cherikha-ye Fadai-ye Khalq*' ('The PFG Critique'), and Sho'aiyan's rebuttal, '*Juyeshi Piramun-e Yek Naqd*' ('An Inquiry about a Critique'). Articles are individually paginated. A preface and an afterword, written by Sho'aiyan's comrades, also appear in the volume.

11   V. I. Lenin, *Two Tactics of Social-Democracy in the Democratic Revolution* (New York: International Publishers, 1989).

12   'Reaction' designates the Shah's regime, 'colonialism' its imperialist supporters, especially the United States. Should guerrilla operations target both? Following Jazani's theory of 'armed propaganda,' the PFG consistently assassinated high-profile figures of Iranian military, security, and police. Although few in number, these assassinations effectively aimed at specific groups to convey the simultaneous message of warning and support (see Vahabzadeh, *A Guerrilla Odyssey* [op. cit.], pp. 38–41). Lacking such theory, the OIPM carried out assassinations of both American military attachés and Iranian armed forces personnel. Does Sho'aiyan mean to endorse the Mojahedin's tactics (when he says militants must target 'reaction-colonialism'), or is he just being vague?

A REBEL'S JOURNEY

13 See my analysis in Vahabzadeh, *A Guerrilla Odyssey*, pp. 84–91.

14 This is best evidenced by the audiotaped debate between Hamid Ashraf (IPFG) and Taqi Shahram, leader of the Marxist-Leninist OIPM. Even though Shahram insists they are now Marxists and have 'purified' themselves of their previous class elements, Ashraf accuses them of remaining a traditional petite bourgeois group. See Peykar (ed.), *Ketab-e Goftogu-ye Sazman-e Cherikha-ye Fadai-ye Khalq-e Iran va Sazman-e Mojahedin-e Khalq-e Iran* [*The Dialogue of OIPFG and OIPM*] (Frankfurt: Andeesheh va Peykar Publications, 2014).

15 Reza Moradi Ghiyasabadi, 'Matn-e Kamel-e Defa'iyyat-e Khosrow Golesorkhi va Karamatollah Daneshian' ['Complete Defense Statements of Khosrow Golesorkhi and Karamatollah Daneshian']. *Persian Studies* (11 February 2007). Available at: http://ghiasabadi.com/golesorkhi.html (accessed 26 January 2018).

16 Vahabzadeh, *A Guerrilla Odyssey*, pp. 30–4.

17 Ibid., pp. 104–11.

18 Bizhan Jazani, 'Hezb-e Tabaqeh-ye Kargar dar Iran' ['The Working-Class Party in Iran']. *19 Bahman-e Te'orik* 1 (December 1976), p. 30.

19 Jazani and Zia Zarifi, *Thesis of Jazani's Group* (op. cit.), p. 3; original emphasis.

20 Béjar, *Peru 1965: Notes on a Guerrilla Experience* (op. cit.), p. 68.

21 Tudeh Party of Iran-Central Committee, 'Komiteh Markazi-ye Hezb-e Tudeh-ye Iran az Hameh-ye Mokhalefan-e Rezhim-e Teror va Ekhtenaq-e Konuni-ye Iran Da'vat Mikonad' ['Central Committee of Tudeh Party of Iran Invites All Those Opposing the Present Terror and Repression Regime in Iran']. *Donya* 3, no. 4 (June 1976), p. 5.

22 N. Kianuri, 'Hezb-e Tabaqeh-ye Kargar va Mobarezan-e dara-ye E'teqadat-e Mazhabi' ['The Working Class Party and the Activists of Religious Beliefs']. *Donya* 3, no. 9 (December 1976), pp. 2–7.

23 Manouchehr Behzadi, 'Jebheh-ye zedd-e Diktatori—Mokhalefatha va Porseshha' ['The Anti-Dictatorship Front: Criticisms and Questions']. *Donya* 3, no. 10 (December 1976), p. 3.

24 Bizhan Jazani, 'Vahdat va Naqsh-e Estratezhik-e Cherikha-ye Fadai-e Khalq' ['Unification and the Strategic Role of the People's Fadai Guerrillas']. *19 Bahman-e Te'orik* 1 (December 1976), p. 5.

25 See: Bizhan Jazani, *Panj Resaleh* [*Five Essays*]. *19 Bahman-e Te'orik* 8 (December 1976), p. 28; Jazani, *War Against the Shah's Dictatorship* (op. cit.), p. 71.

26 See: Matin[-asgari], *Confederation*, pp. 354–5, 366.

27 For the terms 'relations of equivalence' and 'relations of difference,' see Laclau and Mouffe, *Hegemony and Socialist Strategy*, p. 127.

28 Or to put it in post-Marxist terms, 'we will call *articulation* any practice establishing a relation among elements such that their identity is modified as a result of the articulatory practice. The structured totality resulting from the articulatory practice, we will call *discourse*' (Laclau and Mouffe, *Hegemony and Socialist Strategy*, p. 105; emphasis in the original).

29 Chantal Mouffe, 'We urgently need to promote a left-populism.' *Verso Books* (4 August 2017). Available at: https://www.versobooks.com/blogs/3341-chantal-mouffe-we-urgently-need-to-promote-a-left-populism (accessed 27 January 2018).

6. REBELLIOUS ESSENCE, REBELLIOUS ACTION

1 Mostafa Sho'aiyan, ['Letter to Mazdak'] November 1975 (unpublished; from C. Chaqueri personal archives).

2 Gh. Farhang Forutan (Abbas), telegram messaging with Peyman Vahabzadeh (6 April 2018). Since I have not obtained a copy of this pamphlet I have to postpone confirming Shayegan's position.

3 Momeni, *Not Rebellion* (op. cit.), p. 1.

4 Ibid., pp. 12–13, 15.

5 Ibid., p. 10.

6 Jazani, *War Against the Shah's Dictatorship* (op. cit.), pp. 96–7.

7 Vahabzadeh, *A Guerrilla Odyssey* (op. cit.), pp. 119–21.

8 V. I. Lenin, 'On the Slogan for a United States of Europe,' in *Collected Works of Lenin*, Vol. 21 (Moscow: Progress Publishers, 1974), pp. 339–43.

9 The attentive reader may quite judiciously object to Sho'aiyan's criticisms of Leninism and his reading of the history of Russian Revolution and the Soviet Union. But the point here is that these criticisms, at times inapplicable perhaps, open the path for his own thinking. Clearly, he felt

that he must shut the commonly used conceptual doors before opening his uncommon one.

10   See Vahabzadeh, *A Guerrilla Odyssey*, p. 79.

11   Ahmadzadeh, *Armed Struggle: Both Strategy and Tactic* (op. cit.), pp. 63–4.

12   Jazani, *War Against the Shah's Dictatorship*, pp. 65–6.

13   Ibid., p. 59.

14   Hassan Zia Zarifi, 'Enqelabiyyun Naqsh-e Bozorgi dar Takmil-e Sharayet-e Eini-ye Enqelab Darand' ['Revolutionaries Play a Significant Role in Completing the Objective Conditions of the Revolution']. *Rah-e Azadi* 47 (1996), p. 30.

15   Mostafa Sho'aiyan, ['*Mas'aleh-ye Khalq*'] ('The Question of the People') (nd, unpublished, from C. Chaqueri personal archives). See Appendix.

16   Puyan, *The Necessity of Armed Struggle* (op. cit.), p. 15.

17   Ahmadzadeh, *Armed Struggle: Both Strategy and Tactic*, p. 98.

18   Jazani, 'Unification and the Strategic Role of the People's Fadai Guerrillas' (op. cit.), pp. 1–9.

19   Tricontinentalism is shorthand for Organisation of Solidarity with the People of Asia, Africa and Latin America (OSPAAAL). See Thea Pitman and Andy Stafford. 'Introduction: Transatlanticism and Tricontinentalism.' *Journal of Transatlantic Studies* 7(3) (2009): 197–207.

20   Ernesto Che Guevara, 'Message to the Tricontinental' (1967). *Marxists Internet Archive*. Available at: https://www.marxists.org/archive/guevara/1967/04/16.htm (accessed 7 April 2018).

21   Ibid.

22   Momeni, *Not Rebellion*, pp. 52–3.

23   Ahmad Kasravi, *Tarikh-e Mashruteh-ye Iran* [*History of Iranian Constitutionalism*] (Tehran: Negah, 2013), pp. 851–2.

24   Ibid., p. 563.

25   Ibid., p. 530.

26   Ibid., pp. 460, 462–3.

27   Ibid., p. 519.

28   Ibid., pp. 407, 563.

29   Sho'aiyan, 'Open Letter,' in Momeni and Sho'aiyan, *An Inquiry into the Intellectual or Enlightener* (op. cit.) p. 42.

30   Momeni, *Not Rebellion*, p. 7.

31   Ibid., p. 46.

32   Ibid., p. 48.

33   Ibid., p. 51.

34   Ibid., pp. 54, 55.

35   Ibid., p. 57.

36   Ibid., pp. 114, 123.

37   Ibid., p. 56.

38   In this regard see Claude Lefort, 'Rereading *The Communist Manifesto*,' in *Democracy and Political Theory* (Cambridge, UK: Polity Press, 1988), pp. 149–62.

39   Laclau and Mouffe, *Hegemony and Socialist Strategy* (op. cit.), pp. 122–7.

40   Ahmadzadeh, *Armed Struggle: Both Strategy and Tactic*, pp. 97–8.

41   Che Guevara, 'Message to the Tricontinental.'

42   Fanon, *The Wretched of the Earth* (op. cit.), p. 239. See also Frantz Fanon, *Toward the African Revolution*, trans. Haakin Chevalier (New York: Grove Press, 1994).

43   The attentive reader notices the likeness of Sho'aiyan's thought with Trotsky's concept of 'permanent revolution,' but Sho'aiyan does not acknowledge any connections, as his idea is, by his own admission, inspired by Che Guevara. See Leon Trotsky, 'The Three Conceptions of the Russian Revolution.' *Marxist Readings*. Available at: http://www. internationalist.org/three.html (accessed 6 February 2018).

44   On Jazani's theory of the 'second leg' of the movement, see Vahabzadeh, *A Guerrilla Odyssey*, pp. 44–6.

45   Nili, 'The Honourable Rebel' (op. cit.).

46   It should be noted Sho'aiyan must have read Trotsky's theory in *Jahan-e Naw*: Leon Trotsky, '*Chekideh-ye Te`ori-ye Enqelab-e Modavem*' ['A Synopsis of the Theory of Permanent Revolution']. *Jahan-e Naw* 23, nos 7–8–9 (Autumn 1968): 171–5.

CONCLUSION: THE TWENTY-FIRST-CENTURY REVOLUTIONARY THEORY

1   This has been discussed in the introduction to this book. Houshang Mahrooyan's book thrives on this theme of vicitimisation (Mahrooyan, *Mostafa Sho'aiyan: The Lonely Singular Thinker* [op. cit.]; see also Vahabzadeh, 'Mustafa Shu'a'iyan and *Fada`iyan-i Khalq*' [op. cit.]).

2   For a summary of the revolutionary reversals see Peyman Vahabzadeh,
     'Historical and Conceptual Preparations for a Multidisciplinary Study
     of Social Justice in Iran,' in *Iran's Struggles for Social Justice: Economics,
     Agency, Justice, Activism*, ed. P. Vahabzadeh (New York: Palgrave
     Macmillan, 2017): 9–27.
3   Ernesto Laclau, *On Populist Reason* (London: Verso, 2005).

APPENDIX: THE QUESTION OF THE PEOPLE

1   This unpublished note was found in the personal archives of Cosroe
     Chaqueri who provided me with a copy. It offers a summary of Sho'aiyan's
     theory written by him. The note has no date or title, and the present title
     is mine. Given that Sho'aiyan's contact with Chaqueri was established in
     the last two years of his life, this note must have been written between
     1974 and February 1976, possibly closer to the latter date. As such,
     it represents some of Sho'aiyan's last thoughts on the subject. This
     note shows the potential connection between Sho'aiyan's thought and
     contemporary theory, as discussed in this book.

INDEX

315

INDEX

317